Upgrading & Fixing PCs For Dummies, ® 5th Edition

W9-BEB-196

Always Remember These Things

Turn off and unplug your computer before taking off its cover. Please. This one's the most important step. You can damage both yourself *and* your computer if you forget to turn off and unplug it.

The red (or colored) wire is positive. Look for a little + sign on the socket that the wires plug into. The red or colored wire plugs into the pin marked by the + sign.

The positive/red wire connects to Pin 1. Look for little numbers printed along the edge of a socket.

The positive wire — always the red or colored wire — always fits on the pin marked as number 1. Can't see the number 1? Then push the plug into the socket with the red wire facing toward the *low* numbers on the socket.

The two black wires almost always go next to each other on a motherboard's power connector. When pushing power-supply cables into the motherboard's sockets, arrange the two cables so that the two black wires are next to each other.

Steps for Working on Your PC

1. Copy any important information on your hard drive to a safe place for safekeeping. (To be really safe, back up the whole hard drive.)
2. Read any instructions that came with your new part.
3. Close any running programs, turn off your PC, and unplug it from the wall.
4. Clean off the desk or table space next to your computer.
5. Put your tools next to the computer.
6. Remove your PC's cover.
7. Touch an unpainted part of the computer's case to discharge any static electricity that may have built up. This keeps static electricity from damaging your computer's sensitive internal parts. (If you work in a particularly static-prone environment, buy a *wrist strap* or *grounding mat* from your computer store to help discharge static.)
8. Remove the old item and insert the new one.
9. Plug in the PC, turn it on, and carefully test the new part to see whether it works.
10. Turn off the PC, unplug it, and put the case back together.
11. Plug in the PC and put away your tools.

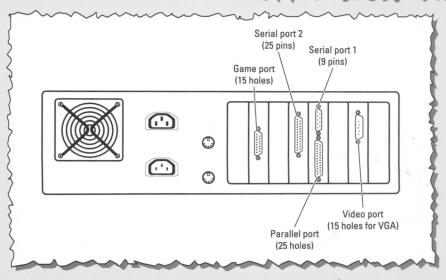

Serial port 2 (25 pins)
Serial port 1 (9 pins)
Game port (15 holes)
Parallel port (25 holes)
Video port (15 holes for VGA)

For Dummies®: Bestselling Book Series for Beginners

Upgrading & Fixing PCs For Dummies,® 5th Edition

How to Remove a PC's Case

1. Turn off the computer, monitor, and peripherals (printer, digital camera, Palm Pilot cradle, and so on). Make sure that everything normally attached to your computer is turned off and unplugged. Your computer's easier to move around that way.

2. Unplug your computer from the wall. Unplug the power cord from the back of your computer, too. (Some cases don't come off until the power cord is removed the computer.)

3. Remove the screws from your PC's back or outside edges. The older your PC, the more screws you find. Some PCs have a screw in each corner, as shown in the following figure. Turn each of those screws counterclockwise to loosen them, and lift off the case. The case on many "upright" models is often held in place with one knob, which you can easily twist off with your fingers.

   Place the screws in a safe place where you can find them later (and where they won't fall and lodge themselves in your PC's cracks).

4. Slide off the cover. On some computers, the cover slides toward the front. You may need to pull pretty hard. Try lifting up a little on the cover from the back. On other computers, the cover lifts up and off. (Squeeze in on any little plastic latches that might be holding the cover in place.)

5. Clean inside the computer and cover. Use a can of compressed air to blow out all the dust while you're in there. Don't do this on white carpets. Clean away the gross dust remnants clinging to the outside vents of the power supply.

To replace the cover, reverse these steps.

For Dummies®: Bestselling Book Series for Beginners

Upgrading & Fixing PCs

FOR DUMMIES®

5TH EDITION

by Andy Rathbone

Hungry Minds™

Best-Selling Books • Digital Downloads • e-Books • Answer Networks • e-Newsletters • Branded Web Sites • e-Learning

New York, NY ◆ Cleveland, OH ◆ Indianapolis, IN

Upgrading & Fixing PCs For Dummies,® 5th Edition

Published by
Hungry Minds, Inc.
909 Third Avenue
New York, NY 10022
www.hungryminds.com
www.dummies.com (Dummies Press Web site)

Library of Congress Control Number: 00-101253

ISBN: 0-7645-0719-2

Printed in the United States of America

10 9 8 7 6 5

5O/RV/QS/QS/IN

Distributed in the United States by Hungry Minds, Inc.

Distributed in the United States by Hungry Minds, Inc.

Distributed by CDG Books Canada Inc. for Canada; by Transworld Publishers Limited in the United Kingdom; by IDG Norge Books for Norway; by IDG Sweden Books for Sweden; by IDG Books Australia Publishing Corporation Pty. Ltd. for Australia and New Zealand; by TransQuest Publishers Pte Ltd. for Singapore, Malaysia, Thailand, Indonesia, and Hong Kong; by Gotop Information Inc. for Taiwan; by ICG Muse, Inc. for Japan; by Intersoft for South Africa; by Eyrolles for France; by International Thomson Publishing for Germany, Austria and Switzerland; by Distribuidora Cuspide for Argentina; by LR International for Brazil; by Galileo Libros for Chile; by Ediciones ZETA S.C.R. Ltda. for Peru; by WS Computer Publishing Corporation, Inc., for the Philippines; by Contemporanea de Ediciones for Venezuela; by Express Computer Distributors for the Caribbean and West Indies; by Micronesia Media Distributor, Inc. for Micronesia; by Chips Computadoras S.A. de C.V. for Mexico; by Editorial Norma de Panama S.A. for Panama; by American Bookshops for Finland.

For general information on Hungry Minds' products and services please contact our Customer Care Department within the U.S. at 800-762-2974, outside the U.S. at 317-572-3993 or fax 317-572-4002.

For sales inquiries and reseller information, including discounts, premium and bulk quantity sales, and foreign-language translations, please contact our Customer Care Department at 800-434-3422, fax 317-572-4002, or write to Hungry Minds, Inc., Attn: Customer Care Department, 10475 Crosspoint Boulevard, Indianapolis, IN 46256.

For information on licensing foreign or domestic rights, please contact our Sub-Rights Customer Care Department at 650-653-7098.

For authorization to photocopy items for corporate, personal, or educational use, please contact Copyright Clearance Center, 222 Rosewood Drive, Danvers, MA 01923, or fax 978-750-4470.

For information on using Hungry Minds' products and services in the classroom or for ordering examination copies, please contact our Educational Sales Department at 800-434-2086 or fax 317-572-4005.

Please contact our Public Relations Department at 212-884-5163 for press review copies or 212-884-5000 for author interviews and other publicity information or fax 212-884-5400.

Hungry Minds™   is a trademark of Hungry Minds, Inc.

About the Author

Andy Rathbone started geeking around with computers in 1985 when he bought a boxy CP/ M Kaypro 2X with lime-green letters. Like other budding nerds, he soon began playing with null-modem adapters, dialing up computer bulletin boards, and working part-time at Radio Shack.

In between playing computer games, he served as editor of the *Daily Aztec* newspaper at San Diego State University. After graduating with a comparative literature degree, he went to work for a bizarre underground coffee-table magazine that sort of disappeared.

Andy began combining his two interests, words and computers, by selling articles to a local computer magazine. During the next few years, Andy started ghostwriting computer books for more famous computer authors as well as writing several hundred articles about computers for technoid publications like *Supercomputing Review, CompuServe* magazine, *ID Systems, DataPro,* and *Shareware.*

In 1992, Andy and the *DOS For Dummies* author/legend Dan Gookin teamed up to write *PCs For Dummies.* Andy subsequently started the *Windows For Dummies* series, and *Windows 3.1 For Dummies* won Best Introductory How-To Book by the Computer Press Association in 1994.

Andy's written the *Upgrading and Fixing For Dummies* series, the *MORE Windows For Dummies* series, the *Dummies 101: Windows* series, *MP3 For Dummies*, and several other *...For Dummies* books. With more than 11 million books in print, he's reached the *New York Times* bestseller list.

Andy lives with his most-excellent wife, Tina, and their cat in southern California. When not writing, he fiddles with his MIDI gadgets and tries to keep the cat off both keyboards.

Dedication

To that sense of satisfaction felt when fixing it yourself.

Author's Acknowledgments

Special thanks to the cat, for staying off the keyboard this time.

Publisher's Acknowledgments

We're proud of this book; please send us your comments through our Online Registration Form located at www.dummies.com.

Some of the people who helped bring this book to market include the following:

Acquisitions, Editorial, and Media Development

Project Editor: Rebecca Whitney

Acquisitions Editor: Steven Hayes

Senior Editor, Freelance: Constance Carlisle

Proof Editors: Teresa Artman; Dwight Ramsey

Technical Editor: Jeff Wiedenfeld

Editorial Assistant: Candace Nicholson

Production

Project Coordinator: Maridee Ennis

Layout and Graphics: Amy Adrian, Karl Brandt, Joe Bucki, Angela F. Hunkler, Shelley Norris, Barry Offringa, Tracy K. Oliver, Jill Piscitelli, Brent Savage, Brian Torwelle, Erin Zeltner

Proofreaders: Laura Albert, John Greenough, Susan Moritz, Marianne Santy, Charles Spencer, Ethel M. Winslow, York Production Services, Inc.

Indexer: York Production Services, Inc.

Special Help: Beth Parlon

General and Administrative

Hungry Minds Technology Publishing Group: Richard Swadley, Senior Vice President and Publisher; Mary Bednarek, Vice President and Publisher, Networking; Joseph Wikert, Vice President and Publisher, Web Development Group; Mary C. Corder, Editorial Director, Dummies Technology; Andy Cummings, Publishing Director, Dummies Technology; Barry Pruett, Publishing Director, Visual/Graphic Design

Hungry Minds Manufacturing: Ivor Parker, Vice President, Manufacturing

Hungry Minds Marketing: John Helmus, Assistant Vice President, Director of Marketing

Hungry Minds Production for Branded Press: Debbie Stailey, Production Director

Hungry Minds Sales: Michael Violano, Vice President, International Sales and Sub Rights

Contents at a Glance

Cartoons at a Glance

By Rich Tennant

page 7

page 109

page 179

page 275

page 329

Fax: 978-546-7747
E-mail: richtennant@the5thwave.com
World Wide Web: www.the5thwave.com

Table of Contents

Introduction

You're no dummy; we both know that. But something about computers makes you feel like a dummy. And that's perfectly understandable. Unlike today's kids, you didn't start browsing the Internet while at the day-care center.

You haven't missed much, though. Computers are still as cryptic as they were the day you first saw one. They haven't gotten any friendlier, either. A bank's ATM rewards its users with a $20 bill after they've figured out which keys to press. Computers just *take* your money.

In fact, your computer's probably asking for some more of your cash right now, and that's why you're flipping through this book's Introduction.

Most of today's computer owners face at least one of the following problems:

- Somebody says that you "need more RAM."

- You can't afford to replace your aging Pentium, but you're too scared to replace your computer's motherboard. You need a different way to speed things up.

- It's time to join the Internet and send e-mail to relatives.

- You know that you need a *faster* CD-ROM drive, but you wonder whether a readable/writable drive or a DVD drive would be a more versatile replacement.

- You keep losing at computer games because your graphics card's too slow. Do you need a CPU with MMX? An AGP video card? Both?

- You wonder why you should pay the repair shop $75 an hour to install a part that costs only half that much.

About This Book

That's where this book comes in handy. With this book in one hand and a screwdriver in the other, you can repair your own computer or add new parts to it. Best yet, this book doesn't force you to learn anything during the process.

Instead, this book is a reference filled with nuggets of information — sort of a mini-encyclopedia. For example, if your floppy drive starts acting weird, just flip through to the section dealing with weird-acting floppy drives. There, you find simple instructions for jump-starting your floppy drive back into action.

Floppy drive still doesn't work? Then follow the clearly numbered steps to pull out your old floppy drive and stick in a new one. You won't find any technobabble blocking the way, either. Instead, you can just jump to the details you need to know now: Which screws do you need to remove? Which cable plugs into which hole? How do you put the computer back together? And what happens if you lose an important screw in the shag carpet?

Unlike other computer repair books, this book steers clear from headings like "Integrated I/O Circuitry on the Mainboard" or "Procedures for Measuring Capacitor Flow." Who cares?

How to Use This Book

Suppose that your keyboard's on the fritz. Don't know how a healthy keyboard's supposed to act? Head to Chapter 3 for a quick rundown. (That chapter explains the computer stuff everybody thinks you already know.)

When you're ready, flip to Chapter 5, the keyboard chapter, to hear about common keyboard foul-ups as well as tips on how to make your keyboard work again. In that chapter, you find fixes for problems like these:

- ✔ "When I turn on my computer, the screen says `Keyboard not found — Press <F1> to continue` or something equally depressing!"

- ✔ "Some of the keys stick after I spilled a Hansen's Natural Raspberry Soda over them!"

- ✔ "My arrow keys don't move the cursor — they make numbers!"

- ✔ "My keyboard doesn't have F11 and F12 keys, and Microsoft Word for Windows uses those keys!"

If your keyboard's truly beyond repair, head for the Chapter 5 section "How Do I Install a New Keyboard?" There, you discover which tools you need (if any) and how much money this setback will cost you. Finally, you see a list of clearly numbered steps explaining everything you need to do to get that new keyboard installed and ready for hunting and pecking.

Type This Stuff Here

If you need to type anything into your computer, you see the text you need to type displayed like this:

```
C:\> TYPE THIS IN
```

Here, you type the words **TYPE THIS IN** after the C:\> thing and then press the Enter key. If things look awkward, a description of what you're supposed to type follows so that there's no confusion (well, as little confusion as possible, anyway).

Words or commands that appear on the screen appear in the book like this: These words appear on the screen.

Read These Parts

If you're lucky (and your computer's healthy), you won't have to read very much of this book. But, when something weird happens, this book can help you figure out what went wrong, whether it can be repaired, or whether you have to replace it.

Along the way, you may find helpful comments or warnings explaining the process in more detail.

You find tips like this scattered throughout the book. Take a look at them first. In fact, some of these tips may spare you from having to read more than a paragraph of a computer book — a worthy feat indeed!

Don't Read These Parts

Okay, I lied a little bit. I did stick some technobabble in this book. After all, I'm a computer geek. (Whenever I sit down in a restaurant, my palmtop computer shoots out the top of my back pocket and clatters on the floor.) Luckily for you, however, I have neatly cordoned off all the technical drivel.

Any particularly odious technical details are isolated and posted with this icon so that you can avoid them easily. If a computer nerd drops by to help with your particular problem, just hand him or her this book. With these icons, the computer nerd will know exactly which sections to look for.

How This Book Is Organized

This book has five major parts. Each part is divided into several chapters. And each chapter covers a major topic, which is divided into specific sections.

The point? Well, this book's indexer sorted all the information with an extra-fine-tooth flea comb, making it easy for you to find the exact section you want when you want it. Plus, everything's cross-referenced. If you need more information about a subject, you can figure out exactly which chapter to head for.

Here are the parts and what they contain:

Part I: Biting Your Fingernails

You find the basics in here. One chapter explains your computer's basic anatomy so that you'll know which parts are *supposed* to make noise. Another chapter helps you figure out which part of your computer isn't working right. Plus, the very first chapter offers a few ego-boosting tips. Yes, you *can* upgrade and fix your computer by yourself.

Part II: The PC Parts You Can See (External Peripherals)

Here you find fix-it information on the parts of your PC that are in plain sight: your monitor, for example, as well as your printer, keyboard, and other stuff you have to wipe the dust off of every once in a while. Each chapter starts off with repair tips and — if the thing still doesn't work right — detailed instructions on how to yank parts out and stick in new ones.

Part III: The Stuff Hiding Inside Your PC

Your PC's more mysterious parts lurk inside its big case, hidden from sight. Tilt down the brim of your safari hat as you rummage through the inside of your PC to replace floppy drives, add memory chips, or add fun computer toys like read/write compact disc drives.

Part IV: Telling Your Computer What You've Done

If anybody's a dummy here, it's your computer. Even after you've stuck a new part in its craw, your computer often doesn't know that the part is there. This part of the book explains how to tell your computer that it has just received a new part and that it should start groping around for it.

Part V: The Part of Tens

Some information just drifts away when it's buried deep within a chapter, or even within a long paragraph. That's why these tidbits are stacked up in lists of ten (give or take a few items). Here, you find lists like "Ten Cheap Fixes to Try First," "Ten Ways to Empower an Aging Pentium," "The Ten Easiest Upgrades," and other fun factoids.

Icons Used in This Book

This book's most exceptional parts are marked by icons — little eye-catching pictures in the margins:

This icon warns of some ugly technical information lying by the side of the road. Feel free to drive right by. The information is probably just a more complex discussion of something already explained in the chapter.

Pounce on this icon whenever you see it. Chances are that it marks a helpful paragraph worthy of a stick-on note.

If you've forgotten what you were supposed to remember, keep an eye toward the margins for this icon.

Better be careful when doing stuff marked by this icon. In fact, it usually warns you about stuff you *shouldn't* be doing, like squirting WD-40 into your floppy drive.

Sometimes, computer parts don't live well together. Computer upgrades that sometimes lead to even *more* repairs or purchases are pegged with this icon.

Still pounding the keys on an ancient hand-me-down? Picked up a lumbering oldster at a garage sale? This icon flags specific fixes and tips for people stuck with those old monsters.

Auto mechanics can find the most helpful sections in their manuals by just looking for the greasiest pages. So, by all means, draw your own icons next to the stuff you find particularly helpful. Scrawl in some of your own observations as well.

Where to Go from Here

I'm not going to kid you. You won't be able to replace or fix *every* part in your PC. For example, most repair shops don't fix broken monitors or power supplies. Those items are just too complicated (and dangerous) to mess with. You almost always have to buy new ones.

Instead, this book tells you which parts of your PC you can fix *yourself* (most of them) and which parts are probably over your head. That way, you know which repairs you should parcel out to the technoweenies in the shop. You won't have to worry about attempting any repairs that are simply beyond your mortal abilities.

Finally, your path will be easier if you're briefly familiar with your PC. Thumb through Chapter 3 for basic explanations of your computer's parts, how they talk to each other, and how you can eavesdrop on their conversations to figure out what's going on.

Need more information about your Windows software? First, check out Chapter 17 for an analysis of Windows' built-in troubleshooting tools. If you need more basic information, pick up a copy of *Windows 98 For Dummies* or *Windows 95 For Dummies* (both written by me). They'll help you figure out when your problem lies with Windows — *not* with your computer.

Ready to go? Then grab this book and a screwdriver. Your computer's ready whenever you are. Good luck.

Part I
Biting Your
Fingernails

The 5th Wave   By Rich Tennant

"WHOA, HOLD THE PHONE! IT SAYS, 'THE ELECTRICITY COMING OUT OF A SURGE PROTECTOR IS GENERALLY CLEANER AND SAFER THAN THAT GOING INTO ONE, UNLESS—UN-LESSS— YOU ARE STANDING IN A BUCKET OF WATER.'"

In this part . . .

Excited about electrolytic capacitors?

All agog over Schottky Integrated Circuits?

Then back up and keep reading those two sentences. You won't find any words like that in the *rest* of this book.

Chapter 1

Are You Nerdy Enough to Do It Yourself?

In This Chapter

▶ Please do this *right now!*

▶ Computers are difficult to destroy

▶ PCs are easier to fix than cars

▶ Can you save money by upgrading instead of buying a new PC?

▶ PCs aren't as scary after you've fixed one

▶ When should you upgrade?

▶ When *shouldn't* you upgrade?

▶ What happens if parts don't work together?

Here's the secret: If you can open a bag of Chee-tos, then you can upgrade and repair your PC. You don't need to be a technoweenie with a vacant stare.

In fact, upgrading a PC is almost always easier than trying to use one. I know a guy who can turn a box of spare parts into a whole PC in less time than it takes to print a three-column page in WordPerfect.

Still not convinced? Then let this chapter serve as a little confidence booster. Remember, you don't *have* to be a computer wizard to upgrade or repair your PC.

Please Do This First!

Please, *please* make a Windows startup disk right now. If you wait until you need one, it will be too late. The Windows startup disk is your saving grace when Windows suddenly refuses to wake up.

When Windows stops working, insert the startup disk into your floppy drive and turn on your computer.

Windows loads itself from the startup disk, and you're able to access a variety of Windows settings. That helps you make the necessary tweaks to put Windows back on its feet. Before reading any further, follow these steps to create the startup disk, and we'll both be happier:

1. **Find an unused floppy disk.**

   Rummage through your spare floppy disk collection until you find one that's either blank or that contains files you no longer need.

2. **Click the Start button and choose Control Panel from the Settings option.**

3. **Double-click the Control Panel's Add/Remove Programs icon.**

4. **When the Add/Remove Programs window appears, click the tab labeled Startup Disk.**

5. **Click the Create Disk button and follow the directions.**

Windows grabs its important files and asks you to insert your floppy disk into drive A. (That's the only floppy disk drive available on most computers.) When you click the OK button, Windows copies those important files to your floppy.

Whew! Whenever your computer refuses to load Windows, insert the startup disk and restart your computer, and Windows 98 will load itself from that disk. (Although Windows 95 isn't savvy enough to load itself from the floppy disk, at least it starts your computer back up so that you or a computer guru can adjust its settings.)

You Probably Won't Kill Your PC by Accident

Are you afraid that you'll mess something up by removing your computer's case? Actually, there's very little that can go wrong. As long as you don't leave a dropped screw rolling around in your computer's innards, you don't have much to worry about. (And I tell you in Chapter 2 how to retrieve the dropped screw.)

Do safety concerns keep you from prodding around inside your PC? Not only is the computer safe from your fingers, but also your fingers are safe from your computer. After you unplug the beasts, computers are safer than an

unplugged blender. You're not going to get a Don King hairstyle by accidentally touching the wrong part. Besides, you can fix many of your computer's
problems without even taking off the case.

Are you afraid that you may accidentally put the wrong wire in the wrong
place? Don't worry about it. Most wires in your PC are color coded. You can
easily tell which wire goes where. The computer designers even catered to
groggy engineers: Most of the cables only fit into their plugs one way — the
right way.

If you can change a coffee filter (even one of those expensive, gold-plated
coffee filters), you can change the parts of your PC.

- ✔ The PC was designed to be *modular* — all the parts slip in and out of
  their own special areas. You can't accidentally install your hard drive
  where the power supply is supposed to go. Your hard drive simply won't
  fit. (Just to be sure, I tried it just now and it didn't work.)

- ✔ Although most computers suck 110 volts from a wall outlet — the same
  as any household appliance — they don't actually use that much electricity. A computer's power supply turns those volts into 3.3 or 5 volts,
  which is less than the amount some freebie Radio Shack flashlights use.
  This amount makes computers much less dangerous.

- ✔ Your PC won't explode if you install a part incorrectly; the PC just won't
  work. Although a computer that doesn't work can lead to serious head
  scratching, it won't lead to any head bandaging. Simply remove the
  misinstalled part and try installing it again from scratch. Then be careful
  to follow this book's step-by-step instructions. (And keep an eye out for
  the troubleshooting tips found in nearby paragraphs.)

- ✔ When IBM built its first PC microcomputer more than a decade ago, the
  engineers designed it to be thrown together quickly with common parts.
  It's still like that today. You can install most computer upgrades with just
  a screwdriver, and other parts snap in place just like expensive Lego
  blocks.

Just as wicked witches don't like water, computer chips are deathly afraid of
static electricity. A little static zap may scare you into dropping your pencil,
but that zap can be instant death for a computer chip. Be sure to touch something metal — the edge of a metal desk, a file cabinet, or even your PC's chassis — before touching anything inside your computer. Live in a particularly
static-prone environment? Some stores sell static-grounding straps: little
wrist bracelets that screw onto your PC's chassis to keep you grounded at all
times.

Shocking information about static electricity

People living in particularly static-prone areas need the greatest protection. To purge static electricity from your body before you reach your computer, buy a special *antistatic* floor mat to place in front of your work area. An antistatic mat may look like a plain old rubber mat, but it's made of special material that grabs the static electricity from your body and sends it running into the ground through a special wire. By the time you touch your computer, you're static free.

Although Radio Shack sells several antistatic mats, most of them are available only through special order. Check out Radio Shack part number 910-4888. It's a 3-inch-by-5-inch anti-static workstation mat that lies on the ground in front of your computer. Unfortunately, antistatic mats aren't cheap, and the Radio Shack model costs around $100.

To see a description of Radio Shack antistatic products, head to www.radioshack.com and search the product list for the word *antistatic*.

Upgrading a PC Beats Working on a Car

Forget about the mechanic's overalls; computers are *much* easier to work on than cars for several reasons. Ninety percent of the time, you can upgrade a PC by using a screwdriver from your kitchen's junk drawer. No need for expensive tools, protective gloves, or noisy wrenches. You don't even have to grunt, spit, or wipe your hands on your pants, unless you already do that stuff anyway.

Also, computer parts are easier to purchase than car parts. Every year, cars use a different kind of bumper or a new air filter. But, with a PC, many parts are the same. You can usually take a mouse off a friend's computer and plug it into your computer without any problem (unless your friend sees you doing it).

With PC repair, you never encounter any heavy lifting. And you never have to roll under your computer either, unless you're laptopping at the beach.

- If you have an old car, you're probably stuck buying parts from a hard-to-find garage in New Jersey. But, if you have an old computer, just grab a replacement part from one of a zillion computer stores, online stores, or mail-order shops. With a few rare exceptions, you don't have to search old IBM heaps for an '87 floppy drive for a TurboChunk 286.

- There aren't any pipes to drop bolts into, like I did when I foolishly tried to replace the carburetor on my '65 VW van. After watching the tow truck haul my car away, I decided to stick with PCs: Computers don't have any open pipes, they don't use bolts, and they smell much better than carburetor cleaner. Plus, PCs don't have as many moving parts to catch your sleeve and drag you perilously close to whirling gears.

✔ Here's one more difference: Car mechanics *repair* stuff. If something inside the engine breaks, the mechanic laboriously takes apart the engine, replaces the bad part with a good one, and laboriously puts the engine back together. But, with PCs, you *replace* stuff. If your PC's video card dies, throw it away and screw in a new one. Much less fuss. And it's almost always cheaper, too.

✔ Finally, you can often fix your PC without even opening the case. Some software automatically probes the innards of your computer, finds the culprits, and fixes them.

Can You Really Save Bundles of Money?

Many people think that they can build their own PCs from scratch and save a bundle. But it just doesn't work that way. Nobody can save money on a Corvette by picking up all the parts at the Chevy dealer's parts window and bolting them together. The same holds true for a PC.

Today's computer dealer buys zillions of parts at a bulk-rate discount, slaps 'em all together in the back room, and sticks the finished product in the store window 20 minutes later. Without all those bulk discounts on the parts, though, a self-made computer usually costs about as much as a brand-new one — often a little more.

Here's another twist. Most new computers come with the latest versions of software preinstalled. Buying all that software for your newly assembled PC adds several hundred dollars to the price tag.

✔ If your computer is so old that you want to replace *everything,* go for it. But replace everything by buying a *brand-new computer.* You save money and time, and you get free, up-to-date software and a new warranty tossed in. It's hard to beat that deal.

✔ It's almost always cheaper to *replace* a part than to *repair* it. Most repair shops charge upward of $75 an hour; a long repair job can cost more than the part itself. And many shops don't even bother trying to repair parts. It's cheaper (and easier) for the shops to just sell you new ones.

✔ So why bother upgrading your computer yourself? Because you can save cash on repair bills. Plus, your computer will be up and running more quickly: It won't be stuck in a backlogged repair shop while you're stuck with no computer. Horrors!

PCs Aren't As Scary After You've Fixed One

When I was a kid, my mom took the car into the shop because it made a strange rattling sound while she turned corners. My mom didn't have any idea what could be causing the problem. The car's rattles and pops *all* sounded scary and mysterious to her. The mechanic couldn't find anything wrong, though, so my mom took him on a test drive. Sure enough, when the car rounded a sharp corner, the rattling noise appeared. The mechanic cocked his ear for a few seconds and then opened the metal ashtray on the dashboard. He removed a round pebble and the sound at the same time.

My mom was embarrassed, of course. And, luckily, the auto shop didn't charge for the fix. But this anecdote proves a point: If my mom had known a little bit more about her car, the rattling sound wouldn't have been scary, and she could have saved herself a trip to the shop.

"So what's your point?" you ask. Well. . . .

✔ After you open your PC's case and see what's inside, your PC isn't as mysterious or scary to you. You see that it's just a collection of parts, like anything else.

✔ After you fiddle with a PC, you feel more confident about working with your computer and its software. Fiddling with PCs doesn't have to become a hobby, heaven forbid. But you won't be afraid that if you press the wrong key, the monitor will explode like it did on *Star Trek* last week (and come to think of it, the week before that, too).

✔ If you're going to bring small rocks back from the desert, put them in the glove compartment. They don't rattle as loudly in there.

When Should You Upgrade?

Your computer will tell you when you need to upgrade. You may have already seen some of the following warning signs:

✔ **When your operating system demands it:** Everybody's using the latest version of Windows, or at least that's what the folks at Microsoft say. And the latest version of Windows works best on one of those big, new, sporty computers with a sexy-sounding CPU (central processing unit), a big hard drive, and large smokestacks. If you want to upgrade to the latest operating system — Windows 2000 or the latest version of Windows 98 — then upgrade parts of your computer as well.

✔ **When you keep waiting for your PC to catch up:** You press a button and wait. And wait. Or if you're using Windows, you click on a button and watch the little hourglass sit on the screen. When you're working faster than your PC, it's time to give the little fellow a boost with some extra memory, a faster CPU, and maybe an accelerated video card. Of course, you'll want a bigger hard drive, too, making you wonder whether it's time to throw in the chips and buy a new computer.

✔ **When you can't afford a new computer:** When you're strapped for cash and can't afford a new computer, buy the parts one at a time. For example, add that additional memory now and add other parts a few months later when your credit card's not as anemic. Besides, prices fluctuate. Time your purchases to grab the lowest price tag.

✔ **When your old equipment becomes tired:** Is your mouse's arrow hopping across the screen? Are the keys on your keyboard stickingggg? Do your disk drives burp on your floppy disks? Is your old hard drive sending you weird messages? Does your computer leave cryptic greeting messages on the screen some mornings? If so, chances are that the parts are saying, "Replace me quick, before I pack my bags and take all your reports, spreadsheets, and high-game scores with me."

✔ **When you want a new part in a hurry:** Computer repair shops aren't nearly as slow as stereo repair shops. Still, do you really want to wait four days for them to install that hot new video card — especially when you have a nagging suspicion that you could do it yourself in less than 15 minutes?

Also, if you're buying your parts through the mail to save some bucks, count on sticking them inside the computer yourself: Mail-order parts don't come with a computer guru to install them.

✔ **When there's no room for new software:** When five people head to the restaurant in a single car, three friends cram into the back seat and ride with their knees in the air. Computer software can't be as neighborly. Each program stakes out its own portion of your computer's hard drive, and it doesn't share. When you run out of hard disk space for new programs, you have three options: 1) delete software you no longer use; 2) buy a hard disk big enough to hold all your programs comfortably; or 3) buy one of the many removable storage systems available to serve as a garage for spare files. (You can use some compression software to pack more software on a hard drive, but that's asking for trouble over the long term.)

When Shouldn't You Upgrade?

Sometimes, you shouldn't work on your computer yourself. Keep your hands away during any of the following circumstances:

- ✔ **When a computer part breaks while your computer is under warranty:** If your computer is under warranty, let *them* fix the part. In fact, fixing a part yourself may void the warranty on the rest of your computer.

- ✔ **When the dealer says, "I'll install the part for free within 15 minutes!"** Fifteen minutes? By all means, take the dealer up on the offer before he or she wises up and starts charging, like all the other dealers. (Make sure that you compare prices with other dealers, however; a higher-priced part may make up for the free installation.)

- ✔ **On a Friday:** Never try to install a new computer part on a Friday afternoon. When you discover that the widget needs a *left* bracket too, most repair shops will be closed, leaving you with a desktop full of detached parts until Monday morning.

- ✔ **When your computer is ancient:** Not all computers can be upgraded. If you're using an XT, AT, 386, or 486 computer (all described in Chapter 3), it's probably cheaper to buy a new computer than to sink more money into sinking ships. In fact, if you're thinking about upgrading a computer that's more than three years old, try this first: Total the amount of new equipment you need (a CPU upgrade, more memory, a bigger hard drive, a faster video card and monitor, a faster modem, a faster CD-ROM drive, and updated software) and compare it with the cost of a new computer. Chances are, a new computer can cost much less. (Chapter 26 describes how older computers can be salvaged or upgraded, if you don't have much cash.)

- ✔ **When you need your computer up and running within 90 minutes:** Just like kitchen remodeling, computer upgrading and repairing takes at least twice as long as you originally thought. Don't try to work on your computer under deadline pressure, or you'll wind up steam-cleaning your ears when your head explodes.

- ✔ **When you haven't optimized your computer's software:** Hey, your computer may not need expensive new hardware in order to run better. You may be able to run some "test and fix" software that ferrets out any software problems and fixes them for you. (Chapter 19 describes some of these.)

Beware of the Chain Reaction

One upgrade often leads to another. Like quarreling office workers, some computer parts refuse to work together — even though they're designed for *IBM-compatible* computers.

For example, you buy a modem, install it, and wonder why it doesn't work with the Internet. Then you discover that you need to sign up for an Internet *service,* which lets your modem talk to the Internet.

Luckily, Internet Service Providers *(ISPs)* are relatively cheap and easy to find these days. When you see the Chain Reaction icon in this book, be aware that you may have to buy yet another part before the upgrade will work.

- Chain reactions can pop up with just about any upgrade, unfortunately. For example, sometimes you have to replace *all* your memory chips rather than just plug in a few new ones, as you had hoped.

- None of this stuff is *your* fault, though. The same chain reaction can happen even if you let the folks at the repair shop upgrade your computer. The only difference is that you hear the sorry news over the phone, just like when the mechanic calls the office saying that you need a new radiator when you only took the car in for a new set of shocks. Yep, those are some shocks, all right.

- If a part doesn't work in your computer, you still have hope. You can almost always return computer parts for a refund just as though the parts were sweaters that didn't fit. If you don't feel like replacing all the incompatible parts, just take back your new part for a refund. As long as you return it within a reasonable amount of time and in good working order, you shouldn't have a problem. (As a precaution, however, always check the return policy before buying a part.)

Chapter 2

The Right Way to Fix Your PC

*W*hen I was a little kid, my sister and I met a guy who lived by the beach and liked to fiddle around with gadgets. One day, he cut the power cord off an old lamp and tied a big nail to the ends of each wire.

Then he stuck one nail in each end of a hot dog and plugged the cord back into the wall. Sure enough, the hot dog cooked. Sizzled, even, and made some sputtering sounds. But we didn't eat the hot dog. In fact, we kind of gave the guy a wide berth after that.

My sister and I knew there was a *right* way to do things and a *wrong* way. This chapter points out the difference between the two when you're working on your computer.

The Ten Steps for Upgrading Your PC

Those technodrones in the back room can charge you $75 an hour for re-placing a part, but they're merely following simple steps they learned at Computer School. Don't care for school and don't think you can flip to these pages when you need them? Then check out the handy Cheat Sheet at the front of this book. It summarizes these ten steps for easy reference:

1. **Back up your hard drive so that you don't lose any data.**

   Whenever you drop a new part into your PC, you run the risk of upsetting its stomach. Your PC probably won't wipe out any information on your hard drive for revenge, but wouldn't you feel like a dweeb if something *did* happen? Make sure that you have a backup copy of everything on your hard drive. Of course, you've been backing up your data every day, so this shouldn't be too much of a chore. (You *have* been backing up your data, haven't you?)

   If you're tired of copying everything to floppy disks, consider buying one of several types of *backup units*. They're special little gizmos that quickly and automatically record all your information on special computerized cassette tapes, disks, or even compact discs. Some can back up your hard drive automatically at the end of each day so that you don't have to remember anything. (Ready to install one? Then head to Chapter 13.)

2. **Read the instructions that come with the part.**

   After you tear open the box, look at the installation instructions. Chances are that the instructions booklet has a page in front labeled "At Least Read This Part." This page is for people who are too excited about their new computer part to wade through the boring manual.

   Next, look for any enclosed computer disks. Find one? Then stick it in your floppy drive and look for a file named README.TXT, README.COM, or something similar. Manufacturers often update their equipment more often than they update their manuals, so they stick the most up-to-date information on the floppy disk. (Double-click on the file's name from within the Windows My Computer or Windows Explorer programs to bring the file to the screen.)

   See any information that might come in handy down the road? Then write it down or print it. Otherwise, head for the next step.

3. **Find your Windows startup disk, exit any programs, turn off your PC, and unplug it from the wall.**

   Don't ever turn off your PC while it has a program on the screen. That's like plucking a kid off the merry-go-round before it stops turning — potentially dangerous and certainly hard on the ears.

   Then make sure that you exit any currently running programs — especially Windows. When Windows says that it's okay to turn off your computer, you can safely head for the off switch. Unplug the computer's power cord from the wall, too, to be extra cautious.

   Don't know how to turn off your computer in Windows 95 and Windows 98? Click the Start button and choose the Shut down button from the list that pops up. Then choose the button labeled Shut down or Shut down the computer to make Windows turn itself off.

Windows, a picky eater, sometimes refuses to come to the screen after being fed a new part. If that's the case, you want an official Windows startup disk, described later in this chapter.

4. **Clean off the counter space next to your computer.**

Dump the junk mail and shelve any stray floppy disks. You need an empty place to set stuff so that you don't have to stack things on top of each other.

Don't keep any liquids near your repair area where you can spill them into your case. A spilled beverage may not destroy your computer, but it certainly won't do it any good.

5. **Find your tools and put them next to the computer.**

After you start to install that new part, the adrenaline begins to flow. You don't want to lose momentum while hunting for a screwdriver, so make sure that all your tools are within reach. What tools? Check out the "What Tools Do You Need?" section, later in this chapter.

6. **Remove the cover of your PC.**

Older models require a screwdriver. You remove screws from the computer's sides or back. Cases from the newer models come off with your fingers: Unscrew the large round bolts holding the case in place. If you're lucky, the case slides off like butter on a hot pancake. Other times, the case sticks like gum under the table. Check this book's Cheat Sheet for more details.

Touch an unpainted part of the computer's case to discharge any static electricity that may have built up. This keeps static electricity from damaging your computer's sensitive internal parts. Consider buying a grounding wrist strap or mat from the computer store if you work in a static-electricity-prone environment.

7. **Pull out the old item and insert the new.**

You may want to take notes on a scratch pad so that you can remember which wires go where. Cables and plugs usually fit only one way, but you may feel more confident if you draw your own picture. (Feel free to take notes in this book as well.)

Have an instant or digital camera? Take a snapshot of the inside of your PC with its case freshly removed. A picture helps ensure that cables are replaced correctly.

8. **Plug in your computer and fire up the gizmo to see whether it works.**

What? Plug in the computer and turn it on when the case is *off?* Yes. Just don't touch anything inside the case, and you'll be safe. For example, if you replace a video card, you can check to make sure that you see stuff on your monitor when you turn on your computer.

If the new part works, head for Step 9. If it doesn't, turn the computer off, unplug it, and start troubleshooting. Perhaps you forgot to connect a cable. Or you may need to flip a switch somewhere, which I describe in Chapter 18.

9. **Unplug the computer and put the PC back together.**

Done? Then check to make sure that you don't have any leftover screws or, even worse, any leftover holes *without* screws. If a forgotten screw is wedged in the wrong place inside the case, your computer may fry like an electrocuted hot dog.

You can find tips on fishing out stubborn screws later in this chapter.

10. **Plug the PC back into the wall and give it a final test.**

The part's installed, the case is back on, and all the cables are plugged back in. Does the computer still work? *Whew.* If not, check the cables to make sure that you pushed them in all the way.

By carefully following these ten steps, you can avoid problems. The key is to proceed methodically, step-by-step. Not watching television at the same time can help, too.

What Tools Do You Need?

All the tools required to fix a PC can fit into a single pocket protector: A small Phillips screwdriver handles 80 percent of the operating-room chores, although a few other tools occasionally come in handy (like the plain old screwdriver in your fix-it drawer).

Feeling particularly sporty? Drop by a computer shop and pick up a computer toolkit. You get most of the tools mentioned in this section and a snazzy, zip-up black case to keep them in. Most kits cost less than $20.

Your computer's documentation

You *did* save all the documentation that came with your computer, didn't you? All that stuff with the fine print and weird drawings? Unfortunately, you may need that stuff when upgrading your PC. The documents describe the parts and model numbers of your PC's innards and how to fix certain things. Keep the manuals in a safe place, preferably sealed in a baggie. Even a receipt helps. It usually contains the model number and brands of your PC's components.

Can't find anything? Then head to your PC manufacturer's Web site. Sometimes your PC has a numbered sticker on the case. If you type the number into the manufacturer's Web site, the manufacturer will tell you that PC's vital statistics. Bought a Dell? Find the PC's serial number and head to www.dell.com for a list of your computer's parts and drivers. (It even tells you whether your PC's still under warranty.)

Small Phillips screwdriver

The Phillips screwdriver needs to be able to handle a screw that's the size of the one shown in Figure 2-1. (Phillips screwdrivers are the kind with the little square cross on their tip, not a flat blade.)

Itty-bitty flat-head screwdriver

Printer cables, monitor cables, and mouse tails all plug into the back of your PC. Some cables can be secured by turning a knob. Other cables have tiny screws to keep them from falling off their plugs. You need a screwdriver to handle screws the size of the one shown in Figure 2-2.

Medium Phillips screwdriver

Sometimes an overeager computer nerd will really bear down on the screws that hold on your computer's case. In that case, a slightly larger Phillips screwdriver can give you better leverage. Check out the size of the screws on your PC's case and shop accordingly.

Paper clip

Believe it or not, tiny elves design and build many computer parts. That's the reason the special switches, called *DIP switches,* are so small. A bent paper clip helps to move these switches back and forth. You often need to "flip a DIP" when adding a new part to your computer. The switches are really as small as they look in Figure 2-3.

You'll find a tiny hole on the front of many CD-ROM drives — a hole much smaller than the headphone jack. If the disc gets stuck, try pushing your bent paperclip into the hole. The hole serves as an Emergency Eject System that extracts stubborn compact discs.

Figure 2-1:
Most of the screws holding your PC together are this size.

Figure 2-2:
The screws holding your cables to the back of your computer are really this tiny.

Figure 2-3:
A bent paper clip comes in handy for flipping tiny switches like these.

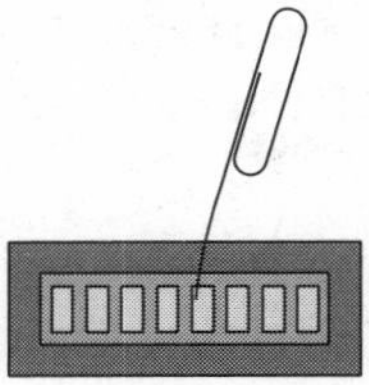

The Internet

A working knowledge of the Internet helps you work on your PC, no doubt about it. The Internet contains information posted by millions of PC users. And some of them have probably gone through the same problems you have. When something's wrong with a part, head to that part manufacturer's Web page. You'll often find a software patch to make things right again. Can't figure out what's wrong? Head for the Internet's newsgroups — there, groups of people post messages about their computer problems and how they solved them.

Diagnosing and fixing your computer through the Internet gets its due in Chapter 4.

Other handy tools

The following items aren't crucial, but feel free to pick them up if you spot them at a garage sale or a Pic 'n Save.

Small flashlight

Some stuff in your computer is jammed in pretty close together. A flashlight helps you read important labels or spot fallen screws. It also helps you read the labels on the back of your computer if it sits only a few inches from a wall.

Magnetized screwdriver

A magnetized screwdriver makes it easier to grab a fallen screw you've just spotted with the flashlight. Just touch the screw with the end of the screwdriver and gently lift it out when it sticks to the end of the screwdriver.

Anything with a magnet can wipe out information on your floppy disk. To avoid problems, don't keep your magnetized screwdriver near your work area. Just grab it when you need to fetch a dropped screw and then put it back on the other side of the room. (Compact discs don't have this problem, by the way.)

Empty egg carton

Most people use a spare coffee cup to hold screws. But an empty egg carton is more fun because you can put screws from different parts into different depressions. Forgetful people label each depression with that part's contents.

Compressed air canister

Your computer's fan constantly sucks in fresh air through your PC's vents. That means it's also sucking in dust, lint, and evil dust mites. PC repair geeks can instantly tell which PC owners have cats by simply looking at the layers of hair inside a PC's case. A cigarette smoker's computer looks even worse.

PC repair shops and art supply shops sell compressed air in canisters so that you can blow all the gross things out of the inside of your PC. Pranksters can also squirt coworkers in the back of the head when they're not looking.

Don't blow with your own breath on your PC's innards to remove dust. Although you're blowing air, you're also blowing moisture, which can be even worse for your PC than dust.

Every few months, pull off the dust balls that clog the air vent on the back of your PC. The cooler you can keep your PC, the longer it will last. (A vacuum cleaner helps here, too.)

Pencil and paper

A pad of paper and a pencil are handy for writing down part numbers — or writing angst-ridden poetry when things aren't going according to plan.

Spare computer parts

A spare-parts collection is something you can build up only over time. Repair shops are filled with extra computers and have stacks of parts lying around in boxes. If a part doesn't work in one computer, the repair person pulls out the part and tries it in another. Through the process of elimination, repair shops figure out which parts are bad.

You don't have that many boxes of parts. Yet. . . .

Making a "Startup," or "System," Disk

Any time you're working on a hard drive, you need a *startup disk,* also called a *system disk* or *boot disk.* Whenever you turn on your computer, it looks for hidden "Who, what, and where am I?" information stored on your hard drive.

If one of your floppy disks is sitting in the disk drive when you turn on your computer, Windows cannot find that hidden information and sends a message like this:

```
Non-System disk or disk error
Replace and press any key when ready
```

Your computer is saying that it couldn't find its hidden information on the floppy disk, so it gave up and stopped working. (Actually, the information was on the hard drive, but most computers are too lazy to look past the floppy.)

However, you can copy that important *system* information to a regular floppy disk. Then you can use that floppy disk to start up your computer, even if your hard drive is on the fritz.

Windows 95 and Windows 98 can create a special type of startup disk for fixing problems. To create one of these essential upgrade/fix tools, follow these steps:

1. **Insert a blank disk (or a disk with information you're trying to get rid of) into drive A and close its latch.**

   The latches usually close automatically on the 3½-inch disk drives. Make sure that the disk matches your floppy drive's capacity — either high or low. Finally, use only drive A. Your computer never bothers to look for its hidden information in drive B unless you make some bizarre internal setting changes.

2. **Click the Windows Start menu and choose Control Panel from the Settings menu.**

3. **Choose the Add/Remove Programs icon and click the Startup Disk tab from the window's top.**

4. **Click the Create Disk button and follow the instructions.**

   Now, twiddle your thumbs. Eventually, the computer wipes its hands on its pants and simply finishes — without telling you that it's finished.

5. **Remove the disk and use a felt-tip pen to write *System Disk* on the label.**

- Using more than one version of Windows? Then make a system disk for each operating system and write the Windows version on each disk. That way, you won't try to start your Windows 98 computer with a Windows 95 system disk.

- Now, if your computer refuses to start some cold morning, you have a weapon: Stick your system disk into drive A and press the computer's Reset button. Hopefully, that will get the computer back on the racetrack.

The Upgrade Do's and Donuts

Over the years, as hungry computer repair technicians swapped tales of occupational stress, they gradually created a list known as The Upgrade Do's and Donuts. The following tips have all been collected and placed here for quick retrieval.

Do upgrade one thing at a time

Even if you've just returned from the computer store with more memory, a CPU upgrade, a new hard drive, and a monitor, don't try to install them all at once. Install one part and make sure that it works before going on to the next part.

If you install all four parts at the same time and your computer doesn't work when you turn it on, you won't be able to figure out which particular part is gagging your computer.

Do watch out for static

You hear this warning several times because it's that important. Static electricity can destroy computer parts. That's why computer parts come packaged in those weird, silvery bags that reflect light like the visor on an astronaut's helmet. That high-tech plastic stuff absorbs any stray static before it zaps the part inside.

To make sure that you don't zap a computer part with static electricity, you must discharge yourself — no matter how gross that sounds — before starting to work on your computer. Touch a piece of bare metal, like the metal edge of your desk or chair, to ground yourself. You also must ground yourself each time you move your feet, especially when standing on carpet, wearing slippers, or after moving the cat back out of the way.

Do hang on to your old boxes, manuals, warranties, and receipts

When you're wrapping up your computer for a move down the street, nothing works better than its old boxes. I keep mine on the top shelf in the garage, just in case I'll be moving. Don't bother hanging on to the smaller boxes, though, like the ones that come with a video card or mouse.

Hang on to *all* your old manuals, even if you don't understand a word they say. Sometimes a new part starts arguing with an older part, and the manuals often have hints on which switch to flip to break up the fight. (You can find even more hints in Chapter 18.)

Don't force parts together

Everything in your PC is designed to fit into place smoothly and without too much of a fight. If something doesn't fit right, stop, scratch your head, and try again using a slightly different tactic.

When trying to plug your monitor's cord into the back of your computer, for example, look closely at the end of the cord and then scrutinize the plug where it's supposed to fit. See how the pins are shaped a certain way? See how the plug's shape differs on one side? Turn the plug until it lines up with its socket and push slowly but firmly. Sometimes it helps if you jiggle it back and forth slightly. Ask your spouse to tickle you gently.

Things that plug directly onto your motherboard seem to need the most force. Things that plug onto the outside of your PC, by contrast, slip on pretty easily. They also slip off pretty easily, so most of the cables have little screws to hold everything in place firmly.

Don't bend stuff that comes on cards

Many of your computer's internal organs are mounted on fiberglass boards. That's the reason there's a warning coming up right now.

Don't bend these boards, no matter how tempting. Bending the board can break the circuits subtly enough to damage the card. Worse yet, the cracks can be too small to see, so you may not know what went wrong.

If you hear little crackling sounds while you're doing something with a board — plugging it into a socket or plugging something into it — you're pushing the wrong way.

Don't use head-cleaning disks

Many new computer owners get head-cleaning disks from well-meaning relatives the following Christmas. Head-cleaning disks look like a regular floppy disk with rice paper inside. Head-cleaning disks are supposed to clean any dirt and oxide deposits from the heads on your floppy drives.

Unfortunately, the disks often do more harm than good. If your floppy drive isn't working, try a head-cleaning disk to see whether it fixes the problem. But don't use head-cleaning disks on a regular basis.

Don't rush yourself

Give yourself plenty of time. If you rush yourself or get nervous, you're much more likely to break something, which can cause even more nervousness.

Don't open up monitors or power supplies

There's nothing inside monitors or power supplies that you can repair. Also, the power supply stores up voltage, even when it's not plugged in.

Don't open your power supply or monitor. They can store electricity inside that may really zap you.

How to Fish Out Dropped Screws

When a screw falls into the inner reaches of your PC, it usually lands in a spot inaccessible to human fingers. The following should call it back home:

- Is it in plain sight? Try grabbing it with some long tweezers. If that doesn't work, wrap some tape, sticky-side out, around the end of a pencil or chopstick. With a few deft pokes, you may be able to snag it. A magnetized screwdriver can come in handy here as well. (Don't leave the magnetized screwdriver near your floppy disks, though; magnets can wipe out the information on them.)

- If you don't see the runaway screw, gently tilt the computer to one side and then the other. Hopefully, the screw will roll out in plain sight. If you can hear it roll, you can often discover what it's hiding behind.

- Still can't find it? Pick up the computer's case with both hands, gently turn it upside down, and tilt it from side to side. The screw should fall out.

✔ If you still can't find the screw and it's not making any noise, check the floor beneath the computer. Sometimes screws hide in the carpet, where only bare feet can find them.

Do not power up your computer until you can account for every screw!

Chapter 3

Where Does This Piece Go? (Basic Computer Anatomy)

*T*his no-nonsense chapter merely points out where your PC's parts live and what they're supposed to do. There's nothing "hands-on" in here and certainly nothing thought-provoking enough to share during dinner conversation. Instead, treat this chapter like a map to Disneyland — something kept in your back pocket but pulled out for reference if you get lost in Frontierland.

Oh, and just as most Disneyland visitors explore more than one of The Mouse's many lands, you may find yourself paging forward or backward through this chapter's many sections. That's because any confusing computer terms, like *CPU* or *motherboard,* get their own sections within this chapter, allowing for a more detailed explanation.

In fact, here's a tip: If you find yourself jumping around in this book to look up the definition of a confusing part, think twice: That particular part influences so many other pieces of your computer that it's probably too complicated or expensive to replace or repair.

Your Computer's Case

The guts of your PC live inside the case, which was almost always beige until a few years ago. Now some executives buy stylish black cases to match their leather chairs. Others buy chartreuse models with smooth lines. Work in the art department? Pop off the case (as described in the Cheat Sheet at the front of this book) and spray-paint it any color you like.

To find out more about your PC, head for the CPU section later in this chapter. It shows how to identify your PC's CPU, discover that CPU's characteristics, and find out whether the CPU can be upgraded.

A big, old, and beat-up case

Just as television sets have shrunk to fit in the dashboards of taxicabs, computers have shrunk, too. If you're stuck with an ancient computer in a huge case (and an ugly monitor that doesn't display color), don't bother upgrading that antique. Buying a new computer is cheaper.

Also, many old computers aren't Y2K compliant. That doesn't mean that they'll blow up or stop working. Usually, it means that they won't keep track of the date correctly. Some people can live with that, or find it to be only a minor annoyance. For others, it's intolerable: Not only are they now stuck with an ancient, slow computer, but also it can't even keep track of the day.

Even though the year 2000 began without major problems, Chapter 4 explains the steps to take to ensure that your computer keeps running without any Y2K problems.

Donate your old computers to charity. Although most charities don't accept anything less than a working 486 — with a working monitor — try making some phone calls to local schools or head to www.microweb.com/pepsite/ Recycle/recycle_index.html for a list of nonprofit groups in your area. The tax deduction may be worth it.

Small cases (also called small footprint)

Smaller than their predecessors, these cases sit flat on your desktop with the monitor on top, as shown in Figure 3-1. Although smaller, the cases hold just as many parts because today's parts have shrunk along with the cases. Any computer older than a Pentium usually lives in these cases.

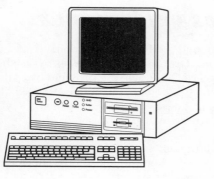

Figure 3-1: Older PCs come in long, flat cases, and the monitor usually rests on top.

Tower

Today, most computers stand up like a *tower* — a regular computer case that's been reconfigured to stand on its side (take a look at Figure 3-2). Tower cases take up less space, yet they're often a little roomier, so you can jam a few extra goodies inside. These cases are popular for Pentium-level computers.

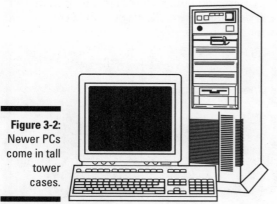

Figure 3-2: Newer PCs come in tall tower cases.

Want to buy and install a new *motherboard?* Buy a new case at the same time so that you know it will fit comfortably inside. Cases are cheap.

Computers stuffed inside monitors

Computer monitors are big enough. Add the computer itself, and you run out of either desk space or legroom. The Gateway Profile series, as shown in Figure 3-3, and the Packard Bell NEC Z1 solve the problem by building the computer inside the base of an *LCD monitor*. Introduced in 1999, the space-saving gadget works well on small desks. Plug the mouse and keyboard into the monitor's *USB* ports, and you're ready to go.

The new design looks pretty darn cool, but all that compactness bears the same problem as laptops: They're rather difficult to upgrade. Most rely on USB connections, and most computer parts still use *serial* ports.

The Gateway Profile series contains *PC card* slots for sliding in extra goodies. But you're never going to be able to upgrade these little tykes like a full-fledged computer.

The Gateway Astro stuffs the computer inside a regular monitor, making the computer easier to set up when removed from the box.

When ordering your new "all-in-one" computer, stock it up with as much power as you can. That's the only time you'll be able to upgrade it with such ease. After a few years, parts will be much more difficult to come by.

Figure 3-3: The Gateway Profile series packs all of a computer's internals into the monitor.

Case Buttons and Lights

Like a car's dashboard, the front of your computer's case comes with lights and buttons (but no coffee cup holder, unfortunately). Figure 3-4 and Figure 3-5 show various lights and buttons you may find on your particular model; they're all described in the following sections.

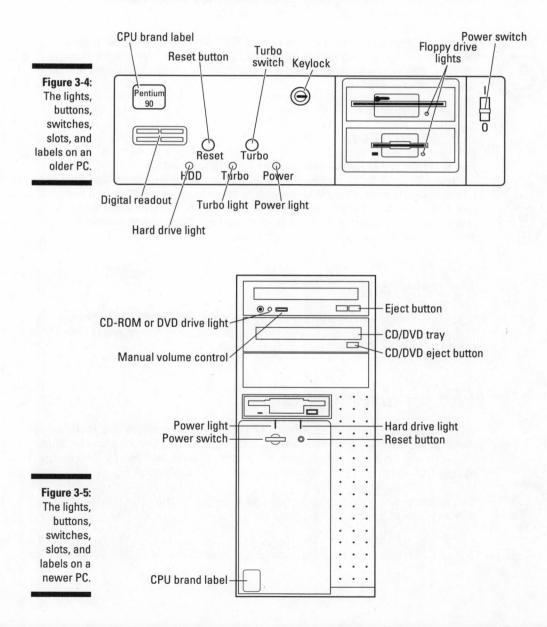

Figure 3-4: The lights, buttons, switches, slots, and labels on an older PC.

Figure 3-5: The lights, buttons, switches, slots, and labels on a newer PC.

Power button

Computers used to be turned on and off through a large, red toggle switch mounted on the back of a PC's case, where nobody could reach it. A few years later, some savvy engineers moved the power switch to the PC's side, which was one step better. After three more years had passed, a core group of designers broke new ground by mounting the switch on the computer's front, within easy reach.

The power switch is rarely labeled On or Off. Instead, a little line means On, and a little circle means Off. Many aren't labeled: If the power light is on, the PC's on. The savviest users listen to their PCs: The humming sound means On, and silence means Off.

Reset button

The reset button is one of the most frequently used buttons and gets the attention of a PC that's frozen solid. Unfortunately, when your PC comes back to life, it drops everything it was working on, which means that you can lose any work you didn't save to a file. Push the reset button only as a last resort. Stuck with a PC that *doesn't* have a reset button? Then you have to turn off your PC, wait 30 seconds, and turn it back on again.

Power light

Some power lights have a picture of a little light bulb next to them; others simply say Power. Either way, the light comes on when you turn on your PC. (And the light is off when the computer is off.)

Floppy drive lights

Floppy drives are those slots in front of your computer where you stuff floppy disks. Almost all floppy drives have a little green or yellow light on the front. The little light turns on when your computer reads or writes any information to the disk, making it easier to tell whether the drive's working.

Don't ever remove a floppy disk from its drive while the little light is still on, or else some of your data may vanish.

Hard drive light

Like their floppy cousins, *hard drives* also flip on their little lights when send-ing information to or from your computer's brain. Sometimes that light is labeled with letters like *HDD;* other computers use a little picture that looks like a can of beans.

If your hard drive's light isn't working, it's an easy fix. Head for Chapter 13 to learn which wires fell off and need to be reattached. (Floppy drive lights can't be repaired as easily, if at all.)

Compact disc or DVD light

When the light turns on, your computer's reading the disc. If the drive's spin-ning when the light's out, don't worry. The drive's spinning in case the com-puter wants to read parts of the disc again. If the computer doesn't read the disc within a few seconds, the disc stops spinning.

Plug your earphones into the little metal-lined hole in the front. Finally, twirl the little wheel to adjust the volume manually — in case you can't find the volume control in Windows.

Modems and network card lights

Network cards and modems, which live inside or outside your computer, also have little lights. A modem's lights blink when it's talking to distant comput-ers through the phone lines or cable. A network card's light blinks when it's talking to other computers on the network. (Networked computers usually aren't very far away from each other.)

Computers with internal modems and network cards force seekers of the lights to bend over and look behind their computers, where all the cables plug in.

Lock and key

The key doesn't start the computer. It doesn't even open a secret storage area in the case where you can find stashed snack foods. The key just disables the keyboard so that nobody can poke through your computer while you're at lunch. Don't feel bad if your key disappears a few months after you buy your computer. Most people lose their keys. Some keys merely lock the case, and many newer PCs have abandoned the "locking PC" concept altogether.

Your PC's Cables and Outlets

The front of a computer is pleasant and clean. A few sculptured air vents may add to the motif. The rear of an older computer, as shown in Figure 3-6, is an ugly conglomeration of twisted cables, plugs, and dust. A newer computer organizes its ports much better, as shown in Figure 3-7. You probably have to pull the PC away from the wall before you can see which cable protrudes from which hole.

Some people call these holes *ports*. Others call them *connectors* or even *jacks*. An older PC's rear should look something like the one shown in Figure 3-6. Newer PCs use a different arrangement like the one shown in Figure 3-7.

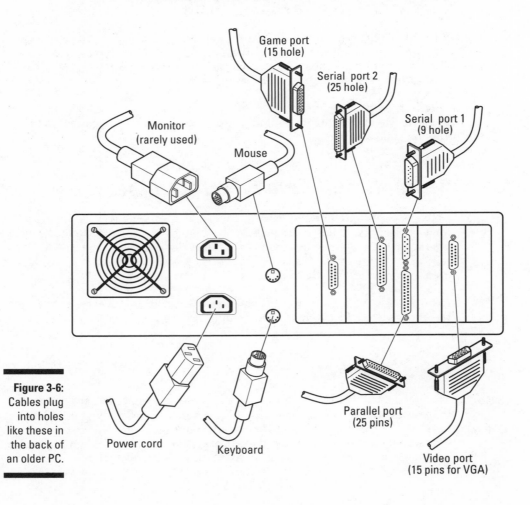

Figure 3-6:
Cables plug into holes like these in the back of an older PC.

Game port
(15 hole)

Serial port 2
(25 hole)

Serial port 1
(9 hole)

Monitor
(rarely used)

Mouse

Power cord

Keyboard

Parallel port
(25 pins)

Video port
(15 pins for VGA)

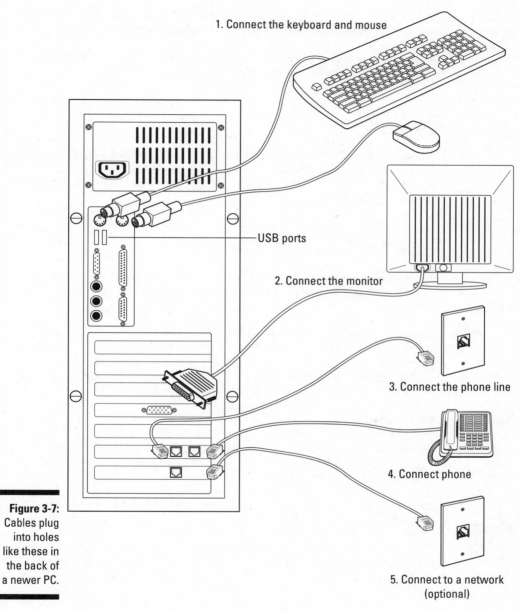

1. Connect the keyboard and mouse

USB ports

2. Connect the monitor

3. Connect the phone line

4. Connect phone

5. Connect to a network (optional)

Figure 3-7:
Cables plug
into holes
like these in
the back of
a newer PC.

It's normal for computers to have a few empty ports on the back. Not every port needs a cable in it in order for your computer to work.

All the cables that plug into the back of your PC fit only one way. If a cable doesn't seem to fit right, try turning it gently back and forth until it slips in.

The following sections show you what these plugs look like and examine what they're *doing* back there, anyway.

Power cord

The power cord almost always plugs into the big D-shaped connector with three pins in the back of your computer. (The power cord is usually the thickest cord coming out of your computer.) It looks like the picture shown in Figure 3-6 or Figure 3-7.

Keyboard and mouse ports

Your keyboard's cord plugs into a little round hole in the back of your computer. An occasional renegade computer has the keyboard hole on the side or even the front.

Your mouse cord plugs into a similar-looking hole called a *PS/2 port,* which is usually located right next to the keyboard port (refer to Figure 3-6 or Figure 3-7). Mouse cords can vary, though, so jump to the section "Mice, Scanners, and Modems," later in this chapter, for more on mice. (Mice actually get their own chapter, Chapter 6; keyboards are covered in Chapter 5.)

Most of today's new computers use identical-looking ports for both the keyboard and the mouse. Look carefully for labels, pictures, or color coding before plugging the keyboard or mouse connector into those two ports. Plugging them in the wrong way doesn't just keep your computer from working; it can fry sensitive parts.

Look carefully for a little raised-plastic line or bump on one side of the keyboard and mouse plugs. On most desktop computers, that little bump faces up, toward the top of the case, when you're plugging in the keyboard or the mouse. On a tower computer, however, the bump may point to the left or right. Look very closely and never force a connector into a port; it fits only one way, and that little mark signifies the correct way.

Serial port

See a little port on the back of your computer that has threatening little pins poking up from inside it? That's a serial port, and most computers have two. You'll find pictures of serial ports in Figures 3-6 and 3-7.

Serial ports are where you plug in cables connected to gizmos that feed the computer information — gizmos like modems, scanners, and even mice. Serial ports are extremely popular; dozens of gizmos want to use them. (Your computer can listen to only two serial ports at the same time, however, creating a bit of madness that's covered in Chapter 18.)

Some manuals refer to serial ports as COM ports. Manuals over the deep end call them RS-232 ports or even RS-232c ports. Nobody will guffaw if you just call yours a serial port, though.

Some gizmos living inside your computer can use a serial port without physically plugging into one. Internal modems are notorious for this practice and, therefore, cause much confusion and gnashing of teeth. My dentist made me add a special section about COM ports in Chapter 18.

Parallel port

Plug the cable from your *printer* into the thing that looks like the parallel port labeled in Figures 3-6 and 3-7. The end of the cable that looks like a grim robot's mouth plugs into your printer, and the end with little protruding pins plugs into your parallel port.

Computers can accept up to three parallel ports, but that rarely happens, for one reason: Each port requires an *interrupt,* a complicated concept described in Chapter 18. Your computer has a limited number of interrupts, and many other devices fight for them, too.

Is your parallel port bi?

For years, parallel ports simply shoveled information to the printer. Since the ports didn't do anything else, the engineers called them *standard parallel ports,* or SPPs. A few renegades called them a *Centronics interface,* named after the company that created the way computers talk to their printers.

A few years later, *bidirectional parallel ports* (BPP) became the rage. A bidirectional parallel port no longer simply shoveled information to the printer. Instead, the information flowed two ways. A printer could even tell the PC when it was low on paper. Taking the concept further,

people attached fancy portable hard drives, videocameras, portable MP3 players, and other goodies to the port and transferred data.

This concept worked so well that computer engineers created two new standards for bidirectional parallel ports: the EPP (enhanced parallel port) and ECP (extended capabilities port). Both toss data around ten times faster than the old standard.

ECP is the fastest, so choose it unless you have problems with it. How? You select ECP in your BIOS, a topic found in Chapter 10.

Game port

Sized midway between a parallel port and a serial port, a *game port* is where you plug in the joystick (refer to Figure 3-6 and Figure 3-7). Most sound cards come with game ports because gamers like to hear explosions.

You don't need two game ports to plug in two joysticks. Just buy a cheap Y adapter cable, usually sold at the same place where you buy computer games.

Also, most sound cards let your game port double as a *MIDI* port. By plugging a weird, boxy thing into your game port, you can plug in music synthesizers, drum machines, cool VG-8 guitar systems, and other things that let you sound like Brian Eno.

The latest sound cards turn your PC into a full-fledged recording studio for creating music. You'll find more about that in my music book, *MP3 For Dummies,* published by IDG Books Worldwide, Inc.

Not even Brian Eno cares that MIDI stands for Musical Instrument Digital Interface

Video port

Although it looks like a fat serial port, a video port is a connector for your *monitor.* Nothing but your monitor fits (unless you use a hammer). The most popular video ports, *VGA* or *SuperVGA* (SVGA), look like the ones shown in Figure 3-6 and Figure 3-7.

Some of those thin, cool-looking, "digital" LCD monitors need special video cards. Those cards have special video ports that accommodate the weird-looking plugs on the monitor's cable.

USB port

For years, computers communicated with the outside world mainly through their two serial ports and single parallel port (both described in the previous sections). But computers soon began talking to more and more things: digital cameras, gamepads, scanners, telephones, robotic toys, and digital joysticks, as well as the usual modems, keyboards, and mice.

When engineers noticed that the two serial ports and one parallel port simply weren't enough, they invented the Universal Serial Bus, or USB port. Most computers released since 1997 have one or two USB ports, as shown in Figure 3-7.

USB will eventually replace your keyboard port, parallel port, game port, and serial port. Instead, you plug one device into a USB port and chain the rest to the same port. For instance, you plug a USB keyboard into the USB port and plug your other USB parts into the keyboard.

It's fast, it's simple, and it has only one problem: It's taking a l-o-n-g time to gather support from manufacturers. Don't invest in an expensive USB part until you know that your system's up to snuff.

Windows 98 and Windows 2000 support USB ports. Windows NT, early versions of Windows 95, and Windows 3.11 or earlier don't support them. More information about USB awaits at www.usb.org.

Be on the watch for the *new* version of USB. Known as USB 2.0, it's compatible with the first version and uses the same connections. However, it's up to 40 times faster, allowing it to support high-performance video and other computer-strangling applications.

"Does my version of Windows 95 support USB?"

To check your Windows 95 computer for USB preparedness, download the Intel USB Evaluation Utility from www.usb.org/faq.html. This handy program determines whether your computer has a USB port, checks for a USB-compatible version of Windows 95, and looks to see whether the proper drivers — including the necessary USBSUPP.EXE file — are installed.

If the Intel utility says that you have a USB port but the wrong version of Windows 95, you're stuck. Only newer computers come with the USB-compatible version of Windows 95 known as 95B. You need Windows 98. (Right-click My Computer, choose Properties, and look under System to see which version of Windows 95 you're using.)

If you have a USB port and the 95B version of Windows but just need the USBSUPP.EXE file, dig out your Windows 95 installation CD. The necessary USBSUPP.EXE is in the OTHER\UPDATES directory, ready to be installed through your Control Panel's Add/Remove Programs utility. Although this Windows 95 trick usually works with most scanners and cameras, it doesn't always work with other USB devices.

Complicated? Yes; that's why most USB users upgrade to Windows 98.

Other ports

Other unidentified ports may peek out from the back of your computer. Some may be network interface cards, letting your computer socialize with other computers. (These look like either fat phone jacks or little metal tubes protruding about a half-inch from the back of your computer.) Other ports may be attached to sound cards, video-capture cards, or special cards that control compact disc drives. (Cards get their due in Chapter 15.) You may even spot a plain old phone jack that is resting on the end of an internal modem.

Older computers wear the marks of older, obsolete technology. Here's a rundown of what you may find on computers older than five years. Figure 3-6 shows what some of them look like.

✔ Many older computers have next to the power jack a second connector that looks almost like the power jack — only with three holes. Years ago, that's where monitors used to plug in to get their power. Today, almost all monitors plug into the wall, but the little connector remains to befuddle the curious.

✔ The old IBM PCs had a second port, identical to the keyboard port: Computer nerds would plug a tape recorder cord in there to store their files because floppy drives were too expensive.

✔ Does your ancient computer have a Turbo switch? Then keep it turned on to Turbo mode so that your computer runs at its fastest. (In the old days, people used the Toggle switch to slow down their computers when playing some action games.)

✔ The second serial port on older computers looks like a parallel port. But instead of holes, the port has pins. Need to plug in a cable with the smaller connector? Pick up an inexpensive adapter at Radio Shack or a computer store. It converts the small serial port to the larger type.

✔ Older monitors plug into ports with only nine holes, unlike the modern ports that have 15 holes.

✔ Having trouble plugging your keyboard's large plug into a newer computer's small outlet? Buy an adapter, available at most computer stores, so that the large plugs fit into the small round hole.

✔ Installed a new sound card in an older computer? The game port on the new sound card will probably argue with any previously installed game ports over who gets priority until you disable one of them. (Jump to the section about jumpers in Chapter 18.)

Keyboards

Keyboards come in zillions of different brands but four basic flavors:

The old XT-style keyboard: One of the oldest keyboards, this 83-key antique doesn't have any little lights on it, making it hard to tell whether you pressed your Caps Lock key.

The AT-style (standard) keyboard: The designers at IBM added little lights to this second-oldest keyboard, as shown in Figure 3-8. They also tossed in a separate numeric keypad on the right side. Some eccentric engineer also added an 84th key, called SysRq, that has never done anything but confuse people. IBM meant to use it for something revolutionary but then forgot which department had come up with the idea. Nobody has used the key since.

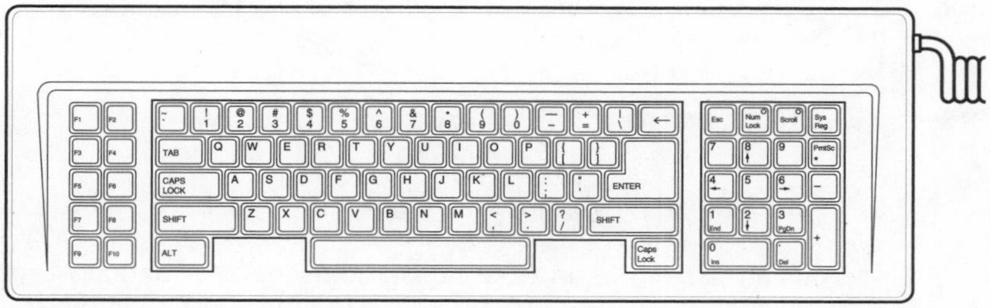

Figure 3-8:
A standard
AT keyboard
(84-key).

The 101-key (enhanced) keyboard: Easily the most popular keyboard today. Also known as the extended keyboard, the keyboard shown in Figure 3-9 has not only a separate numeric keypad but also a second set of cursor-control keys sitting between the keypad and the rest of the letters. It's the most popular of the four keyboard styles. Newer versions of this keyboard may also have Windows keys that function exclusively with Windows 95 and Windows 98. The additional three keys make this, technically, a 104-key keyboard.

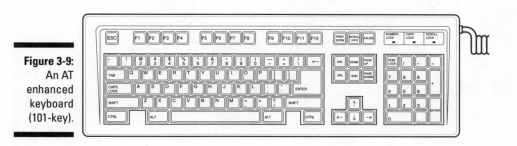

Figure 3-9:
An AT
enhanced
keyboard
(101-key).

The Microsoft Natural Keyboard: Also known as an *ergonomic* keyboard, the keyboard in Figure 3-10 adds a few twists — literally — on the 101-key keyboard. First, the keyboard is bent into a shape that some people find more comfortable for typing. Second, it comes with new function keys for special keystrokes in Windows.

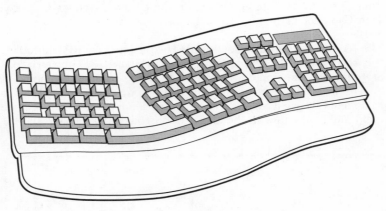

Figure 3-10: A Microsoft Natural keyboard.

If that's not enough keyboard information for you, here's a little more:

✔ You can use either an AT-style keyboard or an enhanced keyboard with your computer. But don't try to reuse your old XT keyboard — those guys used different types of wiring.

✔ The old XT-style keyboards don't work with anything but XTs. But here's a secret: Some manufacturers still sell one keyboard that can work with both types of computers. Check the bottom of your keyboard, and you may find a little switch. Flip the switch to the X side to use the keyboard with an XT computer, or flip the switch to the A side to use it with the AT-style computer. In fact, if your keyboard's not working, check for that little switch and make sure that it's turned the right way.

✔ Some expensive keyboards may have a *trackball* built in: By spinning the little ball, you make the arrow scoot across your screen. When the arrow points to the right button on the screen, click the little button next to the trackball. The button on the screen is selected, just as though you'd pushed it with an electronic finger. It's quick and sanitary and saves you the cost of a mouse.

✔ Notebook computers often use a *touchpad* or a tiny, pencil-eraser-looking device called a *Trackpoint* on their keyboards. The touchpad allows you to drag your fingertip across a small rectangular pad while the cursor mimics your finger's movements on the screen. The Trackpoint acts like a tiny joystick, giving your computer chores a PacMan-esque flavor.

That weird little ridge along the top of most keyboards isn't just there to look sporty. It's designed so you can prop a book against it, leaning it back toward your monitor. That makes copying stuff out of books much easier.

Looking for more ridges? Check out the F and J keys. You'll find little lumps on them, which makes it easier to reposition your fingers if you're typing in the dark. (By contrast, the Apple Macintosh places its keyboard ridges on the D and K keys, which is handy to know if you're playing a game of Stump the Nerd.)

Mice, Scanners, and Modems

Referred to as *input devices* by computer scientists, gizmos like mice, scanners, and modems feed information to your computer. For example, a mouse feeds the computer information about the movements of your hand, and a scanner feeds copies of images to your computer.

Mice

Like all things attached to PCs, mice come in several different breeds:

PS/2 style: Originally found on the older IBM PS/2 series of computers, the PS/2 style caught on quickly and is now used almost exclusively. The tail on a PS/2-style mouse plugs into a tiny, round port with seven holes. Because this breed of mouse doesn't need a serial port, it's easily the most popular mouse.

Serial mouse: The tail from a serial mouse plugs into one of your *serial ports*. Rare.

USB mouse: Computers have sported USB ports for several years, but USB mice are only now hitting the scene. Feel free to pick one up if your old one dies. Don't worry about using up your USB port, either. USB lets you string together more than 100 USB components — and they all still work!

Exotic species: A few other types of mice have hit the scene. For example, cordless mice come in handy for people who are tired of knocking papers off their desk with their mouse cord. Cordless mice not only are more expensive than their tailed counterparts, but they also eat up batteries.

✔ Some mice use feet rather than balls. When a normal mouse ball rolls around, it gathers dust, which rolls up into the mouse's guts. The little optomechanical feet on a "footed" mouse don't roll, so they don't flip dust and hair into any vital organs.

✔ A few people use optical mice, which use light beams to track their movement. Unfortunately, these mice use special, expensive mouse pads. Those fun mouse pads shaped like cows don't work with optical mice.

✔ Some people prefer *trackballs,* which I describe in the "Keyboards" section, later in this chapter. Others think that trackballs are as awkward as dental floss, especially the tiny ones that clip to the sides of laptops.

✔ The Microsoft IntelliMouse has a little spinning wheel mounted between the two buttons. (Windows 98 includes built-in support for the little critter.) Spinning the wheel with the index finger performs various onscreen acrobatics: A page moves up or down the screen, for instance, or your viewpoint into a picture zooms in and out. After you've grown used to one, you never want another.

✔ Some people prefer a *touchpad,* like those found on some notebook computers. This small, flat, rectangular device allows you to control the cursor by simply dragging your fingertip across the surface. You simulate a mouse click by tapping the pad surface. This device isn't for everybody, but it is an interesting alternative to the trackball.

Scanners

Cheap, handheld scanners look like *mice* with anvil heads, as you see in Figure 3-11.

Figure 3-11:
A handheld
scanner.

When you slide the scanner over letters or pictures, the scanner sends a copy of the image to your computer screen, where it can be saved as a file (much to the consternation of copyright attorneys around the world).

Special software lines up the strips of scanned images to produce the full page. Although they work well for people with small desktops and tiny budgets, they're not as efficient as the full-page models.

Who really cares how many buttons a mouse has?

Although mice come in two- and three-button models, few software packages require a three-button mouse. The old version of Windows, Windows 3.1, used mostly one button. Windows 95, Windows 98, and Windows NT use both mouse buttons extensively.

The three-button mouse seems to be a dying breed, so don't feel cheated if your mouse has only two buttons. (Just don't try to use a Macintosh mouse. It has only one button, and it doesn't work with *any* version of Windows.)

The more expensive, flatbed scanners look a little bit like copy machines: You put your paper on top of the glass, shut the door over it, and click the mouse over the right button in the scanner's software to send a copy into the depths of your computer.

Scanners usually come with their own *cards;* plug the card inside your computer and plug the scanner's cord into the card. Most scanners can reproduce color pictures; price depends on picture quality. Handheld scanners often fight against *modems* for available *serial ports;* full-page scanners often use the more expensive and complicated *SCSI cards* instead. Buying a new scanner? Buy a USB model. They're much easier to install.

The latest breed of scanners often comes with *optical character recognition* (OCR) software. That fancy name simply means that the software examines the picture of the scanned-in page and "types" the text into your computer as letters and words. Spell-checker software completes the capture by locating — and fixing — any botched scans.

Modems

These little boxes let your computer connect to the telephone line so that you can call up other computers, meet friends from around the world, and share photos of your cats. You can also grab the news, check the weather, examine stock reports, and swap weird stories about weird people doing weird things. Modems are the '90s equivalent of the '50s shortwave radio, but you don't need a towering network of nerdy antennas that embarrass your neighbors.

Plus, the modem lets you connect to the Internet, a television/card catalog of information, including words, sound, pictures, and video. The engineers are still working out the standards for broadcasting smells.

Like *mice* and *scanners,* external modems plug into *serial ports,* where they're easy to reach and use. An external modem is shown in Figure 3-12.

Figure 3-12:
An external
modem.

Internal modems live inside your computer on little *cards,* where they're hidden from view, which makes them more difficult to control. Actually, internal modems are easy to install but notoriously difficult to set up, especially if your computer's already hooked up to a mouse or a scanner. Most newer computers avoid these difficulties by allowing more than one device to share the same resources (IRQ, DMA, and so on). (Chapter 18 is waiting to explain those acronyms.)

When piecing through boxes of old computer parts for a cheap old internal modem to use with Windows, make sure that the modem uses a 16550AFN UART chip. (You can read the label on the top of the chip.) Slower chips often can't keep up with the heavy-duty data flow.

Most of today's modems can send faxes of information that's already inside your computer. That makes it easy to fax party fliers you've created in your word processor, but impossible to send that newspaper clipping that you know Jerry would get a kick out of. (You need a scanner for that.)

Monitors

A computer monitor may look like a TV, but it's nowhere near as repairable. In fact, you'll probably buy a new monitor after you hear how much money the shop wants to fix the old one. Monitors come in several styles, with the most expensive being the biggest, clearest, and most colorful.

Here are the basic types of monitors:

Hercules, Color Graphics Adapter (CGA), Enhanced Graphics Adapter (EGA): These are the older types of monitors and graphics cards that you want to upgrade because everything on them looks so grainy. Plus, the colors are pretty awful, especially after you've seen a better-quality monitor in the store.

Video Graphics Array (VGA): The industry workhorse of the early '90s, this type of monitor still works well with Windows. It often needs at least a *16-bit or PCI video card* that requires a *16-bit or PCI slot,* so this type of monitor doesn't always work in an XT.

Super Video Graphics Array (SVGA): This type of monitor packs more colors and images onto the same size screen and has replaced VGA as the norm. If you want to watch movies in Windows, you want an SVGA card and monitor.

Extended Graphics Adapter (XGA), 8514/A: This expensive monitor is mostly for high-end (expensive) graphics work.

LCD: Yank the screen off a laptop and put it on an adjustable base, and you have an LCD monitor. Easy to read and space savers, these also cost too much. That's why everybody's not buying them. In five years, they'll replace those regular, "TV" monitors.

LCD monitors come in two flavors: digital and analog. Digital LCD monitors require a special video card; analog models often don't (and they usually have blurrier screens). Also, a 15-inch LCD monitor displays as much information as a 17-inch old-style monitor.

Beware: Your monitor displays only what your computer's *video card* has sent. The two work as a team. That's why it's best to buy your monitor and video card at the same time to make sure that they work well together.

TV sets don't work very well as monitors. They simply lack the resolution, as you discover if you press your nose against the TV screen and then against your monitor. Some fancy video cards let you watch TV on a computer monitor, though.

You can skip buying a computer altogether and opt for WebTV. It's a box, costing much less than a computer, that lets you visit the Internet on your TV set. Unfortunately, that's about *all* it can do. It's not a computer. Plus, the resolution isn't very good, so you can't fit as much information on the screen.

Some gadgets *do* let you use a TV set as a monitor. Known as *VGA-to-NTSC adapters,* they're used mostly for corporate presentations or rabid video gamers. Although these adapters work well for displaying graphics and videos, most of the text is illegible. Chapter 8 dishes up more information.

Because today's software slings lots of graphics onto the screen, 3D and 2D video accelerator cards are the rage. The computer's brain, the *CPU,* was designed to crunch numbers, not to create onscreen cartoon worlds of tennis-playing bananas. To ease the workload, accelerator cards come with built-in graphics chips that help the CPU sling pictures around. Many of these special cards require an *Accelerated Graphics Port* (AGP) that speeds up the graphics.

Printers

Printers take the information from your screen and stick it on paper. They accomplish this feat in a wide variety of ways. Several types of printers use different methods, as described next.

Dot-matrix: One of the noisiest printers, this dying breed creates images by pressing tiny dots against the paper. They're inexpensive, and it shows. Old-timers dump their dot-matrix printers when they break and buy an inkjet or laser printer instead. (Windows still supports dot-matrix printers, but not all programs do. For example, the Fed Ex software for sending packages can't use some old dot-matrix printers because they don't print sharp enough images to create bar codes.)

Daisywheel: These printers are the noisiest by far, and they work like a type-writer, pushing little letters and numbers against a ribbon to leave images on the page. A dying breed, they're found most often in thrift shops. Upgrades? You can just replace the ribbon and add little *wheels* to get different styles of letters. Forget about graphics, though; these can work only like robot-driven typewriters.

Thermal: Pick up a pack of special heat-sensitive paper, or else these won't work. They print by heating up letter-size areas on the paper to create words. Often used by calculators and portable printers, their paper is prone to fades and curls.

Inkjet: Popular for their low price and high quality, inkjet printers squirt ink onto a page, which leads to a surprisingly high-quality image — often in color (see Figure 3-13). You need to replace the ink cartridges every once in a while, which can drain the wallet. However, these printers can be the best buy for the buck.

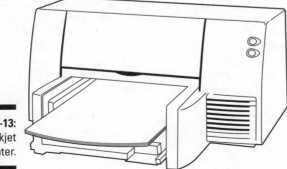

Figure 3-13:
An inkjet
printer.

Bubble-jet: Canon developed this type of inkjet printer, which uses heat to "erupt" the ink onto the page in finely controlled areas. It's very similar in quality to other inkjet printers.

Laser: Laser printers, like the one shown in Figure 3-14, sound dangerous, but their lasers are tiny things buried deep inside. In fact, these printers use the same technology as copy machines — *good* copy machines. You can't find much to upgrade here, although some laser printers let you put more memory into them. With more memory, they can print more graphics on a single page. Eventually, you have to replace the toner cartridge, a job easily handled on your desktop.

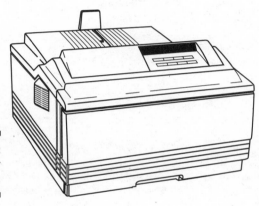

Figure 3-14:
A laser printer.

You can find tips for changing ribbons and cartridges in Chapter 9.

If you have a digital camera, be sure to buy one of the best inkjet or laser printers you can afford, and make sure that it can print in near-photo quality on high-quality paper.

The Sweet Art company in Olathe, Kansas, sells an expensive printer that copies pictures from your computer's screen onto cakes using colored edible icing. The printer also squirts pictures onto cookies and cupcakes.

The Motherboard

Some people call a motherboard a *system board,* but they're the same thing — a sheet of olive green or brown fiberglass that lines one side of your computer's *case.* A typical Pentium motherboard with its parts labeled is shown in Figure 3-15.

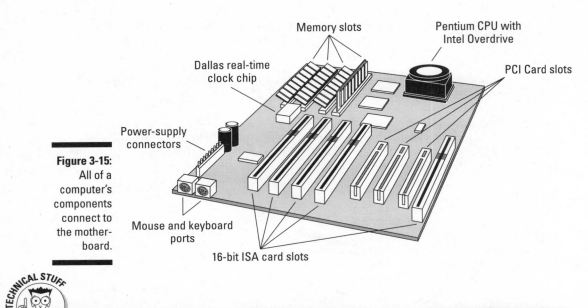

Memory slots

Pentium CPU with
Intel Overdrive

PCI Card slots

Dallas real-time
clock chip

Power-supply
connectors

Figure 3-15:
All of a
computer's
components
connect to
the mother-
board.

Mouse and keyboard
ports

16-bit ISA card slots

PCL and PostScript perplexity

For years, the Cadillac of laser printers was a *PostScript* printer. That meant the printer used the PostScript page-description language — a special way for printers to stick graphics and letters on a page. With PostScript, printers can shrink or enlarge graphics and fonts without creating the jagged edges left by cheaper printers. Desktop publishers quickly embraced the high quality, as did most software programmers.

Plus, a file saved in *PostScript format* can be taken to most professional typesetters, who also use PostScript technology on their mucho-expensive printers. Presto! The Gardening Club Newsletter suddenly looks like a magazine.

Unfortunately, such high class comes at a high price. PostScript printers can cost much more than their competition.

To accommodate the budget-minded crowd, the Hewlett-Packard LaserJet series of printers

provides an alternative, dubbed *PCL: Printer Control Language*. Because not every computer user needs the versatility of PostScript, PCL has grabbed an ever-increasing niche. Today, most laser printers are either "PostScript compatible" or "LaserJet/PCL compatible."

So, which one should you buy? If you do lots of high-end graphics work or desktop publishing, spend the extra money for PostScript. It's more versatile, and the pages look better. If you print mostly text or charts, with a few graphics on the side, PCL printers work fine. Or, if you can't make up your mind, do what I did: Buy a laser printer that can switch between both PostScript *and* PCL modes. The big problem is making sure that you've selected the right printer driver from your program or from the Windows Control Panel before telling the software to print.

By itself, a motherboard is like an empty plate. The important stuff lives on top of the motherboard. The motherboard then acts as a roadway of sorts, pushing information back and forth between all the following residents.

Difficult to repair, ailing motherboards must be replaced — a topic found in Chapter 10.

Your computer's brain: Its CPU

Your computer's brain is its *central processing unit,* or *CPU* (pronounced "see pee you") — a little chip that shovels information back and forth among all your computer's parts. Even though CPUs are small parts of your computer, they're one of the most expensive, often costing hundreds of dollars.

Very old CPUs are named by numbers: 286, 386, or 486. The latest computers get odd names like Pentiums, Xeons, Celerons, AMDs, or Cyrix, which sounds like an experimental vodka.

Actually, CPUs get two descriptors. The first is the model number or name (486, Pentium, or AMD, for example), which measures power or how big a shovelful of information the CPU can move around. The second is the chip's speed in megahertz (90 MHz, 266 MHz, 500 MHz, or 700 MHz, for example), which measures how fast it can sling around those shovelfuls of information.

The different models of PCs described in the next few sections help you identify the beast you've been tapping on. Plus, you discover how (and if) you can give your particular model a little more zip by replacing its internal organs.

Intel advertises its CPU chips on TV the most, so they're listed first. Intel's competitors come next.

A PC's name comes from the name of its brain, or CPU, and the speed of its brain, measured in megahertz, or MHz. For example, a 400 MHz Celeron computer holds a Celeron CPU that runs at 400 MHz.

Don't buy just any old cheap computer at a garage sale, thinking that you can add a new CPU and create a screamer. Computers bearing the names XT, AT, PC*jr*, PS/2, 386, or 486 should be left on the lawn.

Want to know whether your computer's outlived its days? Check out Chapter 26. If your computer's more than five years old, you'll find it described there — in this book's equivalent of the computer junkyard. (At least you'll know what — if any — parts can be salvaged.

Some specially designed motherboards let you pull out the old Pentium CPU and insert a new, faster Pentium chip. Often known as OverDrive chips, these quick-and-easy upgrades get more coverage in Chapter 10.

Here are some fun CPU facts: Most chips are rated by the number of "million hours" they're supposed to last. (One million hours is about 114 years, by the way.) When chips die, it's often because of dust particles that fell into the chip while it was being cooked up on the manufacturing line. With so many tiny wires and electrical passages packed into a little chip, a single dust particle is like a tree falling across a freeway. There's no highway patrolman to stop traffic and pull the tree off the road, so the chip just stops working.

"How do I know what CPU I have?"

Don't bother removing the case. Windows helps identify your CPU when you right-click on the My Computer icon and choose Properties.

A window appears, as shown in the following figure, listing three important things: your version of Windows, the version's registered owner, and your CPU, identified by manufacturer and type. Plus, Windows tosses in the amount of RAM in your system — a helpful tidbit for upgraders.

One caveat: Windows 95, Windows 98, and Windows 98 Second Edition often mistakenly list "Intel Pentium II" when your computer's *really* running a Pentium III or Celeron CPU.

Most CPU makers offer software on their Web sites that identifies the CPU inside your system. Finally, to be extra sure, check your computer's BIOS to identify a CPU: Turn on your computer and press whatever keys are necessary to enter the Setup area. When the BIOS screen arrives, the first page usually identifies the CPU.

System Properties ? X

| General | Device Manager | Hardware Profiles | Performance |

System:
Microsoft Windows 98
4.10.1998

Registered to:
Andy Rathbone

Computer:
GenuineIntel
Pentium(r) Pro Processor
64.0MB RAM

OK   Cancel

What is this CPU socket and slot stuff?

CPUs on the first IBM-compatible PCs lived in a socket on your computer's motherboard, described later in this section. Little pins in the bottom of the CPU fit into little holes in the socket, letting the CPU communicate with the rest of the computer. But as CPU technology advanced, the CPUs needed more pins, requiring larger sockets. Over the years, PCs have used at least eight socket types.

Finally, with the growing needs of its powerful Pentium II, Intel abandoned the socket approach and patented a special slot approach. The CPU lived inside a case that slipped into a special slot on the motherboard. Today's PCs use at least two types of slots.

Overdrive or upgradable CPUs are designed to plug into the same type of socket as the CPU they're replacing. That's why it's important to make sure that you're buying the right upgrade CPU for your system. Otherwise, it won't fit.

Intel abandoned socket 7 when it moved to its patented slot system, hoping to discourage competitors. Competitors stuck with socket 7 for many years because of its versatility: That socket can house either a Pentium, Pentium MMX, AMD K5, AMD K6-2, Cyrix 6x86, or Cyrix 6x86MX. Unfortunately, you need to know all this stuff when buying motherboards, CPUs, and CPU upgrades.

Intel Pentium (1993)

Identifying characteristics: Intel launched a whirlwind media campaign for the Pentium and forced computer makers to stick an Intel Inside stamp on a Pentium computer's case. Beneath the Intel Inside logo sits the word *Pentium*.

After creating the Pentium CPU, Intel created several more powerful models based on the Pentium. Don't confuse the plain old Pentium with the Pentium MMX, Pentium Pro, Pentium II, or Pentium III, described in the next few paragraphs.

Why you should care: Pentiums are slow, and the early versions run almost as hot as waffle irons. (That makes laptop users uncomfortable.)

Upgradability: Three companies let you pop out the old, slow Pentium and replace it with a newer, faster chip for added pep and vigor: Intel, with its Overdrive chips (www.intel.com); Kingston Technology, with its TurboChips (www.kingston.com); and Evergreen Technologies (www.evertech.com) all sell replacement chips for compatible systems.

Socket: 7

Upgrading your computer with a CPU that's twice as fast doesn't make your computer work twice as fast. Your computer's speed comes from a combination of many things: Its hard drive, video card, memory, and motherboard work together. Any one of these components can slow down the entire computer.

Some Pentiums, like the one shown in Figure 3-16, come with the initials MMX tacked on. Although the initials don't mean anything, techies refer to the letters as being "multimedia extensions." Why? Because CPUs with MMX technology contain special codes to speed up graphics. Everybody liked it. So, all future Pentium-level CPUs contained MMX codes built-in. (All of them except for the Pentium Pro, that is.)

Figure 3-16:
Pentiums
with the
initials MMX
have special
graphics-
handling
abilities.
(Photo cour-
tesy of Intel
Corporation)

Intel Pentium Pro (1995)

Identifying characteristics: Unfortunately, the Intel Inside logo labels these CPUs as ordinary Pentiums. Look for the word *Pro* included somewhere in the manufacturer's model name. The Pentium Pro and the Pentium CPUs both lie flat on the motherboard.

Why you should care: Intel optimized the Pentium Pro for Windows NT — the software running mostly on corporate networks and *servers* — computers that dish out information to other computers simultaneously. In fact, it doesn't really add much of a boost to computers still running Windows 95 or Windows 98. It contains some built-in memory called a *cache* that speeds things up.

Upgradability: The latest Intel Overdrive chip (www.intel.com) transforms your computer into a Pentium II. Kingston Technology (www.kingston.com) and Evergreen Technologies (www.evertech.com) both sell replacement chips. Pop out the old CPU and replace it with the new one to add some extra pep and vigor.

Socket: 8

Intel Pentium II (1997)

Identifying characteristics: Whereas earlier chips lay flat on the mother-board like a dropped cracker, the Pentium II comes enclosed in a miniature card that plugs into a slot on the motherboard, as shown in Figure 3-17. The chips often hide beneath bulky cooling devices, so check the Intel Inside logo for the words *Pentium II* to be sure.

The Pentium II's little card is called an SEC, short for Single Edge Cartridge.

Why you should care: The Pentium II is a Pentium Pro with the Intel MMX multimedia goodies tacked on. That makes it a natural for motion video and 3D images.

Upgradability: Intel hasn't announced any Overdrive products for a Pentium II, but the Evergreen Technology (www.evertech.com) Performa series claims to double the speed of some older Pentium IIs, allowing them to run Windows 2000. And no, you can't yank your Pentium II and replace it with a newer CPU, like the Xeon, Celeron, or Pentium III.

Slot: 1

Figure 3-17: Starting a new trend, the Intel Pentium II fits in a casing that plugs into a slot and sits upright on the mother-board. (Photo courtesy of Intel Corporation)

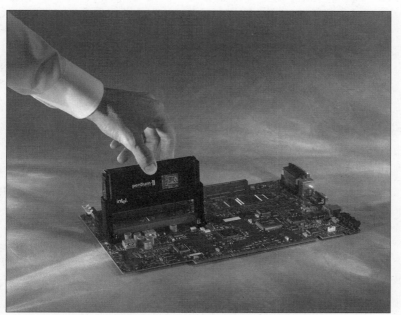

Intel Pentium II Xeon (1998)

Identifying characteristics: The flashy Intel Inside logo spells out the name of its trademarked CPU.

Why you should care: Intel designed the speedy Pentium II Xeon for the business market, where corporations can link together as many as eight CPUs. This makes for not only some powerful data processing but also exciting computer games during lunch breaks. These chips gain much of their power from extra memory — a RAM *cache* — built directly into the chip.

Upgradability: Don't bother upgrading these CPUs. They're probably the fastest part of your computer.

Slot: 2

Intel Pentium II Celeron (1998)

Identifying characteristics: The Intel Inside logos simply say "Celeron," without any mention on the front of the computer's case. The latest of these CPUs is simply called Celeron, without the Pentium II moniker.

Why you should care: The Xeon CPUs, described previously, cost too much. So, Intel decreased the built-in memory — the *cache* — from the CPU and called it a Celeron. It's not quite as fast as its brethren Pentium IIs, but hey, it's cheap enough to make up for it.

Upgradability: Don't bother. Pentium IIs are still plenty fast. Intel dropped the words *Pentium II* and now just calls these CPUs "Celeron."

Slot: 1 for the first models. When slots became too expensive for cheap machines, Intel went back to sockets; new Celerons use Socket 370.

Intel Pentium III and Pentium III Xeon (1999)

Identifying characteristics: Look for the Intel Inside sticker on the computer's front side, as shown in Figure 3-18. Intel usually refers to the Pentium III as a "Pentium !!!" to make everybody both excited and confused.

Why you should care: Intel added more multimedia circuitry to the Pentium II, sped it up, stamped each one with an individual identifying serial number, and called it a Pentium III. The Pentium III Xeon works just like its Pentium II little brother, but it has the extra multimedia circuitry, extra speed, and serial number (see Figure 3-19). Xeons provide power for workstations, but at a high, corporate-level price.

Figure 3-18: The Intel Inside logo, here from a Pentium III, tells owners what CPUs live inside their computers. (Photo courtesy of Intel Corporation)

Figure 3-19: The Intel Pentium III Xeon. (Photo courtesy of Intel Corporation)

Upgradability: Don't bother upgrading. Pentium IIIs are still top notch.

Slot for Pentium III: 1

Slot for Pentium III Xeon: 2

"Can hackers find my Pentium III's secret code?"

In a startling development, Intel added an individual serial number to every Pentium III CPU. Why the Big Brother stuff? Intel thought that the serial number would help identify computers during online shopping, help preserve Internet security, and let people identify stolen computers.

Consumers saw the secret computer code as a blatant invasion of their privacy. In response to the uproar, Intel shipped its CPUs with the serial numbers disabled.

The number still sits inside the CPU, however, even though its tracking mechanism is turned off. To make sure that your Pentium's serial number is disabled, head to your Pentium III's BIOS and make sure that the serial number is listed as Disabled. If the number isn't disabled through your BIOS, malicious hackers can steal it while you're online.

You'll find more about the BIOS listed in Chapter 10.

Intel Itanium (2000)

Identifying characteristics: The Intel Itanium is a biggie for Intel, breaking new ground. You won't miss the TV commercials, blimps, and freebie toys at fast-food restaurants. It even has an exciting new sticker for the computer, as shown in Figure 3-20.

Figure 3-20: The Itanium is the fastest Intel CPU yet.

Why you should care: Whereas the Pentium Pro, Pentium II, and Pentium III chips hail from the same family, the Itanium breaks new ground. Simply put, its mouth is twice as big, letting it move stuff around in bigger chunks. That makes it faster and more powerful.

Its mouth is twice as big? Well, computerized information must pass through a CPU to be processed. Earlier Pentiums processed information in 32-bit chunks. The Itanium processes information in 64-bit chunks — twice the amount, making it faster than its predecessors.

Upgradability: This is the top of the Intel line, so there's nothing to upgrade.

Slot: M (Yep, the Itanium wants its own, newly designed slot.)

AMD K5 (1996)

Identifying characteristics: Check your computer's BIOS to identify these CPUs. Windows often ends up scratching its head.

Why you should care: Designed to run like the Intel *Pentium,* these chips drop into the socket normally designed for a Pentium, providing a cheaper alternative. Since the chips run so hot (temperature wise), AMD rethought the design and created the popular K6.

Upgradability: In theory, you can replace this CPU with the K6, described next, to beef it up. To be practical, though, your motherboard often complicates matters. Some motherboards can handle a faster CPU and accommodate its power needs; others can't. Pull out your motherboard's manual to check its limits. If the motherboard supports a faster CPU, you still may need to update the BIOS (see Chapter 10). Also, some slow motherboards will accept the K6 CPU, but won't run at its fastest speed, limiting its effectiveness.

Socket: 7

AMD stands for Advanced Micro Devices.

AMD K6 (1997)

Identifying characteristics: Look at the CPU itself, as shown in Figure 3-21, check your computer's BIOS, or run the AMD CPU identifying software found on the www.AMD.com Web page.

Why you should care: Designed for serious competition with the Intel Pentium II, the AMD K6 CPU supports MMX multimedia codes for faster graphics and boasts enough memory for powerful performance.

Figure 3-21:
The AMD K6
competes
head-to-
head with
the Intel
Pentium II.
(Courtesy of
AMD)

Upgradability:. Head for your motherboard's Web page. If your motherboard has the correct voltage and BIOS support, the K6-2 or K6-3 microprocessor (described next) should slip right in. Since those CPUs prefer different sockets, however, you can't use all their new features. Also, if you're running an early version of Windows 95, upgrade with all the Windows 95 Service packs on the Microsoft Web page (www.microsoft.com).

Socket: 7

AMD K6-2 (1998)

Identifying characteristics: Your best guess comes from looking at the top of the CPU itself. If it's already installed, check your computer's BIOS or run the AMD CPU identifying software found on the www.AMD.com Web page.

Why you should care: Like its predecessor, this chip handles the Intel MMX fast-graphics technology, but it's faster and cheaper. Compaq snapped it up for its home-based systems, like the Presario. Best yet, this CPU added even more graphics whoop-dee-doo with its 3D-Now! technology. It won't replace your 3-D graphics board, but the two work together for the fastest multimedia applications.

Upgradability: This CPU, as shown in Figure 3-22, runs plenty *fast*. Think about upgrading your computer's video board or adding more memory before replacing the CPU.

Slot: Super 7

The AMD Super 7 adds support for AGP (Accelerated Graphics Port) and the faster, 100 MHz bus. It requires a special, Super 7 motherboard.

Figure 3-22:
The AMD
K6-2 han-
dles speedy
graphics,
moves data
quickly,
and is
inexpensive.
(Courtesy of
AMD)

AMD K6-3 (1999)

Identifying characteristics: Check your receipt or the top of the CPU, if you can see it. If it's already installed, check your computer's BIOS or run the AMD CPU identifying software found on the www.AMD.com Web page.

Why you should care: Designed to compete against the Pentium III, the AMD chip runs even faster — at a cheaper price. Like its K6-2 predecessor, the K6-3 (shown in Figure 3-23) uses the AMD 3DNow! technology.

Upgradability: None to speak of. The AMD Athlon, described next, doesn't work in this CPU's Super 7 socket.

Slot: Super 7

Figure 3-23:
The AMD
K6-3 com-
petes with
the Intel
Pentium III
by providing
faster
speeds and
a lower
price.
(Courtesy of
AMD)

AMD Athlon (1999)

Identifying characteristics: Check your receipt. If you don't trust the receipt, check your computer's BIOS or run the AMD CPU identifying software found on the www.AMD.com Web page.

Why you should care: In the race to create the fastest CPU in the world, AMD created the Athlon, as shown in Figure 3-24.

Upgradability: It's top of the line, so there's nothing to upgrade it with — yet.

Slot: Slot A

Figure 3-24: The AMD Athlon fits into a slot, like the top-of-the-line Pentium IIIs. (Courtesy of AMD)

To incorporate even more features into its CPUs, AMD ditched its Super 7 socket and copied the mechanics of the Intel Slot 1 motherboards. Although the slots look the same, they use different electrical connections. This allows AMD to weasel past the patented Intel slot design and expand the available circuitry for its CPUs.

Cyrix 6x86 (1995)

Identifying characteristics: Check the CPU itself or your computer's BIOS.

Why you should care: The first Pentium-compatible CPU to hit the shelves, it costs too much, runs too hot, and can't handle math as well as its competitors. That means it flops with math-intensive programs and gamers who need the math required for high-powered computer games.

Upgradability: It uses the popular Slot 7, so check your motherboard's manual to see what other chips it can take.

Slot: 7

Cyrix 6x86MX or M2 (1997)

Identifying characteristics: Check the CPU itself or your computer's BIOS.

Why you should care: Cyrix added multimedia enhancements to its earlier CPU to create this chip, designed to compete against the multimedia-packed CPUs from the Pentium MMX series and the AMD K6. Unfortunately, it didn't do as well as its competition. In fact, AMD's popularity relegated Cyrix to second best. Taiwan's Via Technologies, Inc., bought out Cyrix in early 1999, so the company might make a comeback — especially with its upcoming "Joshua" CPU.

Upgradability: It uses the popular Slot 7, so check your motherboard's manual to see what other chips it can take.

Slot: 7

Transmeta Crusoe (2000)

Identifying characteristics: Bursting from a shroud of secrecy at a jumbo computer trade show, the Transmeta Corporation unveiled its low-power, software-enhanced CPU that's compatible with the Intel breed of chips.

Why you should care: Transmeta touts three big features. The CPU doesn't need much power, and it runs cooler. It adjusts its power consumption based on its task, raising the level when you're crunching numbers and lowering the level when you're staring at a crossword puzzle. Plus, it's compatible with Intel chips. So what? That means it's designed mainly for laptops that need to conserve power.

Upgradability: You can't pull out your old Intel or AMD CPU, pop in a Transmeta model, and own the trendiest new computer. These will make their entrance in computers designed specially for the Crusoe CPU.

Slot: These newsters require their own, specially designed motherboards.

Math coprocessor

The math coprocessor, a chip like the *CPU,* acts as a calculator of sorts. It pipes up with quick answers to math questions, like that wiseguy in Mrs. Jackson's class. By listening to the math coprocessor's answers, the CPU can work more quickly.

For years, coprocessors were optional because they only sped up math problems: Most people don't calculate logarithms too often. Now, all Pentium-level CPUs come with built-in math coprocessor circuitry, so you don't have to worry about whether you need it.

Upgrading a notebook or laptop computer

Many notebook computers are surprisingly upgradable. If the manufacturer doesn't offer any upgrades, head for the Internet and start searching. Plenty of mail-order shops sell additional RAM, batteries, and other laptop essentials. Of course, notebook upgrades usually cost much more than the desktop-size equivalents.

Another way to upgrade your notebook is to add *PC cards* — little credit-card-size cards that slide into special slots on a notebook. Today, extra memory, hard drive space, modems, sound synthesizers, and even digital cameras all come on those little PC cards, which slide into the side of the laptop like an ATM card (see Figure 3-25).

Figure 3-25: A PC card inserted into a notebook computer.

PC card components still cost more than their desktop equivalents, although the prices are dropping quickly.

Unfortunately, it's almost impossible to upgrade the CPU in a laptop or notebook computer.

PC cards used to be called PCMCIA cards, which stands for Personal Computer Memory Card International Association.

BIOS

If the *CPU* can be described as the computer's brain, then the BIOS can be called its nervous system. Short for Basic Input/Output System, the BIOS handles computing chores in the background, kind of like our nervous system keeps us breathing, even when we forget to.

The BIOS handles the bare grunt work of a PC: how *floppy disks* grab data or what happens when you press a key on the *keyboard:*

✔ The BIOS comes written on a special little chip or chips, called *ROM* chips, that live on the motherboard of all IBM-compatible computers. When you first turn on your computer, you see which company's bunch of nerds wrote your computer's BIOS and in what year. For example, American Megatrends, Inc., wrote the information for my Pentium Pro 200.

✔ Why should you care? Well, an older BIOS sometimes can't handle a newer product (or vice versa). That often means that you need to buy new BIOS chips (which are often difficult to locate), or you can bite the bullet and buy a new motherboard, complete with already upgraded BIOS chips.

✔ There's a third option. Some newer computers come with upgradable BIOS chips. Just pop in the new BIOS software, and the program copies the new BIOS to the old chips. The software can often be downloaded for free from the Internet.

✔ Today, it's more important than ever to check your BIOS. Some BIOS chips can't handle the changeover from 1999 to 2000 correctly. (That Y2K thing is covered in Chapter 26.) Also, some can't handle today's large hard drives on the market.

✔ The BIOS works jointly with your computer's CMOS — hashed out in Chapter 18.

✔ If your BIOS can't be upgraded, either by replacing the chip or using special Flash software, you're out of luck. You're better off buying a new computer. To see whether your BIOS is upgradable, check your computer's manual or the Web site of the computer's manufacturer. Still no luck? Then watch the BIOS version number as the computer boots up. Head to the BIOS maker's Web page for possible upgrade solutions.

Expansion slots and cards

A motherboard has a little row of parking spaces called *slots*. The slots are for little computer gadgets that come on *cards*. Together, they make upgrades a breeze: Pop off the computer's case, push a card into an empty slot, fasten down the card with a single screw, and stick the case back on.

Cards look like miniature motherboards — daughterboards, so to speak. Such a simple design has to have a problem, however: Those slots and cards come in several different sizes and styles. The right-size card needs to be matched up with the right-size slot. Here's the rundown on the slots probably living inside your Pentium-level computer:

A 16-bit *ISA (Industry Standard Architecture)* card has two little tabs protruding from its bottom that match up with the two little slots it fits into, as shown in Figure 3-26. (Any card that says *16* in its name — SoundBlaster 16, for example — probably needs a 16-bit slot.) A 16-bit ISA slot sits in a row with your other card's slots. The workhorses of the industry for many years, 16-bit ISA cards are slowly being replaced by PCI cards, described next.

Quick identifier: Sixteen-bit slots are almost always black.

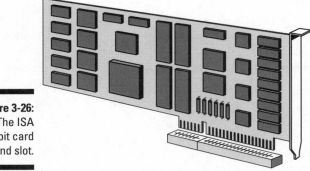

Figure 3-26:
The ISA
16-bit card
and slot.

A *PCI (Peripheral Component Interconnect)* card also has two little tabs protruding from its bottom, as shown in Figure 3-27. How do you tell it apart from a 16-bit ISA card? First, the PCI card's tabs are almost half as long and are set a bit farther back on the card. Second, the slots are set back a little farther from the motherboard's edge. (Check out Figure 3-15 to see how the two slots differ in size.) Speedy PCI cards and slots let Pentiums fling information around as quickly as possible.

Quick identifier: PCI slots are almost always white.

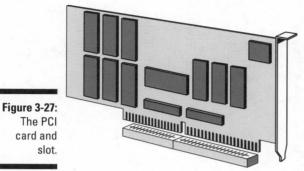

Figure 3-27:
The PCI
card and
slot.

An *AGP (Accelerated Graphics Port)* was designed by Intel for fancy graphics cards. This card outperforms PCI slots for graphics, allowing more speed and realism for games and multimedia programs without slowing down the rest of the computer.

Quick identifier: AGP slots are brown and smaller than the others. Computers have only one AGP slot by design.

Don't be confused by other slots on your motherboard — they're not all expansion slots. Expansion slots sit together in a large row. A single large slot is usually for a newer CPU, like the Pentium II, Pentium III, or Athlon. Also, memory chips come on cards that slide into slots, but those slots are much thinner. The memory cards are rarely more than one inch tall.

✔ Computer gurus refer to the row of slots as your computer's *expansion bus.*

✔ Some people refer to cards as *boards,* but they're both the same thing: little goodies that slide inside your computer to make it more fun.

✔ Before shopping for cards, peek inside your computer's case (or its manual) to see what sort of slots live on its expansion bus. Not all cards work in all types of slots.

Your computer's expansion bus shuttles information between the cards and your computer's CPU. A 16-bit slot can send information along a bigger roadway than its 8-bit slot predecessor, so it's faster. PCI slots are 32-bits, so they're even faster. AGP slots are the fastest, but they work only for graphics.

Remembering all this card stuff can be as tough as remembering whether a straight flush beats a full house at poker. So, Table 3-1 explains the name of the cards and their slots and the pros and cons of each variety as well as its compatibility level and identifying characteristics. Still confused about which cards your computer contains? Check out the dates when the card was used.

Table 3-1   The Card Table

Card Name and Slot	Era and Pros/Cons	Compatibility	Identifying Characteristics and Its Slot
ISA 8-bit (Industry Standard Architecture)	1982–1988; designed for the original XT PCs, it slowly became replaced by more powerful models.	This slot accepts only 8-bit ISA cards; an 8-bit ISA card fits into a 16-bit slot.	A single protruding tab on the card fits into a single black slot. Rare except for very old computers.
ISA 16-bit	1984–today; designed for the AT (286), this slot moved information around much more quickly than it had been before.	This slot accepts 8-bit and 16-bit cards.	Commonly found today, its two protruding tabs fit into a long, black slot (refer to Figure 3-26).
EISA (Enhanced Industry Standard Architecture)	1988; designed for some 386 and 486 computers, this technology never caught on. It requires special software to set up the cards.	This slot accepts 8-bit, 16-bit, and EISA cards.	Rare except in ancient Compaq models, these have two protruding tabs, like 16-bit cards, but both tabs have funny notches in them.
MCA (Micro Channel Architecture)	1987; designed by IBM for its PS/2 386 and 486 computers, this technology died quickly. It wasn't compatible with older technologies.	These slots only accept MCA cards, and the cards only work in MCA slots.	If new cards won't work in your old IBM PS/2 computer, you probably have MCA slots. Bummer.
VESA Local Bus (Video Electronics Standards Association)	1992; a special group of video techies created this standard to speed up graphics. It died when the PCI slots arrived.	VESA cards work only in VESA slots. The slots also accept 8-bit and 16-bit cards, though.	Rare. This card looks like a 16-bit ISA card, but it has another notched tab protruding near its back end.

Card Name and Slot	Era and Pros/Cons	Compatibility	Identifying Characteristics and Its Slot
PCI (Peripheral Component Interconnect)	1992–today; Intel and other techies created this competing standard that's still commonly used.	PCI cards work only in PCI slots and vice versa. Computers now use mostly PCI slots but toss in an occasional 16-bit slot for the oldsters.	These slots are usually white; 16-bit slots are black. PCI cards have two tabs but are much smaller than the 16-bit cards (see Figure 3-27).
AGP (Accelerated Graphics Port)	1997; Intel and other techies created this port for speedy video cards. It's very common today.	Only AGP cards work in AGP slots and vice versa.	Look for a single, small, brown slot sitting farther back than the other slots.
CPU slots	1999; the newest CPUs no longer rest flat on the motherboard. They're attached to cards that slide into slots.	Each type of CPU requires its own special slot. Nothing else fits into the slot.	This long slot sits by itself away from the rows of other slots. This isn't for expansion cards, it's only for CPUs.
Memory	In the early 1980s, memory chips came fastened to a small card for easy insertion.	Only memory cards fit into their own, specially designed slots.	Slots for memory cards are thinner than expansion slots.

What cards does your computer have?

Get this: Several of those *ports* you plug cables into at the back of your computer are actually cards. They're the *tail ends* of cards, as you see when you open your computer case for the first time.

In fact, your computer probably came with these cards already inside:

Video card: Your monitor plugs into this one. This card tells it what to put on the screen. Newer computers use AGP cards to plug into the special AGP slot. Some video cards also sport a cable TV jack for displaying television stations on your monitor. (Many even capture TV shows for later playback, too, provided your hard drive is large enough to handle the file.)

Sound card: Does your computer have speakers? Then they plug into your computer's sound card. Most sound cards include a *game port* for plugging in the joystick or gamepad as well.

These other cards sometimes pop up inside computers as well:

Modem card: See a phone jack or two on one of the cards? That's probably an internal modem card. The telephone line plugs into one, and a telephone plugs into the other. (Look closely to see whether the jacks are labeled — the cords can't go into the wrong jacks.)

Network card: An option for many years, many new computers now come with this card preinstalled. By routing cables from card to card, computers can talk to each other, sharing files and messages. Network cards usually have one or two ports: One may be a little tube sticking out, and the other looks like a wide phone jack.

Controller card: See a card with *no* visible jacks on an older computer? Older computers used a controller card to talk with your disk drives. Cables connected the card to the drive. Today, the controller electronics come built into the motherboard. The cables plug directly from the drive into the motherboard.

I/O card: This is a fancy name for the card with your *serial port* and *parallel port*. Newer computers skip this card and build the port circuitry right on the motherboard, along with ports for your *mouse, keyboard,* and *USB*. That leaves more open slots for plugging in other goodies. Ports built on a motherboard simply stick out the back of the computer's case, ready for their cables.

Battery

Believe it or not, your PC has a battery, just like your smoke detector. The battery sits on the *motherboard* and usually lasts more than three years. Most batteries are easy to replace. You'll know that yours has died if your computer loses track of time, asks you what time it is, or forgets what type of *hard drive* you own and then refuses to operate. You can find out the sorry symptoms (and battery replacement instructions) in Chapter 10.

Memory (Random Access Memory, or RAM)

If you've talked to people about your computer problems, you've probably seen them rub their jaws, narrow their eyes, and say, "Sounds like you might need more memory." Adding more memory is one of the most popular upgrades today. It's also one of the cheapest and easiest upgrades, depending on the friendliness of your computer.

When your computer's *CPU* is telling all your computer's parts what to do, it doesn't have a scratch pad for taking notes. So the CPU stores its information in your computer's memory. The more memory the computer has to work with, the more complicated stuff it can do. And the faster that memory can move information around, the less time you spend waiting for your computer to catch up with your work.

If you're using Windows — and just about everybody is these days — you can probably use more memory. The question is, what kind? Computers complicate matters by using different types of memory.

No matter what type of memory your computer uses, it comes on *chips,* just like your CPU. Just as CPUs are rated by their power and speed, memory chips are rated by their storage and speed. (You can find more about this in Chapter 11.)

Although all the memory serves the same purpose, it comes in several different packages. How do you know which type you need? Your motherboard holds the answer. Memory chips plug into different-size sockets, so be sure to choose the memory that fits into your motherboard. Here's a rundown on the types of memory your motherboard holds:

DIP: *(Dual In-line Package)* Era: Early '80s. DIP stands for *dual in-line package,* but everybody just calls it DIP. (This DIP is no relation to DIP switches, which are little rows of switches you can flip on or off.) DIPs look like antennaless cockroaches, as shown in Figure 3-28. These chips plug into sockets straight on the motherboard, where they lie down in neat little rows like graves. Some old video cards used this memory as well.

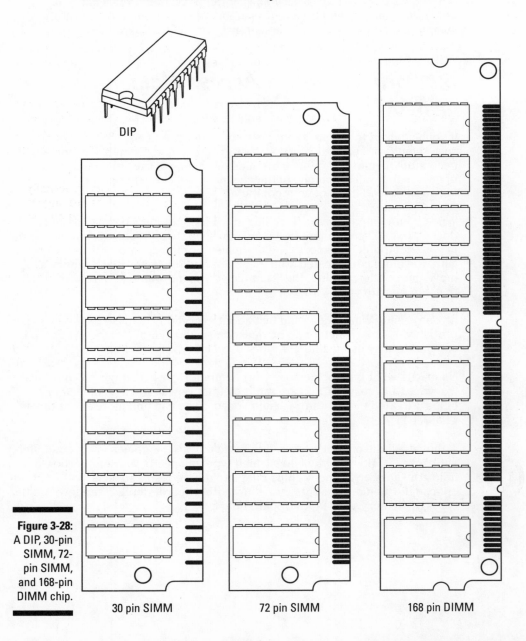

Figure 3-28:
A DIP, 30-pin SIMM, 72-pin SIMM, and 168-pin DIMM chip.

DIP

30 pin SIMM　　　　　72 pin SIMM　　　　　168 pin DIMM

SIP: *(Single In-line Package)* Era: Early '80s. A SIP is pretty much like a SIMM: a tiny little card with a bunch of DIPs on it. But whereas a SIMM has a long flat edge that pushes into a slot, a SIP has a bunch of little prongs that push into a bunch of little holes. It looks kind of like a cat's flea comb. Hardly anybody sells replacements, so if yours go bad, you're out of luck.

SIMM: *(Single In-line Memory Module)* DIPs and SIPS worked fine for years, except for two things: People kept breaking off their little legs when trying to push them into their sockets. Plus, because they lie flat on the motherboard, the chips hogged up too much room. So, some spry engineer took a leftover strip of fiberglass from a motherboard, fastened the little DIP chips to it, and called it a SIMM.

SIMMs come in two sizes, and each size requires a different-size socket. Pre-Pentium computers use the smaller size, which has 30 pins and holds comparatively small amounts of memory: 1MB, 2MB, or 4MB. Later computers use a 72-pin SIMM, bringing larger RAM capacities of 8MB, 16MB, 32MB, 64MB, or more. Both sizes are shown in Figure 3-28.

Don't confuse a memory bank's slots with *expansion slots.* They're actually very different: The SIMM's slots are tiny things; expansion slots are huge in comparison, as shown in Figure 3-15. There's no way to get slapped by accidentally putting the wrong one in the wrong place.

SIMMs come in several varieties. Some have three DIP chips on them; others have eight or nine. Don't mix varieties if you can help it. In fact, some computers won't run if you try to mix.

DIMM: *(Dual In-line Memory Modules)* To meet the increased memory demands of newer Pentiums, designers created DIMMs. With 168 pins, the powerful DIMMs resemble larger SIMMs, as shown in Figure 3-28. (That's why DIMMs cost more and work only in special, custom-designed DIMM slots; regular SIMM slots won't do.)

Although SIMMs must be used in pairs, DIMMs can be used singly. Both types slide or snap into their own tiny slots.

If you're not sure what kind of memory you have, count your number of slots, pluck out your chips, put them in a plastic baggie, and bring them to the memory chip store. The person in the T-shirt behind the counter can then sell you the right kind (and perhaps buy back some of the old stuff that won't fit anymore when you add the newer chips).

Rambling about types of RAM (and ROM)

For the most part, you're not breaking any computer etiquette rules when you say, "I need some more RAM for my computer." But here are the nerdy distinctions:

SRAM (Static Random Access Memory) is fast and expensive. Little snippets of SRAM live in a special place on your motherboard. Whenever the CPU dishes out information to a computer part, it sends a copy of that information to the SRAM. If any computer parts ask for the same information, the CPU just grabs it from the SRAM and dishes it out again, saving time.

DRAM (Dynamic Random Access Memory) is slower than SRAM but a little cheaper. When people say that you need more RAM, they're talking about the DRAM mounted on the chips shown in Figure 3-28.

SDRAM (Synchronous Dynamic Random Access Memory) combines the best of SRAM and DRAM. Basically, it's DRAM that grabs more information than requested, in the hopes that the CPU will ask for it next. (It often does.) If or

when the CPU asks for it, the chip already has the information and can pass it along very quickly.

RDRAM (Rambus Dynamic Random Access Memory) was created in the late 1990s by Rambus, Inc. This superfast memory first appeared on accelerated video cards. Backed by corporate giant Intel, RDRAM first showed up on motherboards as main memory in 1999. True fact: Nintendo uses RDRAM in its 64-bit game consoles.

ROM (Read-Only Memory) differs from all the preceding types of memory. Normally, a computer moves information in and out of RAM as it works. But a ROM chip holds on to information and doesn't ever let go. For example, your computer's *BIOS* comes on ROM. Because your computer's BIOS doesn't normally change, it's stored permanently on a ROM chip. ROM chips are not only a convenient way to store information but also a safer way: Your computer can't accidentally erase the information.

All those other little parts on the motherboard

Who cares about all those other little chips sitting on the motherboard, like the 8253 Programmable Interval Timer (U34)? Very few people, that's for sure. So ignore the rest of the little lumpy things sitting on your motherboard.

Even if those other little chips break, you won't be able to fix them or even tell which one's broken. Leave that job to the folks in the shop, who hook the chips up to expensive instruments with flashing lights and probe around while wolfing down mouthfuls of Atomic Fireball candies.

Disk Drives

Computers use memory chips for doing immediate work: running programs or putting pictures on the screen. But when you're done working and want to save the fruits of your labors, you put your data on disks. They come in three basic flavors: floppy disks, hard disks, and compact discs.

Floppy disks are the portable square things that slide into floppy drives, which read the information off them. A hard disk, often called a *hard drive,* lives hidden inside your computer. And a compact disc, also called a CD, is the round, shiny thing that slides into your computer's CD-ROM drive. Some CD-ROM drives play DVDs as well as CDs.

Your computer sucks and slurps information from the drives through a special controller that lives either on the motherboard, inside the drive itself, or on a card.

Floppy drives

Remember back in the old days of wide-spaced parking lots when you could easily back a car in and out of your parking space? Unfortunately, shop owners figured that they could cram *lots* more cars into the same-size lot by making each parking space a little smaller.

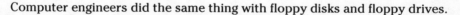

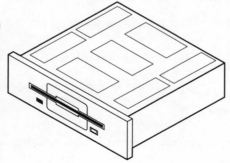

Computer engineers did the same thing with floppy disks and floppy drives.

The early years of computers used big, chunky boxes called *full-height drives.*

In the past ten years, computers used drives about half that size, so they're called *half-height drives,* as shown in Figure 3-29.

Figure 3-29:
Half-height
floppy
drives are
found on
most
computers
today.

But, although half-height drives take up half the space as their ancestors, they're up to four times as filling — they're *high-density drives*. That means they can pack your data onto disks more tightly, allowing the disks to hold more information. (Luckily, if you've stored any information on low-density floppies, the high-density drives can still read them.)

If you're stuck with those big, square, black disks that are slightly bendable, they won't fit in the drives found in today's computer. Ask around at the computer stores for local data-transfer shops. They specialize in moving data between different types of computers and storage mediums.

Table 3-2 shows the amount of information that the low- and high-density drives can hold.

Table 3-2	Floppy Drive Sizes and Capacities	
Drive Size	*General Era*	*Storage Room*
5¼-inch, low-density	Early '80s	360K
3½-inch, low-density	Mid '80s	720K
5¼-inch, high-density	Late '80s	1.2MB
3½-inch, high-density	Current	1.44MB
3½-inch, extended-density	Early '90s (rare)	2.88MB

Almost all computers encountered today use 3½-inch, high-density disks that hold 1.44MB of data.

I don't wanna read about dead floppy drives!

Floppy drives die the quickest when people smoke around them or use the cheapest disks they can find. You know how bad your jacket smells the morning after you've had a night out at the Blue Bayou? Those same smoke particles coat the disk drive's little heads, which read information off the disks. The cheapest floppy disks are made of cheap materials, which can coat the disk drive's heads with a substance known technically as *gunk*.

Keep your computer in the nonsmoking section and don't feel so bad about spending an extra dollar or two for a box of higher-quality disks. Your floppy drive will thank you for it.

Hard drives (hard disks)

Hard drives live inside your computer where they can't fall in the crack behind the wall and your desk. Hard drives can hold thousands of floppy disks' worth of information, making them quite annoying when they finally wear out. Whether it's called a *hard disk* or a *hard drive,* it's just that big can of information that becomes your C:\> drive.

The hard drive has a friend inside your computer: a *drive controller.* Some drive controllers are integrated into the motherboard, and others are expansion cards. Like any other card, it plugs into a *slot.* The card grabs information from your computer's *CPU* and routes it through cables to your drives.

Hard drives not only come in several varieties, they're also controlled by different devices, all described next:

EIDE: Currently the most popular type of drive in new PCs, EIDE stands for *Enhanced Integrated Drive Electronics.* Engineers figured out a way to hot-rod the previous standard, the IDE drives, so that they work in sizes greater than 540MB. (They're also a few times faster at reading and writing information.) These drives still work in older PCs when connected to yesteryear's IDE controller cards, but not nearly as quickly. Engineers have improved EIDE four times, leading to four different standards. Today's drives hold around 40 gigabytes or more.

IDE: The most popular type of drive in the early '90s, these drives are called *Integrated Drive Electronics* because they also have many of the electronics that used to live on the controller card. In fact, many IDE drives don't need a controller: They can plug right into special connectors built into the latest motherboards.

If your motherboard doesn't have a special slot, you can still use an IDE drive by buying an IDE controller card. It's cheaper than the average controller. Unfortunately, the IDE controller card is not as compatible with older hard drives.

MFM and RLL: These older hard drives, known as Modified Frequency Modulation and Run-Length Limited drives, are probably the ones you'll replace with the sexier new IDE drives.

The problem? Well, you can't mix IDE drives with these older drives: The two drives don't get along because they each like different kinds of controllers.

So, you can use all IDE drives or use all MFM/RLL drives. Just don't try to mix the two. As always, the newer technology (EIDE) is the better choice if your budget allows.

ST-506, ST-412, and ESDI: These old-school drives and controllers are what you'll replace with the newer IDE or SCSI drives. Why mention them at all? So you know that the stores don't sell those same types of drives anymore. Go for the EIDE or SCSI drives instead, and make sure that you pick up a new controller as well. (You can find lots more information in Chapter 13.)

SCSI: Pronounced "scuzzy," SCSI stands for Small Computer System Interface. SCSI drives, like MFM and RLL drives, use a controller card. They're expensive, so EIDE is the preferred standard. But some people like SCSI drives because they can chain stuff together.

For example, after installing the SCSI *card,* you can run its cable to your SCSI hard drive. From there, you can run the cable to your CD-ROM drive, where it can head over to a tape backup unit or yet another SCSI toy, as long as all the parts get along with each other. By chaining all the doodads together, you can control them all through one card, which grabs only one slot — often a scarce resource on PCs.

Other ways to store data

The following sections describe data-storage methods that have strayed from the traditional hard drive path, but mostly for good reasons.

Compact disc drives

CD-ROM drives are fun because compact discs are so versatile: They hold great gobs of information, allowing you to listen to music CDs, watch movies, read encyclopedias, or watch special multimedia CDs, which combine sound and pictures to create multifun.

- ✔ Most CD-ROM drives can only *play* stuff — not record stuff. You can't store your own information on them; compact discs come with the information already in place.

- ✔ The capability to store information on compact discs is rapidly changing, though. Drives known as CD-RW drives stuff 640MB of information onto a compact disc costing about $2. Slightly more expensive discs known as CD-RW (read-write) discs can write information on a $20 CD, erase it, and write information on it again — letting CD-ROM drives overcome their last limitation.

✔ CD drives, like modems, can be mounted inside your computer like a floppy drive or outside your computer in their own little cases. If your computer doesn't have room for the internal CD drive, the external drive works just as well. (You need a spare power outlet to plug its power cord into the wall, though, unlike with the internal drive.)

✔ Most CD drives come with audio jacks in the back. You can't just plug in speakers, though; the sound needs to run through an amplifier before you can hear it. To combat this nonsense, some people hook up their players to *sound cards;* others hook their players to their home stereo system. Others forget about the speakers and simply use headphones, which don't need amplifiers.

✔ Some CD-ROM drives require a SCSI *controller,* and others utilize EIDE or IDE controllers. Some drives come with the card, and sometimes you have to pay extra for the card. You'd better check the side of the box to find out. If you're lucky, you can simply connect it to the existing cable leading to your hard drive.

✔ Many sound cards come with a built-in drive controller. Make sure that the port is compatible with the drive you're after, though. (A few sound cards aren't 100 percent compatible with all drives.)

✔ CD-ROM drives can move data around faster than a floppy drive but slower than a hard drive. When shopping, look for something called *access time.* A drive rated at 24X is faster than one rated at 12X.

DVD drives

Yep, these drives let you watch movies on your computer — if you'd want to. Most people will see a much bigger picture on their TV sets.

DVDs (digital versatile discs or digital video discs) come in several capacities, with 4.7GB the most popular. That's enough for a full-length motion picture. Because they're able to read regular CDs, they're quickly becoming standard equipment on new computers.

DVD technology is expanding, and new, second-generation drives (DVD-2) will not only hold 17GB but also be able to read CD-R and CD-RW disks.

The next feature? DVD drives that can write to DVDs themselves are in the works, allowing you to back up your entire hard drive on a single DVD.

Detachable hard drives

Detachable hard drives don't fit inside your computer. Instead, they come inside a little box. The box's cable then plugs into your computer's *parallel port* (the same place where your printer cable lives). After you install a software driver (described in Chapter 18), you see your new drive on the screen. It works just like any old hard drive after that, but you can carry it around from computer to computer, making it great for backups.

Don't forget to check out Chapter 13 for information on Zip drives (shown in Figure 3-30), a popular way to back up your information.

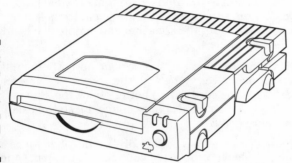

Figure 3-30:
A Zip drive can back up your information quickly and easily.

Weird technical words on the CD drive box

Compact disc manufacturers all started sticking information on discs in different, incompatible ways. Rather than reach a consensus, they just made compact disc players that support all the different standards. Here's a rundown of the weird words you may see:

MPC: Drives with this label can handle multimedia discs with pictures and sound. Almost all compact disc drives can handle these.

ISO-9660/High Sierra: Almost all CDs adhere to this standard, which makes sure that they store information in ways that DOS computers can recognize.

Kodak Photo CD: When you take your pictures to be developed, some developers can stick the pictures on a compact disc, too. Kodak Photo CD-compatible drives can display these pictures on your computer's monitor. Look for a multisession drive, which lets you stick all your pictures on the same disc; single-session drives make you use a new disc for each roll of film.

CD-R: CD-RW drives let you write to these discs until you've filled their 640MB of available space. You can erase information from the disc, too, but that simply deletes the data; it doesn't regain the deleted space.

CD-RW ReWritable Disc: Great for backing up important information, these can read, write, and erase information on the same CD, giving it the benefits of a huge floppy disk. After you've erased the information, you regain the space, letting these discs be used over and over.

Compact disc technology changes so fast that you probably need to read the newsstand computer magazines to keep up with the latest formats and details.

Tape backup units

Back in the 1970s, computer users recorded their files on a plain old tape recorder using a plain old audiocassette — a time-consuming process. Today, specialized tape backup units can store gobs of files. Some internal tape backup units slide into a computer's front, just like a floppy drive; external backup units live in a box next to your computer. Tape backup units have been around for more than 20 years, so you can find two decades' worth of standards on the market. The current tape drive types include AIT, DLT, DAT, SLR, and Travan.

When shopping, look for a tape backup unit that can store as much information as you have on your hard drive. Then buy a bunch of tape cartridges that support your tape backup unit's particular format.

The Power Supply

PCs would be whisper-quiet if it weren't for their power supplies. Power supplies suck in the 110 volts from the standard American wall outlet and turn the 110 volts into the 5 or 12 volts that your computer prefers. This simple task heats up the power supplies, however, so they cool off with a noisy, whirling fan.

The fan also sucks any hot air out of your computer's case and blows it out the hole in the back. In fact, if you keep your computer too close to the wall and don't move it for several years, the fan will leave a round, black dust mark on the wall.

Extra fans are available as add-ons. They can be a lifesaver if your computer is failing due to heat buildup, which can happen if your motherboard uses a *Pentium-level* chip.

For some reason, power supplies seem to die faster than most computer parts. Luckily, they're one of the easiest parts to replace. They vary in size, but a typical power supply and its wires appear in Figure 3-31.

Power supplies vary in size. Your best bet is to remove your old power supply and take it to the store so that you can get another one that's the same size.

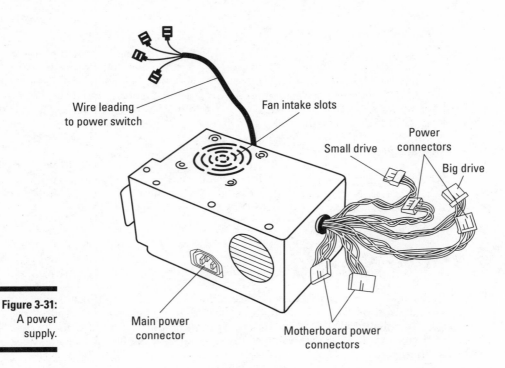

Wire leading to power switch

Fan intake slots

Small drive

Power connectors

Big drive

Figure 3-31:
A power supply.

Main power connector

Motherboard power connectors

Don't ever open up the power supply to try to fix it. Doing so can cause serious bodily harm, even if the computer's turned off and unplugged.

✔ After you find a power supply that's the right size, check its wattage. Older XT computers can get away with the cheaper 130-watt models. If you're using a 386, 486, or early Pentium, buy a model rated at 200 watts or higher. Even 250 watts isn't too much for a relatively new computer with lots of internal toys: internal modems, tape backup drives, compact disc players, DVD drives, and other power-eating devices.

✔ If you live in an older area where the power fluctuates a lot, consider buying a *surge suppressor*. Basically, it plugs into the wall and conditions the power before it enters your computer. Many power strips come with a surge suppressor built in. Power strips wear out, though, so for extra protection, replace them every six months or so. But most higher-priced power strips have indicator lights to let you know when the suppressor has worn out.

✔ An uninterrupted power supply (UPS) goes one step further: If the power dies suddenly, it kicks in, keeping your computer up and running. Most uninterrupted power supplies last for only 5 to 15 minutes, but that's usually plenty of time to shut down your computer, grab a soda, and feel good about your foresight while waiting for the lights to come back on. The drawback? A UPS wears a huge price tag compared to a surge suppressor.

"How Do I Know Which Parts I Have?"

It's not always easy to figure out which parts are inside your computer. Computers really *do* look the same. Your best bet is to look around for your old manuals. They often have a hint to which parts live inside your PC's case.

Sometimes your sales receipt can be a better gauge, however. Dealers occasionally hand out the wrong manual, but they're usually a little better about putting the right part on the receipt.

If you picked up your computer at a garage sale or if it's a hand-me-down from the office, you may have to do a little exploring on your own.

Windows 95 and Windows 98 users can easily figure out what parts live inside their computers. Right-click the My Computer icon and choose Properties from the pop-up menu. Windows lists the computer's CPU and amount of RAM on that page. Click the Device Manager tab along the top, and Windows opens the closet doors, as shown in Figure 3-32.

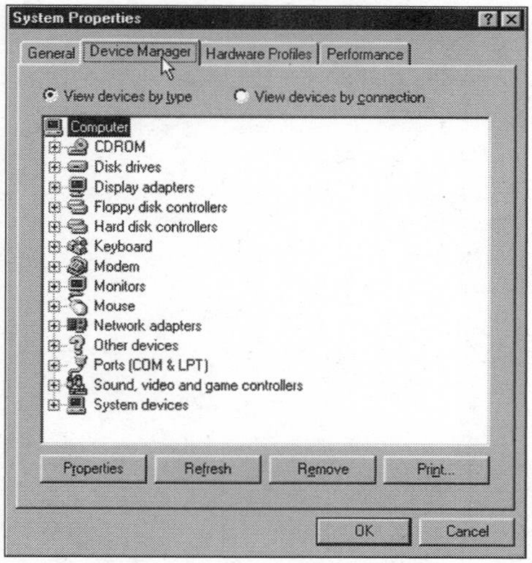

Figure 3-32:
The Device Manager tab in Windows can usually identify all the parts living inside your computer.

Chapter 17 explains more about how Windows identifies its parts and lets you fiddle with the things stuffed inside your computer. (*Hint:* Follow these steps. Click the Start button and weasel your way through these menus: Programs, Accessories, and System Tools. Finally, open the System Information program.

Still using DOS? Then type the following line at any prompt and press Enter:

```
C:\> MSD
```

Still confused? Take off the computer's case (an occasionally laborious process described on the Cheat Sheet in the front of this book) and start looking at the parts described and pictured in this chapter. You find a product name and number stamped on the most important ones.

Computers often boast about their CPUs when first turned on. Watch carefully when any words start flashing by. Your computer usually displays the name of its video card first and then its BIOS, which often contains the CPU number.

Some computers come with a diagnostics disk. If you haven't lost yours yet, put it into your floppy drive and run the program. The diagnostics disk can often identify what stuff's hiding inside your computer's case.

Chapter 4

Figuring Out What's Broken

● ●

In This Chapter

▶ Figuring out what's wrong with a computer

▶ Finding any recent changes

▶ Spotting clues when your PC is first turned on

▶ Listening for warning signals

▶ Using diagnostics programs

▶ Buying replacement parts

▶ Troubleshooting your computer through the Internet

▶ Calling technical support

● ●

*W*hen PCs aren't casting you in the role of the anguished user, they're making you play the detective in The Case of the Broken Part. Your computer's dead: Who dunnit?

At the PC repair shop, nerdy technodetectives wield expensive curly-wired probes that make accusatory blip sounds when they uncover the guilty part. You're merely armed with a cheap screwdriver.

If you already know what your computer needs — a bigger hard drive, for example, or a faster CPU — head for that particular chapter. No need to stop here.

But if you're still searching for the culprit, this chapter can help you figure out which computer part has gone bad. After you finger the culprit, head for the chapter that describes the broken part in more detail.

Finally, if you're having problems with your Windows 95 or Windows 98 software — or you're not sure *what* the problem is — head for Chapter 17. It's devoted to finding and fixing Microsoft's mistakes.

It Doesn't Work Anymore!

PCs don't die very often. Unlike a car, a PC doesn't have many moving parts, leaving fewer things to wear out. When computers do start to cause problems, usually just one small piece has gone bad, spoiling the rest of the experience (kind of like finding gum under the table at a fancy restaurant).

The hardest part isn't fixing the problem. It's simply *finding* the problem. Is the software acting up? Your disk drive? Both? Or is it some complicated mystery part you've never heard of?

Before you whip out your screwdriver, give the tricks in the following sections one final shot.

Make sure that the computer is plugged in and turned on

This one sounds so obvious that many people overlook it. However, a vacuum cleaner or stray foot can inadvertently knock a power cord out of place. Give it one last check for the Gipper.

Make sure that the cables are fastened securely

Make sure that the PC's power cord nestles snugly between the back of your computer and the wall outlet. While you're rummaging around beneath the desk on your hands and knees, check the monitor's power cord as well. Finally, check the monitor's second cord — the one that runs to the back of your PC. Some monitor cords can come loose on both ends — from the back of the monitor as well as from the back of your PC.

Turn the computer off, wait 30 seconds, and turn it back on again

This sounds odd, but if it works, who cares? Turning the computer off and waiting a few seconds before turning it back on has solved many of my PC problems — although it always wipes out any information sitting on the screen at the time. This trick has even fixed my laser printer a couple of times, too. Be sure to wait 30 seconds before turning the computer back on, though.

Flipping a computer off and on quickly can send damaging shocks to its sensitive internal organs.

Does your monitor say something like

```
Non-System disk or disk error
Replace and press any key when ready
```

This message usually means you've turned on your computer with a floppy disk sitting in drive A. Push the disk drive's eject button, press your spacebar (or any other handy key), and wish that all your problems were this easy to fix.

If none of these quick fixes works, move on to the next section.

Narrowing Down the Problem

Technogeeks talk up a storm in the locker room, but it's just talk. There *isn't* an easy way to figure out why your computer has gone kaput. It doesn't take much at all to send a PC running in circles. Maybe your software can't find a crucial piece of itself. Or maybe some tiny chip got tired of playing chambermaid.

The only way to find a cure is to keep narrowing down the problem. Does the computer act weird only when a certain program is running? Or does it just act up when trying to print the eighth page? Do you hear a funny whine from inside the case?

When confronted with a real head scratcher, ask yourself the following questions or try the following suggestions.

Have you added new software lately?

Sometimes, newly installed software not only doesn't work right but also keeps everything else on your computer from working right, too. No easy solutions here.

Try opening the Control Panel, choosing Add/Remove Programs, and uninstalling the suspect program. If that doesn't repair the damage, try reinstalling the suspect software. This time, however, answer some of the installation questions differently.

Did you discover and then delete a weird file or program that didn't do anything?

Some of the most important files on your PC have the weirdest and most inconsequential-sounding names. Unfortunately, there's no easy way to tell the truly important files from the truly technoid trash.

If an adventurous urge caused you to delete a useless file and now your software doesn't work, you have two choices:

Choice 1: Beg a computer guru to figure out what you've done wrong.

Choice 2: Reinstall the software that's not working right.

Using Windows? Whew! You're lucky enough to have a third choice. You can probably retrieve that deleted file that you thought was useless. You see, Windows hangs on to files for a little while after you've deleted them from your hard drive. (Files from floppies or networks get the axe immediately. No same luck.) Here's how to make Windows 95 or Windows 98 regurgitate your swallowed file without harm:

1. **Open the Recycle Bin icon.**

   Either a click or double-click on your desktop's Recycle Bin opens the program window; inside, you see a list of your most recently deleted files.

2. **Choose Arrange Icons from the Recycle Bin's View menu and then choose by Delete Date.**

   The Recycle Bin then sorts your files in the order you deleted them, with your most recently deleted file at either the top or bottom of the list.

3. **Choose View and then choose Details to see more information about the files.**

4. **Right-click the deleted file and choose Restore from the pop-up menu.**

   The Recycle Bin pulls the file back from the dead and places it back in its original home — the folder where it was deleted.

Never delete an unwanted program by simply deleting its files from your hard drive. That often leaves problem-causing remnants of the program. Instead, use the Control Panel's Add/Remove Programs icon to delete programs. The Control Panel method removes *all* parts of the program — even the invisible parts spread out in different areas of your computer.

A scary "bypass" setting lives inside your Recycle Bin, waiting for mischief. If your deleted files don't appear in the Recycle Bin, right-click on the Bin's icon, choose Properties, and make sure that no check mark exists in the box labeled Do not move files to the Recycle Bin.

Have you moved any files or directories around? Changed any of their names?

When a program installs itself, it often tells the computer where it's living on your hard drive. If you subsequently move that program from one Windows folder to another folder (or from the Fish folder to the new Tuna folder *inside* that Fish folder), your computer may not be able to find it again.

Windows programs are notorious for this situation, leading to big trouble if you move files around, change a folder's location, or simply change some names. The fix? Try to remember which files or folders you moved and move them back. Change the filenames back to their originals, too. If the program still doesn't work, your best bet is to run the troublesome program's uninstall programs and reinstall the program.

It's bad luck to delete unidentified files, because they often turn out to be important. Don't delete a file unless you have a compelling reason. If in doubt, grab a computer guru the next time one shuffles down the hall. A guru can usually delete the right files — or repair the damage if something awful happens.

Have you changed the computer's location on your desktop?

Did you pull your computer out from the wall a few inches to plug in the joy-stick? Did the janitor move the desk slightly to clean beneath it? Did the cat find another warm place? Cables often fall off or loosen themselves when the computer's case is moved, even just a few inches here and there.

If a *swivel-mounted* monitor swivels too far in one direction, the monitor's cables often come loose. Leave a little slack in the cables so that they don't get yanked around. Often, loose cables don't dangle or give other visible warning signs. When in doubt, give them all a little push inward for good measure.

Many cables that plug into your computer's case have little knobs. Turn the knobs until they're screwed down tight into your computer. They stay attached much longer that way.

Try a different part

Here's where repair shops have you beat. If you don't think that your hard drive is working right, you can only flap your neck wattles in exasperation. At the repair shop, the nerds will pull out your computer's hard drive and stick it inside another computer to see whether it works.

If it works in that other computer, your hard drive must be okay. Something else inside your computer is making it act weird. Or, if your hard drive *doesn't* work, the nerds will sell you a new hard drive.

Even if you don't have a test-drive computer, you can try some of the same tricks. If your floppy drive is acting up, try using a different floppy disk. (Maybe the disk was bad.) Computer doesn't get any power? Try another wall socket.

By combining part swapping with other clues, you can continue to narrow down your PC's problem.

Look at the PC's Device Manager

Windows often tells you exactly what piece of hardware's causing problems — if you know where to look. In this case, right-click on the My Computer icon and choose Properties from the pop-up menu. When the System Properties window appears, click the Device Manager tab.

Windows kindly displays all the hardware it finds in your machine. Best yet, it tells you which pieces are working fine, disabled, or not working. To find clues, head for the section in Chapter 17 about finding device conflicts in Windows 98. The chapter contains other methods to make Windows uncover its own troubles (and to make Windows fix them, if you're lucky).

Watch the screen when your PC wakes up

Whenever you turn on your PC, it sits still for a while, flashes some words and numbers on the screen, and then belches out a beep or two before letting you get some work out of it.

Those aren't idle yawns and stretches. Your computer's using that time to examine itself and is trying to figure out what you've been able to afford to attach to it and whether everything is working up to snuff.

This series of wake-up checks is called the *power-on self test,* dubbed POST by the acronym-happy engineers. By watching and listening to your computer during its POST, you can often pick up a clue about what's bothering it.

✔ When you find a cockroach in your slippers, you shriek. When the computer finds something it doesn't like, it beeps. This may sound like something straight out of a Captain Crunch commercial, but it's true. Listen to the number of beeps when you turn on your computer, and you'll know whether your computer is happy or sad. (You hear more on this musical weirdness in the next section.)

✔ Sometimes your PC displays a cryptic code on your screen when the PC is first turned on. It rarely says anything really helpful, like The mouse became unplugged. Instead, it says something like Error Code 1105, forcing you to flip to Chapter 23 to find out what your computer is complaining about this time. Some newer computers mention a faulty part's manufacturer when they're first turned on, so that's a start.

✔ Most POST errors happen after you've installed on a card something the computer didn't like. (If the word *card* has you stumped, head for Chapter 3 for a quick refresher.)

✔ When your computer's battery dies, your exhausted computer probably won't be able to find your hard drive. The POST message may say ERROR Code 161. That's usually a pretty simple fix. You can find the explanation in Chapter 10.

✔ The POST makes sure that your keyboard is plugged in — that's the reason your keyboard's lights flash when you first turn on your computer. The lights on your disk drives flash, too, as your computer checks to see whether they're *really* there.

✔ The most visible part of the POST comes with the *memory check*. Your PC first counts all its memory and then checks to make sure that all the memory works. If you have *lots* of memory, you'll be drumming your fingers on the table as your computer adds it all up on the screen for you.

Tired of twiddling your thumbs while your computer counts its memory? Head for Chapter 10 to read about changing your BIOS settings. By tweaking the BIOS settings, you can often tell the computer to skip the memory count and get back to work more quickly.

CHAIN REACTION

Cures for quarreling cards

If you have recently replaced an old card or added a new card, your POST may alert you to a potential problem or, worse yet, a chain reaction of replacements. Card problems leave four possible fixes:

✔ Fiddle with the settings on the new card so that it doesn't interfere with the old card (see Chapter 18).

✔ Fiddle with the settings on the old card so that it doesn't interfere with the new card.

✔ Buy a different brand of card.

✔ Replace the older card that's conflicting with your new card. (Unfortunately, doing so leads to the chain reaction talked about in this book's Introduction.)

Listen to the beeps, Luke!

That single beep you hear just after you turn on your computer is a happy beep. It means that the computer has found all its parts, given them a little kick, and decided that they're all working as they should.

If you hear more than a single beep, though, your computer is often trying to tell you some bad news. See, the PC designers figure that if PCs are so smart, they should be able to tell their users what's wrong with them. But because computers speak a bizarre language of numbers, the beep system is the best they can manage.

By counting the number of beeps and looking them up in Chapter 24, you can figure out what your computer is trying to tell you. Here's a summary:

✔ POST messages and beeps sound serious and look befuddling. But they're not always that bad. Sometimes, just a loose cable can start your PC beeping and weeping.

✔ Beeps come from your PC's built-in speaker, not through a sound card. That means all PCs' beeps sound pretty much the same, no matter how much their sound cards cost. Even laptops beep.

✔ By combining your computer's beep clues with any accompanying error message, you can figure out which chapter to scurry toward for more information.

✔ Some computers, especially some made by Compaq, make two beeps, not one, when they're happy. So much for standards.

Call in Doctor Software

In the old days, people bought software for normal, functioning PCs. Then some sly programmer made millions by designing software for computers that *didn't* work. Today, some of the most popular software merely helps you figure out why your PC has suddenly stopped walking the dog.

Windows comes with some built-in troubleshooting software; that capable armada is described in Chapter 17, although you find a tidbit of advice in the next section.

Many new PCs come bundled with a disk that says *diagnostic* or *DIAG* somewhere on its label. If you're lucky, that disk contains a helpful program designed to help you figure out what's wrong with your PC.

If you can find your PC's diagnostics disk, stick it into drive A and push your computer's reset button. The diagnostics program will try to take over, scrutinizing your system and offering clues to what's ailing the beast. If you can't find any kind of disk like this, try the following:

✔ Microsoft tossed in a helpful diagnostic program with the release of Windows 3.1 and MS-DOS 6. Type **MSD** at any C:\> prompt, and the program leaps into action, letting you know what parts are attached to your computer. For example, the program lets you know whether your computer knows that you've just added a new mouse. Best yet, the program is free. (Head to Chapter 17 to see what the newer Windows versions have to offer.)

✔ If you didn't get a diagnostic disk with your computer, head for the Utilities aisle of your local software store. The Norton Utilities program, for example, offers stealth-like information similar to the Microsoft MSD program. Other Norton programs can salvage the wreckage from damaged hard disks and other disasters.

✔ Some utility and diagnostics programs are better left for the computer gurus, however. Some of these programs dish out information that's detailed down to your PC's bare ribs. Then they delve into complicated technical specifics, like bone composition, blood type, and DNA swirls. Much of the information these programs dish out doesn't make much sense. Still, the programs may be worth a try in some desperate cases.

Buying Replacement Parts

After you finger the bad part, you have to decide how to replace it. Should you replace the bad part with a part of the same brand and model? Or should you buy something a little better? Only you can decide. Keep the following points in mind, though:

- **Avoid the cheapest parts.** They're made of shoddy material and are put together cheaply. Feel free to avoid some of the most expensive stuff, too. You'll pay for the name, the advertising, and the fancy package. Shoot for somewhere in between.

- **Buy from dealers with the friendliest return policy.** If your new part doesn't work, can you take it back? If you're having trouble installing it or getting it to work, can somebody tell you over the phone which buttons to push?

- **Mail-order parts work well for computer geeks who know exactly what they want and how to put the parts together after they get them.** If that's not you, you're probably best off shopping at the friendly local computer store.

- **The good parts come with a standard one-year warranty covering parts and labor.** Watch out for the ones that don't.

- **Some places charge a 15 percent restocking fee if you return a product because you didn't like it or it didn't work right in your computer.** Avoid these places whenever possible.

- **Check out some of the newer, upgradeable computer parts.** For example, many modems come with a special socket inside. When modems become faster, you can plug the new, speedy miracle chip into that socket. Voilà! Your six-month-old modem is instantly transformed into state-of-the-art stuff. Other modem chips can be upgraded to faster speeds by running some software; keep in touch with your modem company's Internet site to see whether it has any upgrades scheduled.

Troubleshooting Your Computer through the Internet

When your computer runs a little strangely or some error message leaves you puzzled, the Internet often holds advice. Sometimes, it even contains detailed instructions for fixing your problem. The problem, unfortunately, is finding that particular piece of information amongst all the Web sites devoted to chat rooms and MP3 files.

The next few sections show how to extract the right informational tidbits for your specific needs.

Hitting up the manufacturer

If your modem's working, rummage around in the box's paperwork for your computer manufacturer's World Wide Web site on the Internet. Head for the Web site, find the Technical Support area, and type in your questions. Chances are that either a techie or a passing stranger will leave you an answer.

To find a company's Web site, head to a search engine like www.yahoo.com. Type the name of the company in the Search box and click Search. Yahoo searches the Internet and returns with a list of Web sites pertaining to that company or its products.

Some companies, like Dell, go all out on their Web sites. When you type your computer's system serial tag (it's printed on a sticker attached to your computer), a Web page dishes up a copy of your computer's vital statistics, as shown in Figure 4-1. The page shows your purchase date, parts, warranty information, Y2K compliance, spare parts availability, and other information pertaining to *your* particular computer. Best yet, the page lists any updated drivers for you to download.

Figure 4-1:
The Web page for Dell computers shows personalized statistics about your computer.

Finally, click on the Dell Knowledge Base to see any issues that have come up regarding your computer model.

When finding important information on the Internet regarding your particular computer model, be sure to tell your browser about it. Either *bookmark* the page with the Bookmark command or choose Add to Favorites so that you find it easier when you need it.

Using the Microsoft Knowledge Base

Microsoft collects all the information it finds about its programs' faults and compiles them into a mammoth search engine named the *Microsoft Knowledge Base*. Start there for software questions, especially if you suspect a Microsoft program — or your operating system — to be involved in the snafu.

To put the Knowledge Base to work, head for `http://support.microsoft .com/search` and start describing your problem. Let's say that Windows 95 displays the error message `Error: Invalid VxD` whenever you turn on your computer. Then it stops working completely. What's the beef?

Head to the Knowledge Base and follow these steps:

1. **Choose Windows 95 from the My search is about drop-down menu.**

   Of course, you can choose any Microsoft product from the drop-down menu. In this case, however, the problem relates to Windows 95.

2. **Type** Invalid VxD **in the box labeled My question is.**

   If some other issue is giving you problems, type words relating to that problem instead.

3. **Leave the Keyword search using All Words option as is, and click the Go button, as shown in Figure 4-2.**

   The Knowledge Base dishes up a page of references explaining why Windows 95 might spit out the words *Invalid VxD*. Scroll down the page, and wham! As shown in Figure 4-3, item number 13 seems to be the answer.

4. **Click on the item that most closely relates to your problem.**

   In this case, click on Number 13 because the headline describes your problem most accurately.

5. **The Knowledge Base explains the symptoms of the Invalid VxD problem and its cause and explains how to resolve the problem.**

   As shown in Figure 4-4, your problem relates to an incompatible type of mouse. Microsoft recommends contacting the mouse's manufacturer for an updated driver.

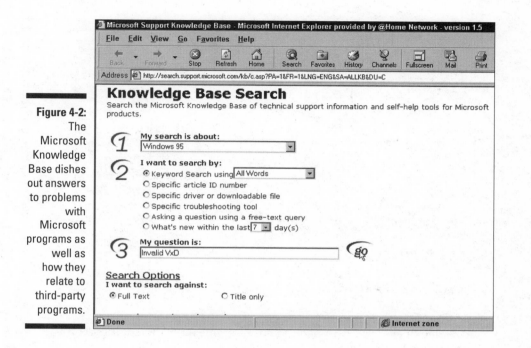

Figure 4-2:
The
Microsoft
Knowledge
Base dishes
out answers
to problems
with
Microsoft
programs as
well as
how they
relate to
third-party
programs.

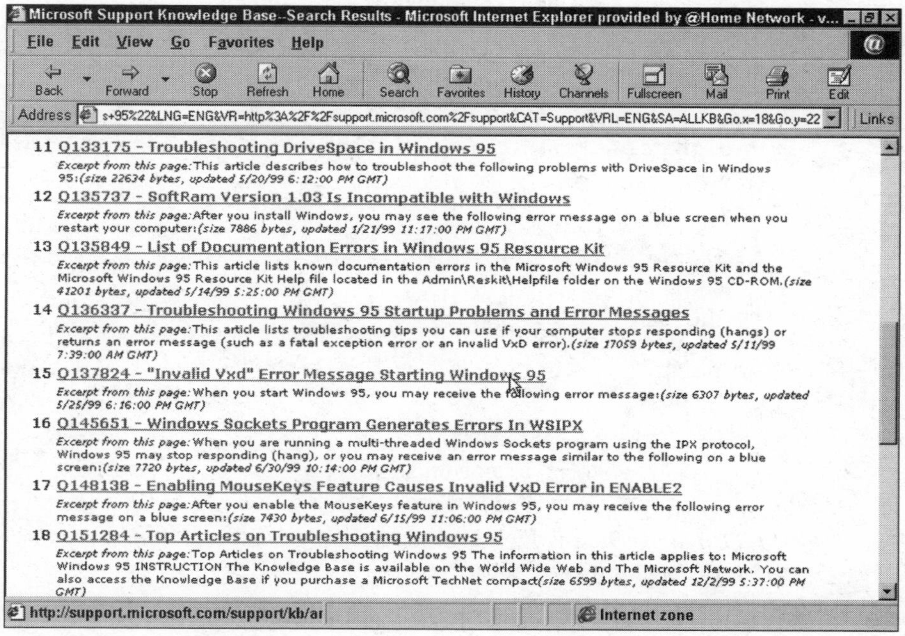

Figure 4-3:
The
Knowledge
Base finds a
reference
to your
particular
problem.

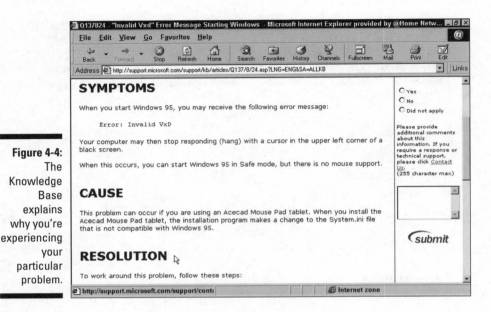

Figure 4-4:
The
Knowledge
Base
explains
why you're
experiencing
your
particular
problem.

Available to everyone through the Internet, this nifty Microsoft tool often provides clues to your Windows problems. By varying your search terms, you often find the answers to your problems quickly.

Having difficulty coming up with a solution in the Knowledge Base? Don't search for a specific program, like Windows 95. Instead, choose the All Microsoft Products option, near the top of the list. The Knowledge Base then searches through its entire stash of solutions while trying to solve your problem.

Using search engines

The Microsoft Knowledge Base provides some answers to Microsoft's problems, but it's not your only recourse. Many Web sites search through the entire Internet — not just Microsoft's own collection of information. But rooting through several different search engines takes lots of time.

To save time, head for a search engine named Dogpile, at www.dogpile.com. Dogpile isn't a normal search engine. Instead, it searches through a large collection of search engines, asking each one about your requested information. As Dogpile digs through each search engine, it spits out any matches that may solve your problem.

Confused about whether your USB (Universal Serial Bus) port works correctly? Put Dogpile to work digging through the Internet. Type the words **universal serial bus support** in the Fetch box, as shown in Figure 4-5, and click the Fetch button. (Don't change any other settings; just type your search term and click Fetch.)

After a few moments, Dogpile brings up its first few Web sites relating to your topic. In this case, you're lucky. It's found a reference to the Universal Serial Bus Web site on the top of the list. Click on the Universal Serial Bus Web Site listing, as shown in Figure 4-6, to find answers to your problem. If you're not so lucky, keep scrolling down the page, clicking the Next Set of Search Engines button. Dogpile will root through more than ten search engines, looking frantically for any references to the problem you've entered.

✔ Dogpile displays the first ten listings or so from each search engine on its list. If you spot one that looks promising, look at the bottom of its list. Click on the button labeled Next Set to temporarily leave Dogpile and head straight to that search engine for more in-depth searching. To return to Dogpile — and your original search — keep clicking your browser's Back arrow.

✔ Didn't find anything interesting? Try rephrasing your search. Type **USB** rather than **Universal Serial Bus,** for instance. Try using the words **Troubleshoot** or **diagnose.**

✔ Dogpile doesn't charge anything extra for its services. The only thing you pay for is your Internet access bill, and most people pay a flat fee for unlimited access to the Internet.

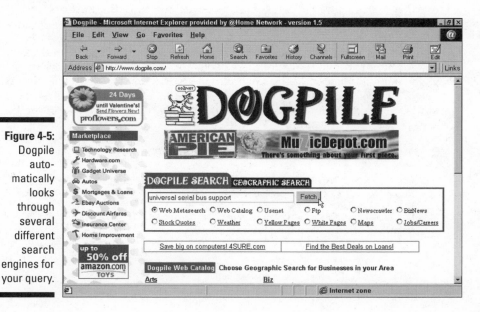

Figure 4-5: Dogpile automatically looks through several different search engines for your query.

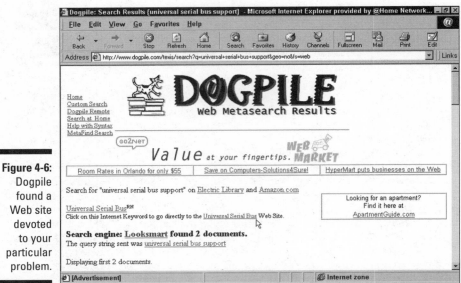

Finding help through the Internet's newsgroups

You're not the only person with your particular computer problem. With millions of people using computers worldwide, many other people have encountered your problem. Best yet, some have even solved it. But how do you reach them?

Your best bet is through the Internet's newsgroups area. And one of the best ways to filter through the more than 20,000 topics of discussion is a search engine named Deja.com. Let's say that you just installed a Umax scanner on your Windows 98 computer, and now you see this error message after the Windows 98 logo: `C:\windows\system\vmm32.vxd: missing/unable to load`. What does it mean?

The Deja Web site offers plenty of clues, as shown here:

1. **Call up your Internet browser and head to** `www.deja.com/home_ps.shtml`.

2. **In the Enter Keywords box, type the name of the problem file:** vmm32.vxd, **as shown in Figure 4-7.**

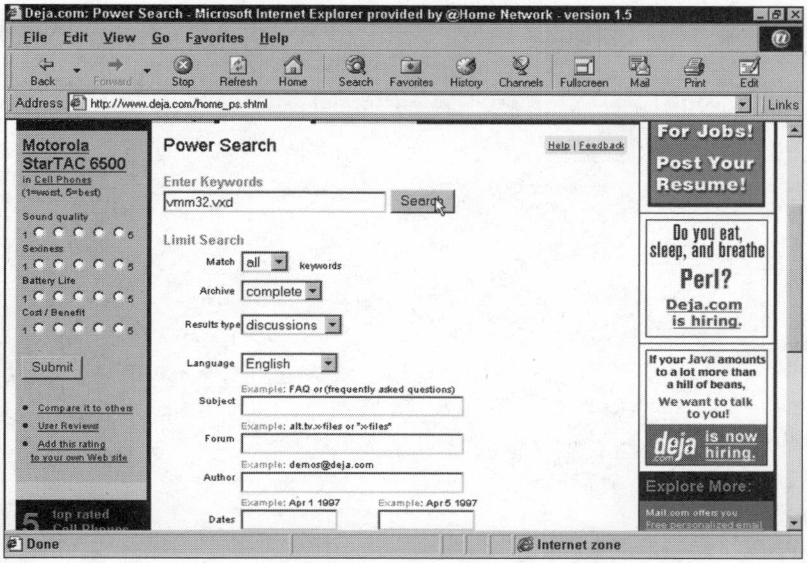

Figure 4-7:
Type the
name of the
problem in
the Enter
Keywords
box.

3. **Before searching, scroll down the page and select your native language from the Language box.**

   Deja searches through messages around the world. Unless you speak more than 30 languages, narrow down the search to your native tongue.

4. **Click the Search button to start sifting through all the messages containing that particular error message.**

5. **Click on a message that seems applicable to your problem and read the answer, as shown in Figure 4-8.**

   In this case, some kind soul has listed the direct link to the Microsoft Knowledge Base, described earlier in this chapter. Click the link, and the Knowledge Base explains that your scanner's current driver isn't compatible with Windows 98 and needs to be upgraded by heading to the scanner's Web site.

Deja often finds thousands of messages pertaining to your error message, making it difficult to find the right answer. To weed out questions and go straight to the answers, click on messages that start with the word Re:. Those messages are responses to previous questions, so they're more apt to contain answers.

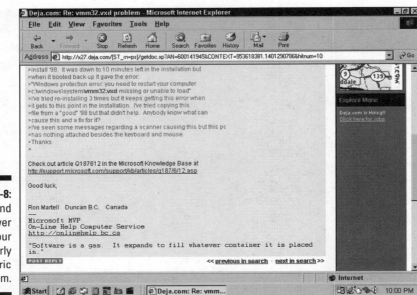

Figure 4-8:
Deja found
an answer
to your
particularly
esoteric
problem.

If you ever post a message to a newsgroup, don't use your real e-mail address. Mean companies use programs to grab all the e-mail addresses found on the newsgroups. Then they sell the addresses to businesses to send junk e-mail *(spam)* to your e-mail account.

Giving up and calling technical support

There comes a time when you should just plain give up. You've installed a new part, and it doesn't work. You've fiddled with the part's switches, you've fiddled with the software, and still the part just sits there looking expensive.

Stay calm. Think of a flock of brilliant-green parrots flying toward you, bringing luscious chunks of island pineapple and a coconut frond for you to weave skillfully into a native hat.

Now, follow the steps listed in the following section.

Preparing to make the call

Before making the call, make sure that you're prepared. Then start rooting through the part's packaging for a little piece of paper with the company's technical support number. It's often on the same paper with the warranty information. Found the number? Then collect the following information before you call the company's technowizards, weed through a Touch-Tone menu, and beg for mercy.

The part's model and serial number

Usually printed on a small sticker, the model and serial number often lurk on the side of the box or somewhere on the product itself. Sometimes, models can have several different varieties; sound cards are notorious for this. You may need to pull the case off your computer and jot down any identifying information printed on the card.

Information about your computer

The nerds on the phone usually try to blame the part's failure on some other company. So write down the names of all the other gizmos installed in your computer.

The version of the operating system

Do you know what version of Windows you're using?

If you have a My Computer icon on your desktop, right-click it and choose Properties. A box pops up, identifying whether the computer uses Windows 95 or Windows 98. Because Microsoft has issued different versions of both Windows 95 and Windows 98, copy all the information listed in the System area.

A printout of your important files

Make a copy of these files and their contents before anything goes wrong; technical-support people love hearing you try to pronounce the complicated words found in these files over the phone. Follow these steps to print your computer's vital statistics:

1. **Right-click the My Computer icon and choose P̲roperties.**
2. **Click the Device Manager tab.**
3. **Click the Pri̲nt button.**
4. **Click the A̲ll devices and system summary option and click OK.**

Calling technical support

If you've gathered all the information I list earlier, in the "Preparing to make the call" section, you're ready to actually place a call to the technical support people. Now load a favorite computer game — if possible — and call the technical support number. You'll probably be on hold for many moons and be routed through several departments.

Hopefully, a helpful person will have an answer and explain why the part's not working or tell you where to send the part for a refund.

Whenever you find helpful people on technical support lines, *ask for their names and direct phone numbers. Then write them in a safe place.* Sometimes, using this information will keep you from waiting on hold the next time you need to call.

Part II

The PC Parts You Can See (External Peripherals)

The 5th Wave · By Rich Tennant

"Hey Dad- guess how many Milk Duds fit inside your disk drive."

In this part . . .

This part of the book deals with the parts of the PC you can see — the parts that aren't hiding from you inside the computer's case.

Here, keyboards, mice, modems, monitors, scanners, and printers all get their due. In each chapter, you'll find a list of the part's symptoms. Next to each symptom, you'll find the fix — whether it's a software tweak, a flip of the a switch, or a gentle, fatherly discussion.

And, if none of those fixes does the trick, you can find explicit instructions for ripping the darn thing out, throwing it away, and installing a replacement that works twice as well.

Chapter 5

The Sticky Keyboard

*T*alk about moving parts — most keyboards have more than 100 of 'em, each moving up and down hundreds of times during the day.

Keyboards don't die very often, but when they start to go, they're easy to diagnose. A few keys start to stickkkk or stop working altogether. And when a water glass hits the keyboard, every key stops working at the same time.

This chapter starts with a list of sick-keyboard symptoms that are followed by a quick fix. If you discover that your tired, old keyboard is ready for retirement, however, head for the "How Do I Install a New Keyboard?" section at the end of this chapter.

"When I Turn On My Computer, the Screen Says 'Keyboard Not Found' or Something Equally Depressing!"

Chances are that your keyboard's cord isn't plugged all the way into its socket. (And pressing F1 won't do anything, no matter what your computer says.) Fumble around in the back of your computer until you find the keyboard's cable. Push it into its socket a little harder.

After you fasten the keyboard's cable more securely, you probably have to push your computer's reset button. Some computers look for their keyboards only once — and that's when they're first turned on. The reset button forces the computer to take a second look. Or, if there's no reset button, turn off your computer, wait 30 seconds, and turn it back on again.

Also, make sure that nothing's sitting on any of the keys, like the corner of a book or magazine. If any of your keys are pressed when you first turn the computer on, the computer thinks that the keyboard is broken.

Still doesn't work? Look for a tiny switch on the bottom of your keyboard and try flicking it the other way. Maybe some nerdy jokester flipped the switch while you weren't looking. (Not all keyboards have this switch, though, so just shrug your shoulders in bewilderment if yours doesn't.)

If your keyboard still doesn't work, check to see whether something gross may have been spilled on it (see the following section).

"I Spilled a Hansen's Natural Raspberry Soda on My Keyboard!"

Your keyboard is probably a goner. But here's the Emergency Keyboard Preservation Procedure: Save your work if possible, turn off your computer, and unplug the keyboard.

With a sponge, wipe off all the spilled stuff you can find. Then sit there and feel foolish for the 24 hours or so that it takes for the keyboard to dry.

If you spill only water, your keyboard may still work the next day. But if you spill anything containing sugar — soda pop, coffee, margaritas, Tang — you'll probably coat the inside of your keyboard with sticky gunk. This gunk then attracts dust and grime — your keyboard starts a slow decline within a few months and dies sooner or later, depending on the tragedy level of the spill.

✔ Luckily, new keyboards are pretty cheap, ranging from the $15 "specials" to the $100 deluxe models with built-in speakers and other goodies.

✔ But if you have lots of spare time and even less spare change, pry off all the keycaps one by one. Start in one corner and work your way across. (Don't bother trying to take off the spacebar because it has too many gizmos holding it on.) When the keys are off, sponge off any stray gunk, dry off the moisture, and try to put all the keycaps back in their right locations. (Figures 3-8, 3-9, and 3-10 in Chapter 3 may help.)

✔ Some people report success and, sometimes, odd stares by immediately taking their wet keyboard to the gas station and squirting it with air from the tire pump to loosen debris. Other people (including me) have cautiously — and successfully — used a hair dryer.

✔ Wait at least 24 hours before giving up on your keyboard. You can salvage many wet keyboards, but only after they are completely dry.

Don't ever give up hope. Erik writes in from Portugal with an old college story about a basketball player who borrowed his computer for video games. Unfortunately, the sportster knocked a cup of spit and tobacco juice into the keyboard. Figuring he had nothing to lose, Erik rinsed off the keyboard at the nearby gym's shower and toweled it off. A few hours later, Erik plugged in the keyboard and the machine rose from the dead.

"My Arrow Keys Don't Move the Cursor — They Make Numbers!"

Look for a key labeled Num Lock or something similar. Press it once. The little Num Lock light on your keyboard should go out, and your arrow keys should go back to normal.

"My keyboard doesn't have F11 and F12 keys, and Microsoft Word for Windows uses those!"

If your keyboard doesn't have F11 and F12 keys, you're using an older 83- or 84-key keyboard. Microsoft Word for Windows and some other Windows programs prefer the more modern 101-key or 104-key keyboard. Buy a 101-key keyboard and try to find a place in the garage to store your old keyboard. (Very few stores take trade-ins.)

Windows still works with an older keyboard, however, and the programs that do use the F11 and F12 keys usually don't make those keys do anything very exciting.

"All the Letters and Numbers Wore Off from My Keys!"

If your rapidly moving fingers wear the letters off, you've probably already memorized all the locations. But if you still want labels, salvage the keycaps from a friend's dead keyboard or ask your local computer store if they sell keycaps by themselves.

If you give up and buy a replacement keyboard, coat the new keyboard's keycaps with a thin layer of clear nail polish. That helps protect the lettering from finger damage, extending the key caps' lives.

"Every Time I Press a Key, the Computer Beeps at Me!"

Are you in a program, possibly filling out some boring form? Some computers beep frantically if they want *letters* and you're typing *numbers* or vice versa. Other times, they beep if you're trying to squeeze some more letters or numbers into a box that's already full.

Can your computer be frozen solid? A frozen computer beeps every time you press a key.

The reason is that your keyboard stores about 20 characters in a special place called a *keyboard buffer.* If the computer doesn't wake up from its icy slumber, the buffer fills up as you pound the keyboard in exasperation. When the buffer's finally full, each character that didn't make it inside beeps in protest.

That's bad news. Your only solution is to hold down your Ctrl, Alt, and Delete keys at the same time. If you're using Windows, often you can close down the bottleneck program and continue to work. (Chapter 17 explores ways to fix Windows problems.)

With Windows 3.1 or DOS, unfortunately, pressing Ctrl+Alt+Del destroys all the work you haven't had time to save. It restarts your computer from scratch.

If the Ctrl+Alt+Del thing doesn't work, push the reset button on your computer's front or just turn the thing off. You still lose all your unsaved work that way, but at least you can get your computer's attention when it starts up again. If the computer still doesn't turn off, get nasty: Unplug the darn thing. Some new computers use power-management systems that occasionally disable the power button.

"How Can I Change to a Dvorak Keyboard?"

The *Dvorak* keyboard strays from the standard key arrangement — the one that spells *QWERTY* along the top row. Instead, the Dvorak keyboard uses a layout that engineers have calibrated especially for speed and finger efficiency. Very few people want the agony of learning how to type all over again, so only a few diehards use the Dvorak keyboard.

If you want to be a diehard, however, Windows comes with a built-in Dvorak keyboard option. If you're using Windows, click the Start button, choose Settings, and then choose Control Panel and double-click the Keyboard icon. Click the Language tab and then click the Properties button. From the Language Properties dialog box, choose your language and then choose Dvorak from the drop-down list (see Figure 5-1). Click OK and then click OK again. Windows will probably ask for its CD to fetch some files.

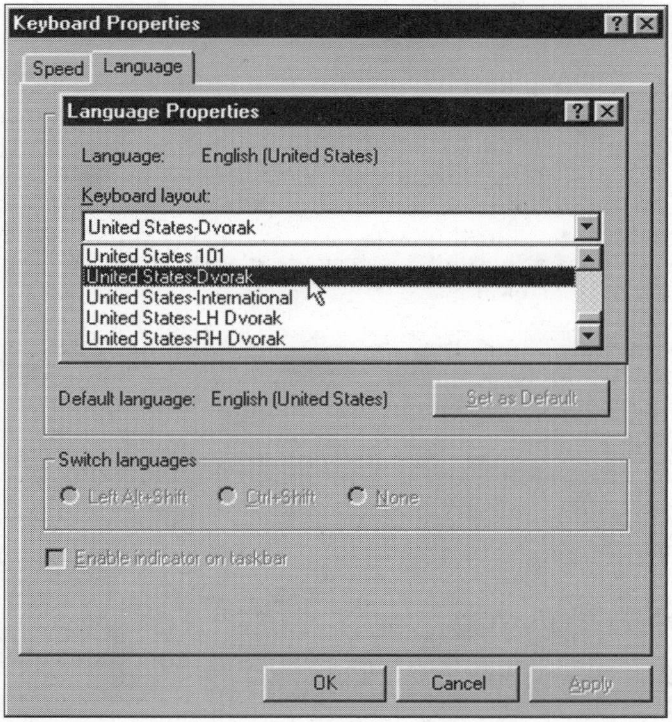

Figure 5-1:
To switch to the Dvorak keyboard layout in Windows, double-click on the Keyboard icon in the Windows Control Panel, click the Language tab, and choose Properties.

In Windows 3.1, head for the Control Panel and double-click the International icon. There, buried under the Keyboard Layout drop-down list (as shown in Figure 5-2), is the US-Dvorak option. You still have to move around all your keycaps yourself, though. (You can pry off and reseat the keycaps fairly easily.)

Figure 5-2:
Double-click the International icon in the Windows 3.1 Control Panel to switch to the Dvorak keyboard layout.

International	
<u>C</u>ountry:	United States	OK
<u>L</u>anguage:	English (American)	Cancel
<u>K</u>eyboard Layout:	US-Dvorak	Help
	Swiss French	
	Swiss German	
<u>M</u>easurement:	US	
	US-Dvorak	
List <u>S</u>eparator:	US-International	

<u>D</u>ate Format
5/13/97   Change...
Tuesday, May 13, 1997

Currency Format
$1.22
($1.22)   Change...

<u>T</u>ime Format
2:04:46 PM   Change...

<u>N</u>umber Format
1,234.22   Change...

Windows NT users can choose the Keyboard icon from the Control Panel and click the General tab. Click the Change button, and Windows NT shows the keyboard models currently compatible with your computer. If the new keyboard came with a disk, put the disk in your floppy drive, click the Have Disk button, and follow the instructions. (They vary with different keyboards.) No disk? Then click the Show All Devices button and choose your keyboard's brand from the master list.

✔ Although the Dvorak layout sounds as promising as solar energy, keep your QWERTY layout memorized. Otherwise, you'll be hunting and pecking at typewriters and terminals in airports, libraries, offices, and just about every other place in the civilized world.

✔ Also, if you're interested in more comfortable keyboards, check out the section on ergonomic keyboards coming up next.

"Do Ergonomic Keyboards Feel As Natural As Soybean Sprouts?"

In the past 50 years, computers have advanced from awkward, room-size primitive calculators into sleek powerhouses that let executives play three-dimensional flight-simulation games during business trips.

The typewriter, by contrast, hasn't changed from its straight, three-row lineup of keys in more than 100 years.

That same typewriter-key layout still lives on most computers, often leading to sore fingers and wrists for people who keep their fingers attached to their keyboards all day.

The solution? First, try several keyboards before buying a new one. The engineers gave more thought to comfort in some models. For instance, *ergonomic keyboards* like the Microsoft Natural Keyboard are sculpted in nontraditional ways so that your fingers approach the keys from different angles.

Ergonomic keyboards don't appeal to everybody, although their users often worship them. To see whether ergonomic keyboards are worthy of worship, check out the picture in the keyboard section of Chapter 3.

A wrist pad — a piece of foam your wrists rest on as you type — sometimes helps deter typing soreness or carpal tunnel syndrome. To see whether you can benefit from one, make a test model from a thin, rolled-up magazine taped shut. Put it along the front of the keyboard and see whether your arms feel better when the magazine lifts your wrists slightly.

"What's That Special Windows Key on a Microsoft Natural Keyboard?"

As a business, Microsoft stays almost exclusively within the software market. Computer programs are relatively inexpensive to make and distribute because they can be sold months before creation and they can be fixed by adding more software when something screws up.

Microsoft trots out a piece of hardware every few years, and the relaxed-looking Microsoft Natural Keyboard is one of the most popular, moving a step beyond the past century's awkward keyboard design. Shaped with angled rows of keys that aim toward a typist's elbows, the Natural Keyboard does something besides comfort the user's limbs: It comes with a special Windows key (shown in the margin) that can perform the mystical tricks listed in Table 5-1.

Today, most keyboards come with the Windows key, ready to puzzle new users.

Table 5-1	Exciting Shortcuts with the Windows Key
Press This	*To Do This*
Win+F1	Help
Win+E	Start Windows Explorer
Win+F	Bring up the Find program
Ctrl+Win+F	Find a computer on a network
Win+Tab	Cycle through taskbar options
Win+R	Bring up the Run program
Win+M	Minimize everything on the screen
Shift+Win+M	Undo the Minimize All command

"How Do I Install a New Keyboard?"

IQ level: 70

Tools you need: One hand

Cost: From $15 to $100 or more for elaborate models with speakers

Stuff to watch out for: If you don't know the difference between an XT computer's 84-key keyboard and an AT computer's 101-key Enhanced Keyboard, flip back to Chapter 3 to make sure that you buy the right one. It's not much of a fuss, though. Almost every keyboard sold today is the 101-key Enhanced Keyboard. Keyboards come with their own circuitry built in, so computers rarely reject them.

Most new keyboards come with small, PS/2-style connectors, as shown in Chapter 3. Older computers and keyboards use different, larger connectors. It never hurts to bring along the old keyboard when shopping for the new one. You can buy an adapter at the store, if necessary. (***Note:*** That same adapter often lets you plug an older keyboard into a laptop.)

Some expensive keyboards come with a built-in *trackball* that works like a built-in mouse. Others let you change the keys around to match your own keyboard tastes. Still others work as a USB "hub:" Plug the keyboard into your USB port, and plug all your USB peripherals into the keyboard's ports. Let your pocketbook be your guide.

Finally, don't buy a keyboard without taking it out of the box and typing nonsense words on it with your own fingers. You'll be working closely with that keyboard for years to come, so don't pick one that feels too hard, too spongy, or just plain unfriendly.

To install a new keyboard, follow these steps:

1. **Save any work you have on the screen, exit your program, and turn off your computer.**

   Don't ever unplug or plug in your keyboard cable while the PC is turned on. Something dreadful is supposed to happen. Besides, the computer recognizes the keyboard only when it's first turned on anyway.

2. **Remove your old keyboard by pulling the cable's plug from its socket on the back of your computer.**

   When unplugging any type of cord, pull on the plug, not the cord. The cord lasts a little longer that way.

3. **Carefully insert the new keyboard's plug into the socket.**

   The plug fits only one way. If the plug has a little plastic lump or ridge on its outside edge, that edge faces up on most desktop computers but sometimes to the side on a tower or mini-tower PC. If there's no lump, try to match up the plug's little pins with the socket's little holes. Then gently push the plug into the socket and turn it back and forth slowly until it begins to slip into the holes. Got it? Push firmly until it's all the way in.

   If that doesn't work, find out whether your keyboard has a PS/2 connector. It's a small plug, about the size of a back molar. A PS/2 connector doesn't fit in the standard-size hole, which is about the size of your thumb. You can buy a converter at most computer shops for about $5.

   Unlike most computer cables, a keyboard's cable doesn't have tiny screws to hold it tightly in place. Just push it in, and friction holds it in place.

   Because no screws are holding a keyboard's cable in place, the cable can sometimes work its way loose, especially during violent typing sessions. If the keyboard's acting up, make sure that the cable's plugged in securely.

4. **Turn your computer back on.**

   One of the first things a computer does when waking up is reach for its keyboard. If the computer doesn't complain, it found the new keyboard and decided that it was appropriate. Hurrah!

   If it does complain, however, head for the three chapters at the end of this book; they're designed to help diagnose strange and depressing startup sights and sounds.

This book's technical editor, Jeff Wiedenfeld, says that if the keyboard connector's little pins become bent, it won't fit into its hole, no matter how hard you push. A little care and needlenose pliers should set things right.

If your computer makes it to Windows before complaining, head for Chapter 17 for some resuscitative medicines. Windows recognizes most new keyboards on touch, but sometimes it needs drivers or special cable connectors for weird models with speakers, calculators, USB ports, or whirlpool controllers.

Chapter 6

Mice in the Pantry

● ●

In This Chapter

▶ Cleaning the mouse ball

▶ Fixing "jerky" or disappearing mouse pointers

▶ Using an optical mouse

▶ Loading a mouse driver

▶ Changing a mouse's pointer in Windows

▶ Choosing a PS/2, USB, serial, or IntelliMouse

▶ Installing a mouse

● ●

Mice all tackle the same computing chore. When you move your mouse across your desk, you subsequently move a little arrow across your computer's screen. By pointing at buttons on the screen and pushing buttons on the mouse, you "push" the buttons on the screen.

Most mice even look pretty much alike. They all resemble a plastic bar of soap with two buttons and a long tail. The confusing part of the mouse kingdom comes when you try to figure out where that tail plugs into the back of your computer. In fact, sometimes several computer devices want to plug into the same place, causing much gnashing of mouse teeth.

This chapter tells you how to referee the fights and tend to the injured. And don't forget that I decipher weird words like *cards* and *serial ports* in Chapter 3.

"My Mouse's Arrow or Cursor Is Starting to Jerk Around"

If you haven't installed any new software or hardware recently, your mouse is probably just dirty. (If you *have* installed new software or hardware, head for the "How Do I Install or Replace a Serial, IntelliMouse, or PS/2-Style Mouse?" section, later in this chapter.) Mouse balls must be cleaned by hand every so often. It's a pretty simple procedure:

1. **Turn the mouse upside down and look at the little square or round plastic plate that holds the ball in place.**

   You usually find an arrow indicating which way to turn a round plate or which way to push a square plate.

2. **Remove the plastic plate holding the ball in place, turn the mouse right-side up, and let the mouse ball fall into your hand.**

   Two things fall out: the plate holding the ball in place and the ball itself.

3. **Set the plate aside and pick all the hairs and crud off the mouse ball. Remove any other dirt and debris from the mouse's ball cavity, too.**

   If you have a Q-Tip and some rubbing alcohol handy, wipe any crud off the little rollers inside the mouse's ball cavity. The rollers are usually white or silver thingies that rub against the mouse ball. Roll the little rollers around with your finger to make sure that there's no stubborn crud you can't see hiding on the sides. Make sure that the crud falls *outside* the mouse and not back into the mouse's guts.

   If some stubborn grunge is on the mouse ball, some mild soap and warm water should melt it off. Never use alcohol on the mouse ball; that can damage the rubber. Also, make sure that the ball is dry before popping it back inside the mouse.

   Mouse balls give off a very disappointing bounce. Don't waste too much time trying to play with them.

4. **Drop the mouse ball back inside the mouse and put the plate back on. Turn or push the plate until the mouse ball is locked in place.**

   This cleaning chore cures most jerky mouse cursor problems. However, the mouse ball stays only as clean as your desk. Computer users with cats or shaggy beards may have to pluck stray hairs from their mouse ball every month or so.

"My Computer Says That It Can't Find My Mouse"

Are you sure that the mouse is plugged in? Grope around until you're sure that the plug on the end of its cable fits snugly into the little socket on the back of your computer. Plugged in tight? Then the problem could be something like the following.

Ever had a soggy bit of lettuce mulch stuck between your teeth after lunch, but you didn't know that it was there until you got home and looked in the mirror? Computers are the same way. Even though a mouse may be plugged into the case, the computer doesn't necessarily know that the mouse is there.

Before the computer can fiddle with your mouse, the computer needs to read a piece of software known as a *driver*. (Drivers are confusing enough to warrant their own section in Chapter 15.)

Here's what may be happening: When you turn on your computer, it finds the mouse's special *driver* software. The driver tells the computer where to look for the mouse. But when the computer turns its head and looks, it can't find the mouse. So, try these fixes, in this order:

1. **Make sure that your mouse is plugged into the back of your computer, and then restart your computer.**

2. **If you just installed another piece of hardware, head for the section in Chapter 17 about finding device conflicts in Windows. The new hardware probably grabbed the mouse's spot, confusing the computer in the process.**

   A mouse often works in Windows programs but not in those old DOS programs (the programs that don't look anything like Windows). That's because Windows has a built-in mouse driver and DOS doesn't.

3. **The solution? Type** \DOS\MOUSE **or just plain** MOUSE **at the DOS prompt, as shown in the following line, before loading your DOS program. This step should load the mouse driver so that the mouse and the computer can start talking to each other:**

   ```
   C:\>\DOS\MOUSE
   ```

   Then load up your program again and see whether the mouse works this time. If it doesn't, you have to contact your mouse's manufacturer for a "DOS" mouse driver.

If you want the DOS mouse driver to be loaded all the time, head for Chapter 15. When you put the MOUSE line in a file named AUTOEXEC.BAT, your computer loads the mouse driver every time you restart your computer.

"My Friend's Mouse Doesn't Work on My Computer"

Chances are that the mouse needs different drivers — software that translates your mouse's movements into something the computer can relate to. Ask for the software that came with your friend's mouse and run its installation program.

Also, some mice are *optical,* which means that they don't have balls like normal mice; instead, they use little sensors that read a special reflective pad with little lines on it. Without that special pad, the mouse won't work. In fact, if you have an optical mouse, you're forever stuck with that special optical pad. You can't use the free one that a computer magazine sends you for subscribing.

The early laptops aboard the space shuttle *Discovery* used the Microsoft Ballpoint *trackball*. The trackball clipped to the laptop's edge so that it wouldn't float around in the aisles.

"I Installed a Modem (Or Scanner or Weird Network Thing), and Now My Mouse Cursor Jerks Around or Hides"

Some mice and most modems squirt information into the computer through something called a *serial port*. Unfortunately, sometimes a mouse and modem try to squirt through the same port at the same time. When stuck with two conflicting sources of information, your poor computer feels as lost as a character in a Franz Kafka novel.

It boils down to this: You need to make sure that all your devices get a serial port all to themselves. This stuff gets pretty grueling, so head for Chapter 18 to see how to break up fights over a serial port.

A serial port is sometimes called a *COM port,* which is short for communications port. Your computer uses the serial port to communicate with other computer parts by moving messages back and forth.

Sometimes, you install a serial modem and a mouse, and suddenly you don't have a serial port left for your other gizmos. This problem is rough enough to send you to Chapters 17 and 18. Serial ports can quickly turn into a complicated and crunchy problem. Your computer can use only two serial ports at the same time, and yet dozens of computer gadgets want to grab one of them.

"My Cordless Mouse Sometimes Acts Weird"

Cordless mice need fresh batteries every so often. If your cordless mouse is acting funny, try replacing the batteries. Some batteries fit in the mouse's receiving unit; others slip into the bottom of the mouse itself.

An *infrared* cordless mouse needs a clean line of sight between itself and its *receiving unit,* the thing that plugs into the back of your computer. But because that clean line of sight will be the only clean spot on your desk, that's the first place you may tend to set down books and junk mail. Try moving your books and junk mail out of the way, and the mouse will probably calm down.

Other cordless mice use *radio* signals. These mice don't need to point in any particular direction. (Except for the battery drawer, unfortunately. These little critters feast on batteries.)

"How Can I Get a Better Windows Mouse Pointer?"

This little perk doesn't apply to older versions of Windows, just Windows 95 and Windows 98.

To get a better mouse pointer in Windows, click the Start button and choose Settings; then choose Control Panel and double-click the Mouse icon. The Mouse Properties dialog box appears. Click the Pointers tab, and Windows displays your choice of available mouse pointers. Click in the Scheme box to see the list of choices, as shown in Figure 6-1.

Then click on your choice from the list that drops down. Windows comes with a few different mouse pointer schemes; some programs toss their own in here as well.

Laptop users should try the Windows Standard (large) scheme; sometimes that makes a small pointer easier to spot.

After buying some new mouse pointers, a friend of an editor at IDG Books switched to a dinosaur for his mouse pointer and then couldn't get his mouse to work. Why? He didn't realize that the *head* of the dinosaur was the pointer. Be sure to try all parts of your new pointer before giving up hope.

Which Mouse Is Better — PS/2, Serial, USB, or IntelliMouse?

At first glance, none of the above. All four breeds of mice scoot the little arrow across the screen in the same way. You can't tell any difference in the mouse's look or feel. So your choice of mouse depends on your computer's needs.

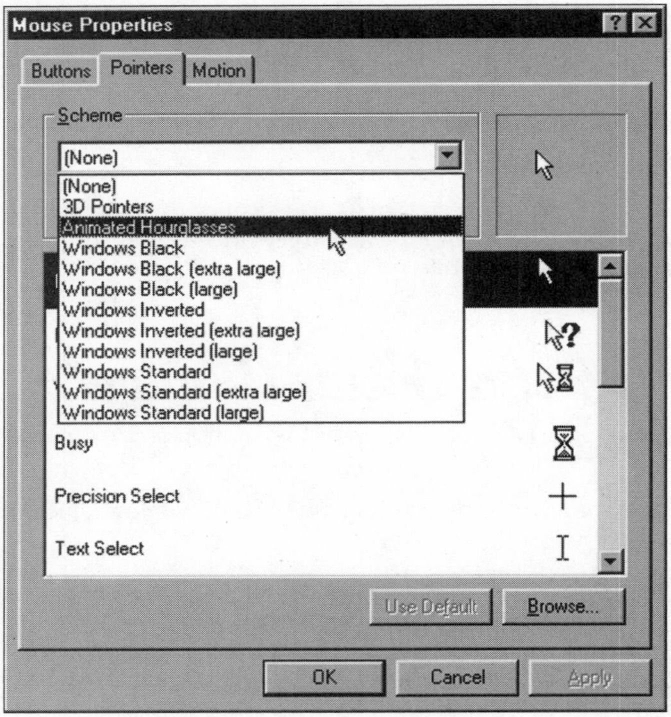

Mouse Properties

Buttons | Pointers | Motion

Scheme

(None)

(None)
3D Pointers
Animated Hourglasses
Windows Black
Windows Black (extra large)
Windows Black (large)
Windows Inverted
Windows Inverted (extra large)
Windows Inverted (large)
Windows Standard
Windows Standard (extra large)
Windows Standard (large)

Busy

Precision Select

Text Select

Use Default | Browse...

OK | Cancel | Apply

Figure 6-1:
Click the
Scheme
drop-down
list to select
a variety of
mouse
pointers.

PS/2 mouse: Most new computers and laptops come with a built-in PS/2 mouse port, so that's the best choice. That port — usually labeled Mouse or PS/2 — lets you plug in most of the mice on store shelves today, including the fancy Microsoft IntelliMouse (the one with the little wheel on its back).

Serial mouse: The cable from a serial mouse plugs into your computer's serial port — one of those protruding outlets along the back of your computer's case. Simple and easy — if you have an unused serial port on your computer's rear. Many PS/2 mice also work in a serial port, as long as you have an adapter that lets the PS/2 mouse's newfangled tail plug into an old-style serial port.

USB mouse: Some mice plug into your computer's wonder port — the Universal Serial Bus, or USB, port. They tend to cost a little more and don't have any huge advantages. If all your other ports are used up, however, USB may be for you.

IntelliMouse: My favorite, the IntelliMouse takes the cheese. It looks like a regular mouse, although the casing on the newer versions warps to the side a bit. But the real identifying feature is a little rollable "tire," or wheel, protruding from the top, between the left and right mouse buttons. When you install the special IntelliMouse software, the wheel comes to life. Spin the wheel with your index finger, and the page scrolls down on the screen. You no longer need to point and click on those awkward bars along the screen's sides. Unfortunately, these mice are pricey.

So, if your computer has a PS/2 mouse port and you're broke, buy a PS/2-compatible mouse. No PS/2 port? Then plug a serial mouse into an empty serial port. Got a little cash? Buy that IntelliMouse for the Cadillac of mice. It's fun, it's useful, and it comes with cool software that lets you calculate how many miles your mouse travels. Best yet, the Intellimouse with the IntelliEye eliminates moving parts and works on any mouse pad. No mouse balls to clean!

Why Is All This COM and Serial Port Stuff So Difficult?

All this port stuff is much easier than it sounds — unless you already have a bunch of toys plugged into your computer. Like a nursing mother, a computer has a limited number of resources. If you try to install more than two gizmos, the extra gizmos have problems talking to your PC.

If you're installing only a mouse and a modem, you'll probably do fine. But if you try to install a third guy — a scanner, a network card, or even a sound card — the potential for problems increases.

It all boils down to the fact that your PC was designed more than a decade ago when nobody could afford more than two toys. Now, with cheap toys everywhere, the PC's antique design is coming back to haunt people.

When Is a Mouse Not a Mouse?

The latest pointing devices are not mice at all, although they still allow you to chase your cursor around the screen. *Trackballs* are, in essence, upside-down mice. Rather than roll the ball around your tabletop, you roll the ball with your fingertips.

Another type of pointing device is a *trackpoint,* or *accupoint.* A few years ago, some notebook computer manufacturers designed a pointing device that looks like a pencil eraser stuck in the middle of your keyboard. This little joystick moves the cursor when you nudge it with your fingertip. Although the trackpoint device was originally designed for notebooks, Lexmark offers this technology in a desktop replacement keyboard.

The newest mouse replacements are *touchpads*. These flat, squarish devices enable you to move the cursor by simply dragging your finger across its surface. Touchpads are more common in notebook computers but are also available for desktops.

"How Do I Install or Replace a Serial, IntelliMouse, or PS/2-Style Mouse?"

IQ level: 80 to 100, depending on your computer's setup

Tools you need: A screwdriver

Cost: Anywhere from $10 to $120

Stuff to watch out for: When buying a new mouse, make sure that your mouse box says "Microsoft mode," "Microsoft compatible," or just plain "Microsoft mouse" somewhere on the package. Most programs prefer that kind of mouse.

Some mice can work in two modes: Microsoft mode and some other weird mode. Increase your chances of success by installing them to work under Microsoft mode. Then, whenever a new program asks what type of mouse you're using, answer "Microsoft."

A mouse comes with its own software and attached cord. You don't have to buy any extras. You can buy serial mice dirt-cheap — often as low as $10. The ones with the better warranties, better parts, and bigger ad campaigns can cost much more.

To replace or add a serial or PS/2-style mouse, follow these steps:

1. **Look at the back of your computer and look at the serial-ports section of Chapter 3 to see where you plug in your mouse. Then follow the instructions listed for that particular port:**

   Your old mouse port: If you're just replacing a dead mouse, take its corpse to the software store and buy another one just like it. That way, you can be sure to plug the new mouse into the same hole and all will be well.

   Small, round PS/2-style port: You're in luck! The plug on the cable of just about every mouse sold today fits without a problem. You can buy a PS/2-style mouse and plug it right in. Most mice today use this port, including the IntelliMouse.

Small serial port: Some mice plug directly into this port; a PS/2 mouse can plug in here through a PS/2-to-serial mouse adapter that costs less than $10.

This smaller port is usually named COM1. The software may ask you about it later in the installation process.

Big serial port: Described in Chapter 3, this port is probably too big for the mouse cable plug, so ask the salesperson for a 9-pin to 25-pin adapter. Some people call it a DB25 female/DB9 male connector. Whatever it's called, it costs less than $10 and lets a serial mouse's small plug fit into a computer's big serial port. This larger port is usually called COM2, which the software may want to know later in the installation process.

If you have a PS/2-style mouse port, by all means use it. By using this port, you can free up one of your serial ports for other computer gadgets.

No empty port: If you don't have *any* visible serial ports or any PS/2 port, look for a USB port. If you're using an older computer that lacks all those options, head to the computer store and ask for a serial card or an *I/O card*. (Installation instructions are in Chapter 15.) In fact, if you're using Windows 98, consider adding a USB card and buying a USB mouse.

If your computer has only *one* serial port and your modem is using it, head back to the computer store and ask for a second serial port for your I/O card.

2. **Turn off your computer.**

   Be sure to exit any of your currently running programs first.

3. **Push the plug that's on the end of the mouse's tail into the port on the back of your computer.**

   Push the plug until it fits tightly. If it doesn't fit correctly, you're probably trying to push it into the wrong port. (You may need one of the adapters that I describe in Step 1.) After you connect the cable firmly, use your tiny screwdriver to screw it in place. Some plugs have protruding thumbscrews, making them easier to screw in; some mice plugs don't screw in at all.

4. **Run the mouse's installation program.**

   Mice usually come with a floppy disk or CD. If you find a disk with yours, stick the disk into your drive and look at the drive's contents. Run any program named SETUP or INSTALL to start things rolling.

   Some installation programs can figure out for themselves where you've plugged in your mouse — they handle everything automatically. Others interview you like a job applicant. Some programs make you tell them whether the mouse is connected to COM1 or COM2. If the program asks, answer with the COM port you remember from Step 1.

The program probably wants to add some information to your AUTOEXEC.BAT or CONFIG.SYS file, even if you don't care what those files do. Feel free to let it continue. You can find more information on those two files in Chapter 16. If you're stuck at that weird COM port stuff, head for Chapter 18.

You may need to restart your computer before the mouse starts working. When the installation program is through, choose Restart from the Start button.

Windows almost always recognizes a new mouse and immediately treats it as a good friend. If Windows runs for the kitchen and starts counting the silver, head for Chapter 17.

Chapter 7

Mucked-Up Modems

● ●

In This Chapter

▶ Figuring out modem language

▶ Assessing your need for speed

▶ Upgrading to a better modem

▶ Calling the Internet and other useful places

▶ Configuring Internet Explorer for an Internet Service Provider

▶ Figuring out 56K, ISDN, DSL, cable, and other fast modem technologies

▶ Troubleshooting your faxes

▶ Installing an external modem

● ●

*A*dding a modem to your computer adds up to a dramatic upgrade. Suddenly, your computing horizons jump from *you + computer* to *you + computer + entire universe*. After you install a modem, you can use the Internet to type a message to someone halfway around the world or fax someone halfway across town — all from the privacy of your worn old PJs.

Here's the chapter that hooks you up to the Net and checks your *e-mail (electronic mail)* — reuniting you with your family, friends, neighbors, and the rest of the known universe.

Oh, and no one calls it a fax–modem anymore. Most modems come with built-in faxing capabilities, so just leave it at *modem*. (But don't buy a modem that can't fax!)

Who Can Understand All This Modem Stuff?

Nobody understands modems, really, but here's enough information so that you can fake it, like everybody else.

The main thing that counts with modems is how fast they spew information back and forth to other modems. Table 7-1 provides a rundown of the most common types of modems.

Table 7-1	Funny Modem Words
This Funny Word	*Means This*
300 baud or bps	Introduced in 1968, these first modems aren't even collectibles — just slow relics to be avoided.
1200 baud or bps	Marginally faster than 300 bps models, these are rowboats among cruise ships.
2400 bps	Peppier than former models, these are little red wagons versus today's luge.
9600 bps	The trendsetter of the 1980s, these are small placeholders in modem-speed history.
14400 bps	Now thought of as agonizingly slow, the 14400 bps model held favor with modem maniacs until the 28800 bps models became affordable.
28800 bps	Yesterday's workhorses, also known as 28.8 Kbps.
33600 bps	Modem makers added an edge to the 28800 bps models that pushed data-transfer speeds up to 33600 bps — but only under ideal conditions. These guys are often referred to as 33.6 Kbps. Many can be updated with software to the next speed, described next.
56000 bps	More often seen as 56K, this much-hyped standard (also known as V.90) achieves its rated speed only when attached to another V.90 modem, and then only under ideal line conditions. That's why you rarely connect at 56K when Web surfing. Still, it's the current workhorse of today's phone lines.

This Funny Word	Means This
ISDN modem	This one runs at 64000 bps and requires a special digital hookup from your local phone company. Most telephone companies offer two ISDN lines, called *B channels.* Although one's intended for voice and the other for data, you connect them to reach 128 Kbps. That's still relatively slow, however, and the technology's fading fast.
DSL	DSL, or a *Digital Subscriber Line,* comes in two speedy flavors: *ADSL (Asymmetric)* and *SDSL (Symmetric).* These formats pack information on regular phone lines, but there's a catch: You need to live near a telephone switching station. ADSL receives data at anywhere from 1.5 to 9 Mbps and sends data at anywhere from 16 to 640 Kbps. SDSL sends and receives at up to 3 Mbps.
Cable modem	Run — don't walk — to sign up — *if* you live in one of the few neighborhoods that offers cable modem service, that is. Why the fuss? Because cable modems grab Internet data at anywhere from 3 to 10 Mbps and send data at speeds as fast as 2 Mbps. Cable modem users *must* read this chapter's section on setting up a firewall, however. Evil computer hackers often target cable modems for attack.

- ✔ The higher the bps number, the faster the modem moves data around the Internet — and the more the modem costs.

- ✔ Thanks to something known as *backward compatibility,* the speediest modems can slow down to talk to the older, slower ones. So a 56K modem can still talk to a 28800 bps modem, which can still talk to a 14400 bps modem, which can still, well, you get the idea.

- ✔ The speeds listed here apply only under optimum conditions. Just because your car's engine can move the car at 100 m.p.h., you can't always drive that fast because of all the stoplights and traffic.

Fast, faster, fastest!

The newspapers are full of stories on cable modems, DSL, and ISDN — faster technologies that hope to speed the masses (that's you and me) onto the Internet. But what's what? Which one's best? And, most important, is the extra speed really worth it?

56K and V.90

In an effort to squeeze maximum speed from our existing *POTS* (Plain Old Telephone Service) copper-wire phone line system, modem companies released 56K models in the mid-1990s. The problem? Modems from 3Com used the X2 standard, and the Rockwell Semiconductor modems used K56flex, meaning they couldn't talk to each other.

After 1998, modem manufacturers switched to a new V.90 modem standard, so all 56K modems could chatter away at 56K, no matter who made the modem. Why should you care? If you're using an older 56K modem, head to its manufacturer's Web site. Chances are, downloadable software will upgrade your old modem to the *new* 56K standard, called *V.90.*

ISDN

For ISDN, you need a special new modem and a special type of phone line. That's because *ISDN* (*Integrated Services Digital Network,* for the terminally curious) takes advantage of the telephone company's digital signaling capa-bilities. After installation, ISDN sends and receives data on two separate channels at speeds up to 64000 bps, with a maximum speed of 128000 bps if you combine, or *bond,* the two channels in a given Internet session.

One cool thing about ISDN is that you can talk on the phone on one channel while you're dialing up your Internet provider on another. (This arrangement seems complex, but it's actually transparent to you.) This complexity makes it important to look for an ISDN modem that includes an analog port, which is where you plug in that phone or fax machine.

For a hefty installation fee, your phone company dispatches a technician to wire your house with a digital phone line; prices vary widely. You supply the ISDN modem; 3Com products rate highly.

Cable modems

Cable modems — the name says it all. They're modems that work through your cable TV connection.

Rather than come through the phone lines, the Internet rushes into your home through the same coaxial cable your cable TV company installed (if you're a cable TV subscriber). And your cable company becomes your Internet provider.

The cable representative drops by your house or office, installs a network card in your computer, splits your cable signal, and hooks it to a special cable modem, which you lease for a nominal fee (just like the phone com-pany used to do with your telephone).

After it's hooked up, your cable modem receives data at speeds up to 10 Mbps — zillions of times faster than today's popular 56 Kbps modem.

Cable modems don't send data nearly as quickly as they receive, however, but that's usually not a big deal: Internet users receive far more data than they send. In fact, the only real drawback to cable modem access is that you probably can't get it — it's available in very few cities . . . so far.

Even the price is right: Most cable modem providers charge between $30 and $50 per month for unlimited Internet access — meaning that you can leave your connection open 24 hours a day if you want. (Although normal Internet accounts cost closer to $20 per month, they also hog the family's phone line, forcing most people to install a second line for a hefty installation charge and an additional $15 or so per month.)

In my area, the local cable company offers three separate usernames and 5 megabytes of Web space for each username.

And, yes, the family can still watch cable TV or listen to cable radio — in every room in the house, if so desired — at the same time you're blazing around the Internet.

When using a cable or DSL modem, make sure that you're not sharing your files with the entire Internet. Open the Network icon from the Control Panel and click the File and Print Sharing button. When the File and Print Sharing window appears, make sure that neither of the two boxes is checked. If you need to check either of the boxes for your own computer network, buy and install a firewall, described in the following sidebar, to block unauthorized outside access.

Cable modems need firewalls

Cable modems can be as dangerous as a high-speed sports car because they function differently from old-school Internet connections. Whenever your computer connects to the Internet, your Internet Service Provider assigns it a number known as an _IP address._ Each time you connect to the Internet, your IP address changes to a different number.

That means telephone-based Internet users are safer from malicious "hackers." Because the number changes with each connection, the hacker has more trouble finding and relocating a particular computer.

A cable modem remains constantly connected to the Internet, so your computer's IP address never changes. After a hacker locates your computer's address on the Internet, he or she can break into it much more easily.

Hackers run special search programs that randomly search the IP addresses assigned to DSL and cable modem users, looking for a computer they can break into. After the hackers break in, they can browse the computer's files or cause damage. They can also take control of the computer's connection, using the computer's address as a launchpad to hack into other

(continued)

(continued)

computers. That preserves their anonymity as they try to "crack" other accounts.

The solution? Use special software, called a *firewall,* to stop hackers from entering your computer. I've been using BlackICE Defender, shown in the following figure, the past few months. It makes your computer invisible to hackers. It notifies you when somebody has tried to break into your computer using a random IP address. Best yet, the program records the hacker's IP address so that you can notify the hacker's Internet Service Provider of their customer's evil deeds.

If somebody directly targets your computer for attack, raise the level of BlackICE's protection so that the invader can't get in.

In a single day, the BlackICE Defender firewall logged eight different attempts to break into my computer.

DSL modems

Digital Subscriber Line technology *(DSL)* is yet another attempt to put off the inevitable day when our plain copper phone lines will be replaced with high-bandwidth fiber lines.

Using digital signal processing to beef up the copper wire's bandwidth, DSL receives data (to you) from 128 Kbps to 1.5 Mbps and sends data (from you) at a rate of up to 768 Kbps.

Although some installations are in place today, the technology is spreading slowly, largely on a trial basis.

The downside? It's expensive, and users must live near a phone-switching station for the stuff to work.

Baud, bps, Kbps, Mbps, and other tidbits

Modem speed is measured in *bps* (bits per second) — the number of bits of information a modem can throw to another modem in one second. Some people measure modem speed in baud rate, a term that only engineers really understand.

Here's where things get sticky. A 300 or 1200 bps modem is also a 300 or 1200 baud modem. But the terms *bps* and *baud* don't stay the same past speeds of 2400 bps.

If, for some strange reason, you find yourself stuck discussing icky stuff like modem speeds, just stick with the term bps. Then you won't have to see the orange stuff between the nerds' teeth when they start laughing.

Oh, and if you see the term Kbps, they're using the metric system to say, "thousands (Kilo) of bits per second." Rather than take the trouble to spell out 56000 bps, folks usually shorten it to "56 Kbps" and even 56K (pronounced "fifty-six kay").

With the advent of new technologies like the cable modem, a new unit of measure arose: 1 Mbps means roughly 1,000 kilobits, or roughly a million bits per second.

Asymmetric DSL, or ADSL, shuttles data at different speeds, whether it's going to or from your house. *Symmetric* DSL moves the data at the same speed no matter which direction it's going.

Soon after spotting the abbreviation DSL, you'll spot a new one: xDSL. When a format branches in different directions, computer gurus stick an *x* next to the format's abbreviation to signify all the different directions. Windows 9.*x*, for instance, means Windows 95 and Windows 98. Similarly, xDSL stands for all the new flavors of DSL: ADSL, SDSL, and any other DSL flavor of the month.

Satellite modems

A Digital Satellite System (DSS) only *downloads* information, giving you a great excuse for not answering your e-mail. It's four to eight times as fast as a 56 Kbps modem. If you want to send information, however, you still need to buy a modem and use a phone line. In fact, that's how the DSS knows what to send you — you send your Web page requests through the modem, and the satellite sends the requested information to your PC.

Which system works the best?

The bottom line? When listening to all the amazing speed claims, consider this: The Internet itself is the slowest part of the connection. The Internet's simply an umbrella term for a vast web of connected computers. Many of these computers still use 56 Kbps modems. That means even cable modem users are often caught twiddling their thumbs, waiting for a slow Web site to spit out its information. Still, cable's the best bet right now, if it's offered in your area and you've installed a firewall.

What Are Modem Standards?

You've already glimpsed a few modem terms, but you're not off the hook yet. One important concept, *modem standards,* comes in handy whether you're upgrading to a better modem or trying to understand the one you have.

Over the years, engineers have roughly doubled modem speeds each year or two. Well, each new speed breakthrough corresponds to a formal modem standard, decided by an actual standards committee. Your 56000 bps modem, for example, complies with the V.90 standard. It also complies with preceding standards, making it backward compatible — able to work with previous models. Finally, modems conform to additional standards that, er, standardize crucial functions like *error control* and *data compression* — functions which ensure that your data arrives intact . . . even when traveling through the noisiest phone lines.

Who cares about standards? You do. Modem marketers often claim impossibly high *throughput,* or transmission speeds, by reporting speeds achieved only when their modems are connected to identical models on the other end. These claims aren't outright lies, exactly — but how many times will you find yourself connecting with your modem's exact twin?

On the other hand, no manufacturer can fake compliance with a modem standard. To make sure that you're getting the best modem, shop *standards* and not just speeds. A modem's package proclaims the modem's standards in the form of vee-dot numbers like V.90 (say "vee-dot ninety") and others. For the history of those complicated-looking vee-dot numbers, check out Table 7-2.

Table 7-2	Keep Your Eye on the Vee-Dot Number
This Vee-Dot Number	*Corresponds to This Feature*
V.90	56000 bps data transfer speeds
V.34	28800 bps data transfer speeds; 14400 bps faxing
V.34 plus or enhanced	33600 bps data transfer speeds
V.42/MNP 2–4	Error control; modem detects and corrects missing bits during noisy connections or other less-than-ideal conditions; be sure that you buy one with *hardware* error control

This Vee-Dot Number	Corresponds to This Feature
V.42*bis*/MNP5	Data compression; uses modem shorthand to squish data and boost the number of bits transferred; specify *hardware* data compression
Class 1/Class 2, Group III	Fax standards which ensure that the modem can talk to the broadest range of fax devices

Keep in mind that no standard can work unless it's supported by the modems on each end of the connection — an important thing to remember. (When you hear the modems wail upon connecting, they're negotiating what standards to use.) When a fast modem calls one that supports a slower standard, for example, they just agree to use the (slow) one they can both manage.

What You Need to Get on the Internet

Most modems come with prefab "Internet Starter Kits," software to help you make your first Internet connection.

Getting on the Internet means that you need to find a company called an *Internet Service Provider (ISP)* and buy access through it, much the same way you call the phone company to start up telephone service.

Many people decide that it's easier to take the Internet plunge by going through an online service like America Online (AOL) or CompuServe. Other users look for national or local Internet providers. Either way, if your new modem fails to include any cool Internet software, peruse the following list to find out what to do next:

- ✔ **AOL or CompuServe:** Obtain and install the free software; most modems include trial offers for both services. After you connect, each service offers a prominent Internet button; just click to start exploring. (No software? Call and have some mailed to you: AOL, 800-516-0046; CompuServe, 800-292-3900.) Or sign up on the Internet at www.aol.com or www.compuserve.com.

- ✔ **Local or national Internet provider:** Request instructions on how to set up Windows to call its computers. Also ask someone there to send you any software you may need. If you're not using Windows 98, demand an up-to-date Web browser — special software that enables you to access the World Wide Web, send and receive e-mail, participate in newsgroup discussion forums, and do other cool stuff.

✔ **Windows 98:** Windows 98 brandishes a folder, named Online Services, right on the desktop. Click it to find icons that take you to Internet providers and online services, such as America Online, CompuServe, Prodigy, and others. In fact, Microsoft leaves its own online service's icon, MSN, right on the desktop — a fact that annoys not only Microsoft's competitors but also the government.

After you're connected, your modem can snag dozens of other Internet-related programs for you that can help you organize your e-mail, streamline your special-interest groups, block your kids' Internet access, and more. Try heading to a Web page called TUCOWS, a good starting point for Internet software, at www.tucows.com.

Will a Modem Replace a Fax Machine?

Ninety-nine percent of all modems can fax, but if you already have a fax machine, don't throw it away! You still need it if you want to fax today's *Dilbert* strip or that take-out menu from Alberto's Tacos — and anything else you can't store on a computer file.

Actually, if you have a scanner, you can scan the Alberto's Tacos take-out menu, save it as a computer file, and then fax it from your fax/modem. Everyone else will have to pop it in the mail, make their buddies drive to Alberto's to get their own darn menus, or find a fax machine.

Also, note that some of the newest, fastest modems — cable modems, for example — can't send or receive faxes. Hang on to your old fax modem (or a fax machine) to round out your telecommunications equipment.

Sending and receiving faxes

Almost any modern 56K modem can fax, but you still need special fax software to make it all work. Fortunately, most modems come with fairly decent software named WinFax Lite. (Windows 95 comes with the MS-Fax program, but, alas, Windows 98 does not.)

If you plan to do much faxing from your computer, splurge for a good commercial-grade program like WinFax Pro, from Symantec.

Although Windows 98 doesn't install a fax program, it hides one on its installation CD. Open the CD's Tools\OldWin95\Messaging folder and double-click the WMS.EXE file. Follow the instructions to install the fax program. It's not fancy, and it's downright confusing, but it's free. If you're willing to stray from the Microsoft fold, head to www.tucows.com or www.winfiles.com for some shareware and freeware fax programs.

Sending a fax

After you install fax software, the fax program appears on the Windows list of installed printers. After creating a document you want to fax, select your word processor or other software's Print command and choose the fax program rather than your usual printer. (You may need to click on the scroll-down button to see the other installed printers.) Your fax software loads, asks a few questions (such as the name and fax number of your recipient and whether you want to fill out a cover sheet), and, with the click of a Send button, your document chugs across the phone lines.

Receiving a fax

Receiving a fax requires a bit of preparation — unless you're sitting right in front of your computer, with fax software loaded and ready.

First, load your fax software — otherwise, your fax program won't hear the modem ring. (Most fax programs can be set up to work in the background and take a call within any number of rings you specify.)

Second, set up your modem and fax software to *auto-answer* an incoming phone call. Fortunately, your modem's manual explains how you can set the modem to pick up only after several rings — so that it doesn't beat you to the phone (six or eight rings works well).

For these reasons, many business owners prefer to keep a fax machine around for receiving unexpected faxes. Then the only hassle comes with those Internet-generated "junk" faxes that are sent indiscriminately and use up all your fax paper!

Fixing the fax

Experiencing faxing frustration? One or more of these tips may prod your computer to behave:

- ✔ Lower the speed by dropping the fax software's *fax receive rate* to a lower bps number.

- ✔ Check to make sure that the fax software's Class 1/Class 2 setting accurately reflects your modem's capabilities (the modem's manual tells you these).

Using a Modem on a Laptop or Palmtop

Depending on the age of your laptop, you can make it modem-ready in several ways. Most laptops come equipped with special PC Card slots that can accommodate credit-card-size PC Card modems. (You may see some older PC Card modems calling themselves PCMCIA modems instead.) Check out Figure 7-1 to eyeball one.

Very old laptops or laptops without slots can always accommodate a serial cable and an external modem. Often, you can find smallish external modems designed for travelers.

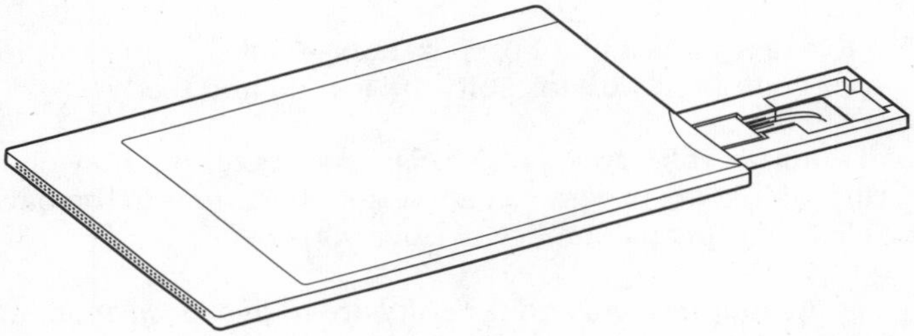

Figure 7-1:
Tiny, credit-card-size modems slide into the PC Card slot on most laptops.

TIP

Windows 95 and 98 automatically recognize and install most PC Card modems these days; still, make sure that the modem says "Plug and Play" on the box.

If your laptop came with a built-in modem but you want to use a faster modem on a PC Card, you may need to go into your laptop's setup files and disable the built-in modem. Your laptop's manual should prove helpful here.

"My Modem Hangs Up Whenever Anybody Calls Me!"

Some popular people have *call waiting* installed on their phone lines. When the person is talking on the phone and somebody else calls, the phone makes a little "beep" sound. The person then interrupts the conversation to say, "Can you hold on a second? I have another call."

But your modem is even ruder than that. If your modem is talking to another modem and a call-waiting beep blasts into the discussion, your modem may simply hang up.

The solution? Dial the four characters ***70,** (that's an asterisk, the number seven, the number zero, and a comma) before dialing the other modem's number. For example, rather than dial **555-1212,** dial ***70,555-1212** to turn off your call waiting on a push-button line. That funky little code tells the phone company to turn off call waiting for your next call. Incoming callers get busy signals. Then, when you finish that call, your call waiting is automatically turned back on.

Note: The ***70,** command works only with the newer tone (push-button) phones. If you're one of the ten remaining people on the planet with the older pulse phone, dial **1170,** (the numbers 1170 followed by a comma).

It's hard to remember to turn off call waiting before each call, so you can tell your modem software to do it automatically. Look for a "dialing command" area in the software. The dialing command is usually set up to say ATDT. Change it to **ATDT*70,** (or change it to **ATDT 1170,** if you have a pulse phone), and call waiting is turned off automatically before each call.

"How Do I Configure My Internet Browser to Work with an Internet Service Provider?"

IQ level: 90 to 110, depending on your ISP's friendliness.

Tools you need: Before connecting to the Internet, round up these three things:

- ✔ **An Internet Service Provider, or ISP:** This is the company that provides a connection to the Internet. Ask a friend, coworker, teenager, or computer nerd for a recommendation. Don't have one? The Internet Connection Wizard will find one for you that's in your own area.

- ✔ **Your username, password, and phone number from your Internet Service Provider:** Write down these key informational tidbits. You need them to configure your Internet browser. Don't have an ISP? If the wizard finds you a service provider, it will dish out those things, too.

- ✔ **A modem:** Most new computers come with a modem lodged in their innards. To see whether one's inside yours, look for telephone jacks on the back of your computer, near where all the other cables protrude. If a cable modem service is available in your area, go for it. It's zillions of times quicker, and you don't need to tie up your phone line. (Plus, you won't need to pay for a second phone line while Web surfing.)

Cost: Most ISPs charge an average of $20 to $40 a month. (Windows includes a free Internet browser.)

Stuff to watch out for: Microsoft realized the difficulty level of making Internet Explorer work with an ISP, so it created a wizard to walk you through the process.

To configure Internet Explorer to work with your ISP, follow this next set of steps.

In fact, whenever you encounter difficulties in getting your Internet connection just right, head here and run through these steps. The Wizard displays your current settings and allows you to change them:

1. **Click the Start button, click _P_rograms, choose Accessories, and load the Internet Connection Wizard from the Communications area.**

2. **Choose one of these three options:**

   • Sign up for a new Internet account.

   Don't have an Internet account? Choose this option, and Windows helps you select one. When you choose this option, the Wizard dials a number to locate Internet Service Providers in your area and displays their rates and options. Chances are, you can sign up with one of several providers, including America Online, Prodigy, AT&T WorldNet Service, and others.

   After you choose a provider, the Wizard makes you fill out your name, address, and credit card information before leaving you at Step 3.

   • Transfer your existing Internet account to your computer.

   Already have an Internet account? Click here to set up your computer to access this account. Your modem still dials a number to find local providers in your area. This time, however, it finds only providers who've signed up for Windows 98 Second Edition's new "automatic configuration."

   Chances are, your provider won't be listed. Tell the form that your provider isn't listed, and Windows guides you through setting up the Internet connection process manually — the same as the next step.

   • Set up your existing Internet account manually or through a network.

   You'll probably work with this step if you're setting up a computer to use an existing ISP. Continue along these steps to introduce your computer to your existing Internet account by filling out forms and punching buttons.

3. **Tell Windows 98 whether you connect through a phone line or a network.**

   If a phone line plugs between the wall and the back of your computer or into a little box near your computer, you're connecting through the phone line and a modem. Choose that option.

   If you use a network, find a technosavvy teenager for help or check out *MORE Windows 98 For Dummies,* which I wrote (published by IDG Books Worldwide, Inc.). Or, if enough people log on to my Web site, at www.andyrathbone.com, and ask me for network coverage, I'll stick it in the next edition.

4. **Enter the phone number for your Internet Service Provider, click Next, and enter the appropriate info in the User name and Password blanks.**

   Your ISP should have given you these three things. If not, call and ask for more information.

5. **Type a name for your Internet provider.**

   Just make up a name for your own reference, or type **My Provider**.

6. **Create a mail account.**

   On the next page, suppose that you want to set up an Internet mail account. On the coming pages, type your name, your username, and your e-mail address — usually your username, the @ sign, and the name of your provider. If your provider is home.com and your username is q-a, for example, type **q-a@home.com**.

   The next page has the most confusing part. Unless your Internet provider tells you otherwise, simply type the word **mail** in the Incoming mail and Outgoing mail server boxes.

   On the next page, type your account name. Still using the preceding example, you'd type **q-a**. Then, type your password in the box below. If you want to log on automatically without entering your password each time, check the Remember password box. Because this eliminates a need for a password, however, anybody can sit at your computer and read your e-mail.

   Check the Secure Password Authentication box only if requested by your Internet provider.

7. **Click the Finish button.**

   You're done. The latest Windows 98 Internet browser, Internet Explorer 5.0, automatically leaps into action and uses your settings to call your Internet provider.

If everything goes correctly, your modem dials, and you are soon logged on to the Internet and ready to browse. Need a place to go for a quick test? Try logging on to www.dummies.com and see what happens.

Some versions of Windows may not have the Internet Connection Wizard listed on your Start menu. To find the wizard, right-click on your Internet Explorer icon, choose Properties, click the Connections tab, and click the Setup button.

"How Do I Install or Replace an External Modem?"

IQ level: 80 to 100, depending on your computer's setup.

Tools you need: One hand.

Cost: Anywhere from $25 to $150.

Stuff to watch out for: Internal modems cost the least, followed by external modems, followed by PC cards. Don't accidentally buy a laptop's PC card modem rather than a desktop modem.

Modems are as easy as mice to install. The hard part is trying to make them do something useful. A mouse's software is pretty much automatic; it works in the background. A modem's software forces you to make all the complicated decisions, even when you're not in that kind of a mood.

Also, mice need special *drivers.* Modems don't. However, external modems need cables. Unlike mice, modems don't come with any cables attached, and most modems don't include any cables in their boxes.

Finally, internal modems come on *cards,* so I cover them in Chapter 15.

To install an external modem, follow these steps:

1. **Locate where to plug in your modem.**

   Look at the back of your computer, and then look at the serial ports section of Chapter 3 to find out the right place for your modem to plug into. Then follow the instructions for that port.

   If you're replacing your old modem, pull the cable off the back of your old modem and plug it into the back of your new modem. Then jump to Step 3.

   Small serial port: A small serial port has 9 little pins in it. Most external modems sport large, 25-pin female ports. So your cable needs a 9-pin female plug on one end and a 25-pin male plug on the other.

   This smaller port is usually named COM1. Your modem software will want to know that port's name in a few minutes.

Big serial port: For this task, you need a cable with a 25-pin female plug on one end and a 25-pin male plug on the other end.

This larger serial port is usually named COM2. Modem software always wants to know these things so that it can find the modem.

Having trouble remembering all that male/female pin adapter stuff? Grab a piece of paper and draw a picture of the port on the back of your modem and the one on the back of your computer. Then bring that paper to the computer store when shopping. (Don't bother counting all the pins or holes. The number is either 9 or 25.) This information helps when shopping for the right cable as well.

No empty port: If you don't have any serial ports, head to the software store and ask for an *I/O card*. (You can find installation instructions in Chapter 15.)

If your computer has only *one* serial port and your mouse is already using it, head back to the computer store and ask for a second serial port for your I/O card. The I/O card will probably be one of the big serial ports I described a few paragraphs back. Or buy an internal modem, which I describe in the next paragraph.

If you have two serial ports and both are being used, sidestep this serial-port stuff altogether by buying an *internal modem*. It comes on a card, so it's covered in Chapter 15.

2. **Connect your cable between the end of your modem and the port on the back of your computer.**

   The cable should fit perfectly at either end. If not, keep perusing Step 1 until you find a cable that fits right. Sometimes it helps to draw a picture. When you've finally plugged the cable in, use your little screwdriver to fasten the two little screws that hold it in place. The more expensive cables have thumbscrews that make screwing them in easier.

3. **Plug the phone line into the back of the modem.**

   If your modem has a single phone jack in the back, plug one end of the phone cord into there and plug the cord's other end into the phone's wall jack. However, if your modem has two phone jacks, the procedure is a little harder. One phone jack is for the phone line cord, and the other is for you to plug a desk phone into. You must put the right cord into the right jack, or the modem won't work.

If you're lucky, the two phone jacks are labeled. The one that says *phone* is where you plug in your desk phone's cord. The one that's labeled *line* is for the cord that runs to the phone jack in your wall.

If the two jacks *aren't* labeled, dig out the manual while cursing under your breath the whole while. Turn the modem upside down first, though. Sometimes you can find helpful pictures or labels on its bottom. If the two jacks aren't labeled and you can't find the manual, just guess at which line plugs into which jack. If the modem or your phone doesn't work, just swap the two plugs. (Having them wrong at first doesn't harm anything.)

4. **Plug the modem's AC adapter into the wall and plug the other end into the modem. Then turn the modem's power switch on.**

   Modems aren't so self-contained. Almost all of them need an AC adapter. Then they need to be turned on. (These are two things that can go wrong.)

5. **Run your modem software.**

   Modems usually don't need complicated *drivers,* like mice do. No, a modem's communications software is complicated enough. You can find it on a disk somewhere inside the box. When you type SETUP or INSTALL, the software takes over and starts asking you questions. You did remember which COM port you plugged your modem into, didn't you?

   The software also asks your modem's speed, so keep that information handy as well. (It's listed on the box.)

   If your modem software complains about IRQ conflicts or COM port problems, sigh sadly. (Sigh.) Then troop to Chapter 18 for help with all the IRQ stuff.

Fast external modems sometimes have a problem when installed in pre-Pentium computers, especially when used with Windows programs. That's because the chip used in the old computer's serial port can't keep up with the data flowing through the speedy new modem. If your modem seems to lose data after transmissions, bite the bullet and buy a new, internal modem. The new models come with the updated chipsets already installed.

I won't leave you hanging. If you're using Windows 95 or earlier, click the Start button, choose Run, type **MSD,** and hit Enter. The Microsoft Diagnostics Program identifies your serial port's chips. Windows 98 users need to remove the case from their computers and inspect the chips — if they're worried about it. Those newer computers usually don't have the same problem.

Chapter 8

Tweaking the Monitor

● ●

In This Chapter

▶ Cleaning dust off the screen

▶ Fixing monitors that don't turn on

▶ Understanding video vocabulary

▶ Adjusting a monitor's screen

▶ Matching monitors with video cards

▶ Buying a 3D accelerator card

▶ Finding missing cursors

▶ Eliminating weird monitor noises

▶ Preventing burn-in

▶ Adjusting a laptop's screen

▶ Installing a new monitor

● ●

Most computer terms sound dreadfully ho-hum: High density. Device driver. Video adapter. Yawn.

But the engineers had apparently just returned from a horror flick when they started coming up with monitor terms: Electron gun! Cathode ray! Liquid crystal! Zounds!

This chapter talks about the thing everybody stares at and puts stick-on notes on — the computer monitor. Plus, you get a few digestible tidbits about your *video card,* which is the gizmo inside your computer that bosses your monitor around.

"The Screen Has Dust All Over It"

Monitors not only attract your attention, but they also attract dust. Thick, furry layers of dust. And that dust is attracted on a weekly basis.

Do not clean your monitor while it is turned on! The static charge that builds up on the surface can wipe out a few little parts in your computer. Wait three to five minutes after you shut off the monitor before you clean it.

Computer salespeople brush dust off quickly with a single swipe of their sleeves. Don't have a beige sport coat? A soft cloth and a little glass cleaner do the trick. You really have only one thing to remember: Spray the Windex on the *cloth,* not on the monitor itself. A monitor won't blow up if its screen gets wet, but the Windex can drip down the screen's front and make the parts inside soggy. If you like fine print, check the manufacturer's recommendations regarding cleaning solutions for your particular monitor's screen.

And don't spray Windex into the monitor's top or side vents, even if you like the burning smell.

"My Monitor Doesn't Turn On!"

Are you *sure* that your monitor is plugged in? Actually, your monitor has four plugs you need to check:

- ✓ Check to make sure that you plugged the power cord securely into the wall or power strip, and make sure that your power strip is turned on.
- ✓ Wiggle the connection where the monitor's cord plugs into the back of your computer.
- ✓ Check the back of your monitor.

  Some cords aren't built into the monitor, leading to loose connections. Push the cord hard to make sure that it's plugged in tight.

- ✓ Check the back of your computer.

  On particularly old models, you plug the monitor's power cord into the back of the computer — not into the wall.

You know how some outlets are wired to wall switches? For example, you flip a wall switch by the door and a lamp turns on across the room. Well, don't plug your monitor (or your computer) into one of those switched outlets. If you use one of those outlets, you may find yourself scratching your head, wondering why the monitor doesn't always work.

"What Do All Those Funny Video Words Mean?"

Video cards and monitors are full of technical buzzwords. But you don't need to know what the buzzwords mean. Instead, just trust your eyes.

Believe it or not, one of the best ways to buy a monitor and a card is to head for the computer store and play Windows Solitaire on a bunch of different monitors. When you decide which monitor looks best, buy it along with the video card that's powering it.

If you're looking for a monitor to watch multimedia movies, ask to see some onscreen videos — somebody sailing a 60-foot yacht or eating crackers while parachuting off the Eiffel Tower. Compare the videos on different screens and trust your eyes.

Some salespeople may gab about *dot pitch* this and *vertical sync* that. But don't buy a monitor and card unless you see them in action. All the technical specifications in the world don't mean anything compared with what you see with your own eyeballs.

If you're still curious about what those video buzzwords mean, check out Table 8-1.

Table 8-1	Awful Video Terms	
This Word	**Means This**	**So?**
Pixel ("PIX-el")	A single little "dot" on your screen.	Computer pictures are merely collections of thousands of little dots.
Resolution	Pixel dots are stacked across your monitor in a grid, like tiny bottles in a wine rack. *Resolution* describes the number of rows and columns your monitor and card can display.	Common resolutions are 640 rows x 480 columns, 800 rows x 600 columns, and 1,024 rows x 768 columns. Bigger numbers lead to smaller rows and columns, meaning you can pack more information on the screen (bigger numbers also mean a bigger price tag).
Color	The number of colors you can see on the screen.	Here, the card is the limiting factor. Most newer monitors can display any number of colors.

(continued)

Table 8-1 *(continued)*

This Word	*Means This*	*So?*
Mode	A combination of resolution and color.	Most cards and monitors can usually display several different "modes." For example, you can run Windows in 640 x 480 resolution with 65,000 colors. Or, you can switch to 800 x 600 resolution with 256 colors. There's no right or wrong mode. It all depends on personal preference.
Dot pitch	The distance between the little pixel dots on the monitor. The smaller the dot pitch, the clearer the picture.	*Tip:* Don't buy a monitor with more than .28 dot pitch, or the picture looks hazy.
Digital	Digital technology once powered older monitors, but it couldn't handle newer cards, so it was phased out. Now it's back, but it powers the flat-panel LCD screens that look so cool.	*Tip:* Check to see whether an old CRT monitor has a "digital/analog" switch. If so, it may still work with some newer cards.
CRT and LCD monitors	Short for *cathode ray tube,* the monitors that look like TV sets. LCD stands for *liquid crystal display.* They look like a laptop's screen.	LCD monitors cost much more than CRT monitors.
Analog	The new-technology way of displaying pictures on the monitors that look like TV sets (most monitors).	Today's video cards all require analog monitors except for the ones that power LCD displays. (Those require digital output.)
Multiscan, Multifrequency, or Multisync	These friendly monitors can switch back and forth to work with a wide variety of video cards.	Because they're the easiest monitors to please, they're also the most expensive.

This Word	Means This	So?
Bandwidth	The speed at which your card can send information to your monitor. Faster is better. It's measured in megahertz (MHz), and 70 MHz is easy on the eyes. (Bigger numbers are faster.)	A monitor has to be able to accept the information as fast as the card can send it. That's why those *multiscanning* monitors are popular: They can accept information at a bunch of different bandwidths.
Refresh rate	How fast your monitor and card can "repaint" the picture.	The bigger the number, the less flicker on the screen.
3D accelerator	These cards have a special chip that helps your computer put pictures on the screen more quickly.	*Tip:* For an easy way to work faster in Windows and other graphics programs, replace your old card with an accelerator card. (These work especially well with games.)
Memory	The amount of RAM chips on your video card. Some cards can be upgraded by adding more memory chips. The higher the card's resolution, the more memory it needs. High-resolution images with lots of colors can require 4MB or more of memory.	Don't confuse video memory with your computer's memory. Video memory lives on the video card; your computer's memory lives on the motherboard. They can never visit each other's houses. *Tip:* Don't buy a video card with a small amount of memory, thinking that you can add more memory later. That usually leads to problems.
Driver	A piece of software that translates a program's numbers into pictures you can drool over.	If you're going to use Windows NT or OS/2, make sure that the card has a Windows or OS/2 *driver. Tip:* Windows 98 and earlier versions work with most popular video cards. OS/2 doesn't.
Interlaced, non-interlaced	Technical stuff that's much too awful to bother with.	Just remember that a non-interlaced display has less flicker and is easier on your eyes.

"I Bought an Expensive New Monitor, but My Screen Still Looks Ugly"

A television merely displays pictures that come through the airwaves, like the Movie of the Week. Even with cable television, you're stuck with whatever's coming over the wire.

The same goes for computer monitors. They display only what is being sent by your computer's video card, which lives inside your computer's case.

Upgrading your computer's display can get expensive — fast. The expense quickly adds up because you usually need a new video card as well as a new monitor.

Basically, card- and monitor-shopping boils down to these simple "make sures:"

- Make sure that your video card and your monitor match in resolution — the number of little rows and columns they can display. The most popular resolutions are 640 x 480, 800 x 600, 1,024 x 768, and 1,280 x 1,024. The best video cards and monitors reach 1,280 x 1,024 or higher.

- If you are looking for SuperVGA performance, make sure that you have a SuperVGA monitor *and* card. A VGA monitor still works with a newer, SuperVGA card, but only in VGA mode. A VGA monitor can't show any of the SuperVGA card's superduper video modes.

- The term "spit roasted" sounds pretty unhygienic, if you stop to think about it.

"The monitor's screen looks washed out"

Just like a television set, a monitor comes with a row of fiddling knobs. Although most people just kind of spin 'em around and squint until things look better, there really is an official way to fine-tune your monitor's picture.

Here's the scoop:

1. Locate your monitor's brightness and contrast knobs or buttons.

The knobs or buttons usually live along the monitor's right edge, where they irritate left-handers. Or they are somewhere beneath the monitor's front edge, where they are often concealed behind a little fold-down plate.

The knobs and buttons aren't always labeled, unfortunately, but they almost always have little symbols next to them, like in Figure 8-1.

Figure 8-1:
These moon
and sun
symbols
usually
appear next
to the
contrast and
brightness
knobs.

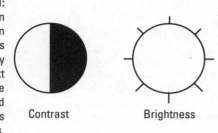

Contrast   Brightness

2. **Open your word processor and put some text on the screen.**

   With characters onscreen, turn the monitor's brightness knob all the way clockwise, which turns the brightness up all the way. A light-colored border glows along the edges of the screen.

3. **Turn the contrast knob back and forth until the letters onscreen look sharp.**

   Look for a clear difference between the dim and bright areas. You may have to fiddle for a bit until it looks just right. Also, try moving your desk lamp around until you find the best picture.

4. **Turn down the brightness until the light-colored glow around the screen's border merges into the blackness.**

   Your screen should be at its best. You may need to repeat the trick after your monitor has warmed up or after a well-meaning coworker fiddles with the knobs.

"The colors look awful in one of my programs"

You can adjust a monitor's brightness and contrast. But, unlike with a television, you can't fiddle with the colors on most monitors. You're spared from the bother of rectifying green newscasters.

Instead, you can change the colors from within your program. Look for the program's *setup screen* or *control panel*. Chances are that the setup screen or control panel will let you change the colors to something more pleasing.

Windows users — and color laptop users — can flip to Chapter 17 to see how to change their desktops' colors from the traditional boring blue to the Egyptian look of carved stone. (You can also find some settings particularly beneficial to laptop users.)

When a monitor has been turned on for several hours, the colors often start to look tired and blurry. Some of the more well-to-do monitors sport a Degauss button, which restores the correct colors, like the monitor's equivalent of a rejuvenating facial. (No Degauss button? Many newer monitors degauss automatically when powered on. Or, leaving your monitor turned off for 15 minutes does the same thing.)

If you're using an older laptop without a color screen, check to see whether the program supports *LCD* or *monochrome* settings.

"Will My Old Monitor Work with My New Video Card?"

New cards can nearly always work with older monitors. However, older monitors usually can't display all the new colors and resolutions that the new cards have to offer.

The only way to tell whether an old monitor and your new card can work together is to get technical. You have to find the old monitor's manual and make sure that your monitor can match your new card's *resolution* and *refresh rates.* You can find those weird words explained in Table 8-1.

Or you can just plug your monitor in, turn it on, and have a look-see.

"What's That Local Bus, PCI, and AGP Video Stuff?"

For years, people simply pushed video cards into the rows of slots sitting inside their computers. Today, the process is a little more complicated. The concept is the same — push the card into the slot — but the slots are trickier.

"My computer doesn't have a video card!"

Some computers don't have a video card. The video stuff is built right onto the computer's motherboard. This setup was the rage in the first days of 486 local bus video — a way to speed up the flow of pictures on the monitor. Unfortunately, these "built-in" video computers have a problem when you want to upgrade: You need to turn off the built-in video before your computer can start using your newly installed card.

You may need to pull out the computer's manual for this one. Some computers want you to move a jumper, an act I describe in Chapter 18. Other computers make you run the setup program that came with the computer.

Finally, some computers are smart enough to know that you've plugged in a new card and that they should turn off their own card. Imagine that — a smart computer!

Computer manufacturers figured that the old-style slots didn't let computers grab information from the cards quickly enough to do fancy things, such as show Alpine skiing movies on the monitor. So they created special slots that grabbed information more quickly. The first, VL-Bus, emerged for the old 486 computers, and the PCI slots took over when Pentiums hit the stores.

The latest computers come with another slot, called AGP. Described in Chapter 3, this slot takes full advantage of your video card to move pictures around onscreen at their fastest.

Before buying a new video card, check your computer's manual or motherboard to see what video slot to use. (Chapter 3 helps identify slots and video cards.) When you know what slot your computer uses, make sure that your video card fits into that slot. Manufacturers make video cards that fit into several different slots, so make sure that your new card has the right type of slot listed on the box.

"Should I Buy a 3D Accelerator Card?"

For years, people bought new video cards to make their pictures look more realistic onscreen. That little green parrot would look more and more like it flew right out of *National Geographic*.

But as video quality improved, the computer had to slow down. Tossing all those hundreds of thousands of colored dots onto the screen takes lots of muscle.

So somebody invented a *graphics accelerator chip*. Rather than strain to toss dots onto the screen, the computer just tosses the chore to the graphics accelerator chip. The chip takes over all the rough graphics, and the computer goes back to doing more traditional computer-oriented stuff.

These accelerator cards come with the accelerator chip built in, so you merely have to install the card. The latest cards, *3D accelerators,* speed up the action in many video games by displaying three-dimensional objects realistically on your two-dimensional monitor. If you play computer games, you need one of these cards.

✔ If you use Windows and you're in the market for a new video card, be sure to buy a 3D accelerator card. That ensures compatibility with future software.

✔ The video boards on many older Pentiums have only 1MB of video memory, yet a Pentium can process more information than that. The fastest video cards now come with 16MB or more of video memory.

Gamers should check out one of today's finest cards: The ATI All-in-Wonder card not only offers 2D and 3D accelerator action, but it can also display the image on a TV set, place a fully tunable TV set on your monitor's screen, and capture images from the screen, saving them as files.

"My Monitor Makes Weird Noises!"

Almost all monitors make little *popping* sounds when first turned on or while warming up. That's nothing to worry about. But they're never supposed to whine, buzz, or make threatening sounds like they're about to blow up.

Monitors are normally one of the quietest parts of your PC. If your monitor ever starts making noise, something is wrong. If those noises are ever accompanied by an odd smell or even smoke, turn off your monitor immediately.

If your monitor is slowly turning into an old creaker, it may pick up a few odd sounds toward the end. Better start saving the cash for a new one.

If you install a new video card and the monitor screams, the card's trying to make the monitor do something cruel and unnatural. Chances are that the two aren't compatible. Try fiddling with the card's software to make it run in a different video mode.

✔ Even if you've had the card and monitor for a long time, changing the card's video mode can make the monitor squeal. Avoid the video mode that's causing the problem. Only power supply fans are allowed to squeal.

✔ If the monitor squeals in only one program, then that program is probably forcing the monitor to display a mode it just can't handle. Color televisions can cheerfully display old black-and-white movies, but monitors can burn themselves out if they're not built for the mode they're receiving. Head for that program's setup area and choose a different video mode or video resolution.

"I Don't Want My Screen to Burn In"

Have you ever seen an old, monochrome monitor that looks like it's running WordPerfect even when it's turned off? That permanent, leftover image is known as *screen burn-in*.

To prevent the burn-in, some wizened computer guru invented a *screen saver*. If nobody touches a computer's keyboard for a few minutes, the computer assumes that the owner has wandered off and turns off the screen to save it.

Today's new color monitors don't have much of a burn-in problem. But some wizened, wacky, and now wealthy computer guru invented a colorful screen saver. Rather than blank the screen while the owner is away, the computer displays a fish tank complete with animated fish (or flying toasters or other colorful images).

✔ Windows comes with a healthy selection of screen savers; the docent waits to describe them in Chapter 17.

✔ Some people like screen savers because prying eyes can't read their screens when they're in the lunchroom getting coffee.

✔ Most people just use screen savers because they're fun. Besides, you never have to scrub the algae off the insides of an onscreen aquarium.

"My Laptop's Screen Looks Weird"

Most laptop screens are temperature sensitive. Whenever I charge the battery in my laptop, for example, the battery heats up and warms the bottom corner of the screen. Then when I turn on my laptop, that bottom corner looks weird until it cools down.

Also, check your program's setup screen. Some programs let you change the colors. Keep cycling through them all until you find the one that is most readable.

Freezing temperatures can damage your display. Also, don't apply pressure to get that mood ring effect, no matter how fun it looks.

"How Do I Install a New Monitor?"

IQ level: 70

Tools you need: A screwdriver

Cost: Anywhere from $150 to $2,000

Stuff to watch out for: Be sure to match your monitor with your video card. Like Donny and Marie, your monitor and video card work as a team. When buying a flat-panel LCD monitor, be sure to buy a video card that works with that particular brand of monitor.

If you're installing a video card at the same time you're installing a monitor, flip to Chapter 15 first. There you find all the card-installing instructions. When the card is in, head back here.

Unless you're installing a new card while adding a new monitor, your new monitor's screen won't look much different from your old monitor's screen.

Finally, don't shudder too violently when looking at that $150-to-$2,000 price range listed. The cheapest monitors are blurry, 14-inch things; the most expensive ones are huge, colorful appliances that can display two full-size pages on the screen at the same time. Although the most common display size purchased today is 15 inches, higher-resolution video settings produce smaller Windows icons. Power Windows users are demanding monitors measuring 17 inches and larger. Power PC gamers are even connecting their computers to their big-screen TVs.

Also, if you've purchased a card that can display TV shows on your monitor, you'll definitely want a large monitor so that you can watch *Dawson's Creek* in the corner of your monitor while having enough room to work around it.

To install a new monitor, perform the following steps:

1. **Turn off your computer and unplug your old monitor.**

   Save your work and exit any programs. Then, after turning off your computer, unplug your old monitor's power cord from the wall. Then unplug the monitor's video cable from its little port on the back of your computer's case. You may need a tiny screwdriver to loosen the tiny screws.

   Remember which little port the monitor cable plugged into. That's where you need to plug in your new monitor's cable.

2. **Remove the old monitor from your desktop.**

   You can either store the old monitor next to the electric wok in your garage's Old Appliance Graveyard or try to sell it to a friend or stranger.

3. **Remove the new monitor from the box.**

   Monitors are packaged pretty securely, so you have to remove lots of Styrofoam balls and plastic wrap. The cable is wrapped up in its own little package.

4. **Place the monitor on your desk and plug it into the video port, as shown in Figure 8-2.**

Figure 8-2: 15 - hole port
Most monitors plug into a port that looks like this.

5. **Plug the monitor's cable into the back of your computer and make sure that the cable is fastened securely on the monitor's end.**

   If the cable is not fitting right, you either bought the wrong monitor or you are trying to plug it into the wrong card.

   Do you have one of those cool *swivel* stands? Then be sure to leave a little slack on the cables. Otherwise, one little angle adjustment can pull the cables loose.

6. **Plug the monitor's power cord into the wall or a power strip.**

   Or, if your monitor's power cord plugs into the back of your computer, plug it in there.

7. **Turn on your monitor and then turn on your computer.**

   Can you see words on the screen as the computer spews its opening remarks? If so, you're done. Hurrah! If it doesn't work, however, keep going through some of the fixes you skimmed in this chapter. The monitor should be pretty easy to fix.

If you bought a fancy monitor with speakers, cameras, or other goodies, you have to perform two more tricks: Plug the cords from the speakers and cameras into their spots in the back of your computer — usually on cards (covered in Chapter 15). Then, if Windows doesn't recognize your new monitor's special features, you probably have to install the drivers that came on the floppy disk that came with the monitor. (Your monitor *did* come with a floppy disk, didn't it?) Either way, Chapter 17 can help out.

Chapter 9

Printers (Those Paper Wasters)

• •

In This Chapter

▶ Understanding printer terms

▶ Fixing paper jams

▶ Understanding fonts

▶ Fixing spacing problems

▶ Curing blotchy pages

▶ Troubleshooting the printer

• •

Most newly installed programs grovel around inside your computer. After some electronic poking and prodding, the programs can figure out for themselves what stuff is hiding in there. But even the smartest programs can't figure out what's on the end of your printer cable.

Windows makes this process a little easier. If your printer is plug-and-play compatible, Windows 95 and 98 automatically detect what kind of printer is on the end of the cable and prompt you through installing the correct software driver. Even if you don't have a plug-and-play printer, you can tell Windows your printer's brand name and model, and Windows will kindly spread the printer's name to any Windows programs that ask.

Even without Windows, printers are getting easier to use every day. The only problem is those odd days. You know, when the margins just don't look right, the letter to the phone company looks like some weird weather map, or the printer won't even turn on.

When your printed pages look funny — or the paper won't even come out of the printer — this is the chapter to peruse.

"I Dunno What All This Printer Stuff Means"

Like monitors, printers have picked up some pretty weird terms over the years. None of these terms sounds really violent, unless *laser* counts. The terms are all just dreadfully boring — unless, of course, the terms are placed in a table that's pleasing to the eye, like Table 9-1.

Need information on different *types* of printers? Head for the "Printers" section of Chapter 3.

Table 9-1	Boring Printer Words
The Boring Term	*What It Means*
Emulation or printer mode	Some printers pretend to be other printers so that they can work with more varieties of software. The most commonly copied printers and designs include IBM, Hewlett-Packard LaserJet, PostScript, and Epson.
Hewlett-Packard LaserJet	One of the most popular laser printers. This printer is also copied a lot. *Tip:* For almost surefire results, set your laser printer to LaserJet mode and choose LaserJet from your program's printer menu.
Epson	When in doubt about what kind of dot-matrix printer you have, choose Epson. Although many IBM and Okidata printers are still floating around, most can be set to work in an Epson emulation mode. And if, by chance, you happen to pick up a genuine Epson dot-matrix printer, you'll have no problems.
PostScript	The Adobe programming language for printers. This language excites artsy graphics people who put peacock feathers on their desks. PostScript printers can handle high-end, professional-quality graphics and great gobs of fancy fonts. *Tip:* If you have a PostScript printer, set it to PostScript mode. Choose PostScript from your program's printer menu.
Printer control language (pcl)	The way a program explains a page to the printer. (See the following entry, page description language.)

The Boring Term	*What It Means*
Page description language (pdl)	Another way a program explains a page to the printer. For example, PostScript and LaserJet use their own pdls.
Pages per minute (ppm)	The number of pages a laser printer can squirt out in one minute. That's the same page, though. If you print several different pages, the pages don't come out nearly as fast.
Dots per inch (dpi)	The number of dots a laser printer can pack into one square inch. The more dots per inch, the better your printed stuff will look.
Driver	This little piece of software translates the stuff on your screen into the stuff you see on the printed page. Windows uses different drivers to talk to different brands of printers. Can't find the right driver for your printer's model? Most printers mimic popular brands, so choose the driver for the printer that your printer mimics. It's probably the Hewlett-Packard LaserJet, PostScript, or Epson. Better yet, if Windows doesn't list the correct driver for your printer, visit the printer manufacturer's Web site and download one for free.
Point size	The size of a single letter. This word uses a bigger point size than this word.
Typeface	Describes a letter's distinctive style. Courier is a different typeface than TimesRoman.
Font	A typeface of a certain size and characteristic. For example, TimesRoman is a typeface, and **TimesRoman Bold** is a font within that typeface family.
Pitch	The amount of space between letters.
Line feed	Flip this switch only if everything is always double-spaced. Or flip this switch if everything is printing on the same line, over and over. Otherwise, ignore it. Note that some dot-matrix printers let you push this button to advance the paper one line at a time.

(continued)

Table 9-1 *continued*

The Boring Term	What It Means
Form feed	On some printers, selecting this button brings up the top of the next piece of paper so that it is ready for printing.
Toner cartridge	This plastic box inside a laser printer holds black powder, known as *toner*. The toner is transferred to the paper electrostatically and melted on by the fuser rollers. Whatever that means.
Skip perforation	Does your dot-matrix printer keep printing on top of the perforation where you tear the paper into pieces? Or does your printer skip the perforation and leave an inch or so between each page? If so, this toggle switch lets you choose to skip or not skip. *Tip:* After changing a printer's settings, you often need to turn your printer off and then turn it on again. (Turn your printer on and off slowly, though. Electric stuff doesn't like quick flicks.)

"My Printer Doesn't Print Anything"

Are you *sure* that the printer is plugged in and turned on?

Check to see whether the printer's little *power* light is beaming merrily. If not, plug a lamp into the outlet to make sure that the outlet works. If the lamp works in the outlet where your printer doesn't, the printer is most likely suffering from a blown power supply. You have to take your printer to the repair shop and hope that the repair folks can fix it within two weeks. If the power light is on, though, keep reading.

 ✔ Does the printer have paper? Is the paper jammed somewhere? Some printers have a little readout that announces "paper jam" when the paper is stuck. With other printers, you have to ogle the paper supply yourself.

 ✔ Is the printer cable plugged firmly into its ports? Be sure that you check the port on the computer and the port on the printer.

✔ Do you have a *switch box* that lets two computers connect to one printer? Check to make sure that the switch box is switched to the right computer. While you're there, give the cables a tug to make sure that they're firmly attached.

✔ Is the printer *online?* Meaning: Is the online light glowing? If not, press the Online button.

✔ Also, try printing from a different program. Maybe your program is messing up, and the printer is perfectly innocent. If the program is messing up, it probably doesn't know what brand of printer you have bought. Head to the following section, "When I Try to Print Something, I Get Greek!"

Laser printers are *supposed* to heat up. That's why you shouldn't put pillow-cases or covers on laser printers when they're running. If you don't allow for plenty of air ventilation, your laser printer may overheat. When you're not using your laser printer, make sure that it has cooled off and then put the cover on to keep dust and dead flies out of it.

"When I Try to Print Something, I Get Greek!"

When you see Greek rather than English (or, for you overseas readers, English rather than Greek), chances are that your printer is working right. It's your *software* that's messing up. The software thinks that you have a different kind of printer on the end of the cable. For example, Figure 9-1 shows what Microsoft Word for Windows prints when it thinks that a PostScript printer is on the line but it's really a Hewlett-Packard LaserJet.

You can reuse your scrap paper. Place it in your printer tray either upside-down or right-side up, whichever way makes your printer use the blank side. You don't want to use scrap paper for important stuff, but use it for stuff you're not going to show other people.

Rather than have Greek come out of your printer, the opposite — having nothing print — can be equally annoying. When Word for Windows prints in LaserJet format to PostScript, nothing at all comes out of the printer.

The problem is that the software is using the wrong *driver*. You need to head for the program's Print Setup menu and then choose the driver that's right for your printer.

```
%!PS-Adobe-3.0
%%Creator: Windows PSCRIPT
%%Title: Microsoft Word - CHAP08.DOC
%%BoundingBox: 13 15 595 778
%%DocumentNeededResources: (atend)
%%DocumentSuppliedResources: (atend)
%%Pages: (atend)
%%BeginResource: procset Win35Dict 3 1
/Win35Dict 290 dict def Win35Dict begin/bd{bind def}bind def/in{72
mul}bd/ed{exch def}bd/ld{load def}bd/tr/translate ld/gs/gsave ld/gr
/grestore ld/M/moveto ld/L/lineto ld/rmt/rmoveto ld/rlt/rlineto ld
/rct/rcurveto ld/st/stroke ld/n/newpath ld/sm/setmatrix ld/cm/currentmatrix
ld/cp/closepath ld/ARC/arcn ld/TR{65536 div}bd/lj/setlinejoin ld/lc
/setlinecap ld/ml/setmiterlimit ld/sl/setlinewidth ld/scignore false
def/sc{scignore{pop pop pop}{0 index 2 index eq 2 index 4 index eq
and{pop pop 255 div setgray}{3{255 div 3 1 roll}repeat setrgbcolor}ifelse}ifelse
/FC{bR bG bB sc}bd/fC{/bB ed/bG ed/bR ed}bd/HC{hR hG hB sc}bd/hC{
/hB ed/hG ed/hR ed}bd/PC{pR pG pB sc}bd/pC{/pB ed/pG ed/pR ed}bd/sM
matrix def/PenW 1 def/iPen 5 def/mxF matrix def/mxE matrix def/mxUE
matrix def/mxUF matrix def/fBE false def/iDevRes 72 0 matrix defaultmatrix
dtransform dup mul exch dup mul add sqrt def/fPP false def/SS{fPP{
/SV save def}{gs}ifelse}bd/RS{fPP{SV restore}{gr}ifelse}bd/EJ{gsave
showpage grestore}bd/#C{userdict begin/#copies ed end}bd/FEbuf 2 string
def/FEglyph{G  }def/FE{1 exch{dup 16 FEbuf cvrs FEglyph 1 exch
putinterval 1 index exch FEglyph cvn put}for}bd/SM{/iRes ed/cyP ed
/cxP ed/cyM ed/cxM ed 72 100 div dup scale dup 0 ne{90 eq{cyM exch
0 eq{cxM exch tr -90 rotate -1 1 scale}{cxM cxPg add exch tr +90 rotate}ifelse}{
cyM sub exch 0 ne{cxM exch tr -90 rotate}{cxM cxPg add exch tr -90
rotate 1 -1 scale}ifelse}ifelse}{pop cyP cyM sub exch 0 ne{cxM cxPg
add exch tr 180 rotate}{cxM exch tr 1 -1 scale}ifelse}ifelse 100 iRes
div dup scale 0 0 transform .25 add round .25 sub exch .25 add round
.25 sub exch itransform translate}bd/SJ{1 index 0 eq{pop pop/fBE false
def}{1 index/Break ed div/dxBreak ed/fBE true def}ifelse}bd/ANSIVec[
16#0/grave 16#1/acute 16#2/circumflex 16#3/tilde 16#4/macron 16#5/breve
16#6/dotaccent 16#7/dieresis 16#8/ring 16#A/hungarumlaut
16#B/ogonek 16#C/caron 16#D/dotlessi 16#27/quotesingle 16#60/grave
16#7C/bar 16#82/quotesinglbase 16#83/florin 16#84/quotedblbase 16#85
/ellipsis 16#86/dagger 16#87/daggerdbl 16#89/perthousand 16#8A/Scaron
16#8B/guilsinglleft 16#8C/OE 16#91/quoteleft 16#92/quoteright 16#93
/quotedblleft 16#94/quotedblright 16#95/bullet 16#96/endash 16#97
/emdash 16#99/trademark 16#9A/scaron 16#9B/guilsinglright 16#9C/oe
16#9F/Ydieresis 16#A0/space 16#A4/currency 16#A6/brokenbar 16#A7/section
16#A8/dieresis 16#A9/copyright 16#AA/ordfeminine 16#AB/guillemotleft
16#AC/logicalnot 16#AD/hyphen 16#AE/registered 16#AF/macron 16#B0/degree
16#B1/plusminus 16#B2/twosuperior 16#B3/threesuperior 16#B4/acute 16#B5
/mu 16#B6/paragraph 16#B7/periodcentered 16#B8/cedilla 16#B9/onesuperior
16#BA/ordmasculine 16#BB/guillemotright 16#BC/onequarter 16#BD/onehalf
16#BE/threequarters 16#BF/questiondown 16#C0/Agrave 16#C1/Aacute 16#C2
/Acircumflex 16#C3/Atilde 16#C4/Adieresis 16#C5/Aring 16#C6/AE 16#C7
/Ccedilla 16#C8/Egrave 16#C9/Eacute 16#CA/Ecircumflex 16#CB/Edieresis
16#CC/Igrave 16#CD/Iacute 16#CE/Icircumflex 16#CF/Idieresis 16#D0/Eth
16#D1/Ntilde 16#D2/Ograve 16#D3/Oacute 16#D4/Ocircumflex 16#D5/Otilde
16#D6/Odieresis 16#D7/multiply 16#D8/Oslash 16#D9/Ugrave 16#DA/Uacute
16#DB/Ucircumflex 16#DC/Udieresis 16#DD/Yacute 16#DE/Thorn 16#DF/germandbls
16#E0/agrave 16#E1/aacute 16#E2/acircumflex 16#E3/atilde 16#E4/adieresis
16#E5/aring 16#E6/ae 16#E8/ccedilla 16#E8/egrave 16#E9/eacute 16#EA
/ecircumflex 16#EB/edieresis 16#EC/igrave 16#ED/iacute 16#EE/icircumflex
16#EF/idieresis 16#F0/eth 16#F1/ntilde 16#F2/ograve 16#F3/oacute 16#F4
/ocircumflex 16#F5/otilde 16#F6/odieresis 16#F7/divide 16#F8/oslash
16#F9/ugrave 16#FA/uacute 16#FB/ucircumflex 16#FC/udieresis 16#FD/yacute
```

Figure 9-1:
This garbage appears when Word for Window prints in PostScript format to a LaserJet printer.

✔ In Windows 98, open the My Computer icon from the desktop and double-click the Printers folder inside. Double-click the Add Printer icon and follow the steps to introduce Windows to your printer. (You can find a more complete description of how to do this task in Chapter 18.)

✔ If you're using a DOS program, you may need to reinstall the program and tell it the name of the right printer this time.

✔ Windows already comes with drivers for most printers.

✔ You can find more information about PostScript in Chapter 3.

If your older-style printer can switch between PostScript and LaserJet emulation, try to make sure to select the correct driver from Windows before you start printing on the printer. Nobody can *always* remember, but you can at least try. Luckily, most newer models are auto-sensing.

"Paper Keeps Jamming in My Laser Printer!"

Sounds like you need to get your printer cleaned by a professional. In the meantime, open the laser printer's top and carefully remove the offending sheet of paper.

Grab hold of the paper stack, hold it loosely with both hands, and flick the edges as though they were one of those little flip-page cartoons. This process loosens up the paper and makes it flow through the feeder easier.

Keep cats away from laser printers. My friend's cat peed in hers, and the printer cost her several hundred dollars to repair.

Don't run labels through your laser printer — unless the label's box says specifically that it's okay. The heat inside the printer can make the labels fall off inside the printer. The labels gum up everything, which makes you feel just awful.

"My Printer Says That It Has 35 Built-In Fonts — Where?"

A printer company's marketing department often plays on the confusion between typefaces and fonts.

A *typeface* is a family of letters. Arial is a typeface, for example. `Courier` is a typeface, too.

A *font* describes a particular *breed* of typeface. **Arial Bold** is a font, and so is *Arial Italic*.

Your printer considers Arial, **Arial Bold,** and *Arial Italic* to be three different fonts. That's why the term "35 built-in fonts" is pretty boring after you see what the letters really look like.

"Everything Is Double Spaced or Printing on the Same Line"

After a printer puts a single line of text on the paper, the printer needs to drop down a line and start printing the next line. But should the printer do so automatically? Or should it wait until the computer says so?

This awful bit of computerized politeness can really mess things up. If your printer and computer *both* drop down a line, everything turns out double-spaced. But, if neither of them speaks up, all your text prints on the same line, over and over.

The solution? If your lines are always double-spaced or all the text prints on the same line, flip the printer's *line feed* switch.

- ✔ After flipping the line feed switch, you need to turn your printer off, wait ten seconds, and turn it back on again. Printers look at their switches only when they're first turned on.

- ✔ If only one of your programs has this problem, *don't* flip the printer's line feed switch. Flipping the switch makes the printer act weird with all your other programs. Instead, tell that renegade program to reverse its line feed setting. You find that setting in the program's setup area or installation program.

- ✔ Some printers change their line feeds with a DIP switch. A *DIP switch* is the size of two ants standing side by side. You need a little paper clip to flick the DIP switch the other way. (That delicate procedure is covered in Chapter 18.) The switch is usually near the back.

- ✔ If your stuff is printing okay, ignore the line feed switch. Otherwise, your stuff won't print okay.

- ✔ Some printers come with software to control line feeds. Rather than search for little switches, you have to search for the right software.

"The Page Looks Blotchy on My Laser Printer"

Sometimes the page looks, well, blotchy. You see big patches of black here and there or big, empty, white spots. Those patches and spots usually mean that it's time for a trip to the repair shop. Your laser printer needs to be poked, prodded, cleaned, and billed by a professional. The next few paragraphs describe some problems and how to fix them.

Black streaks: This problem can mean that you need a new photoconductor — a big, expensive thingy inside the laser printer. Sometimes the repair shop can just clean the photoconductor to bring it back to normal. Or sometimes you need a new toner cartridge — an increasing number of printers now put the photoconductor inside the cartridge.

Faded print: You probably need a new toner cartridge. But, before you buy a new one, try this tip:

When your print looks faded, your printer is probably running out of toner. Open the lid to the laser printer and look for a big, black, plastic thing. Pull it straight out, and then gently rock it back and forth. Don't turn the cartridge upside down unless you want to make an incredible mess. Then slide the cartridge back in the same way. This procedure sometimes lets your laser printer squeeze out a few dozen extra pages.

Creased paper: Keep paper stored in a dry place and not in the bottom corner of the garage or under the coffeemaker. Moist paper can crease as it runs through a laser printer.

Jeff Wiedenfeld, this book's technical editor, notes that a lasagna Tupperware container makes a great airtight paper storage container.

Also, all that laser stuff really heats up a laser printer. If you're running some preprinted letterhead through it, the ink on the letterhead may smear.

Keeping Your Printer Happy

Your printer generally prefers Authorized Service Technicians with white coats to perform repairs. Feel free to perform any of the appropriate tasks listed next, however, to keep your printer happy:

✓ Download the latest software and drivers. Every few months — or when your printer's acting too weird to ignore — head to your printer manufacturer's Web page and download the latest drivers and software. They're two different things. A *driver* is software that lets Windows communicate with your printer when sending pages. The *software* is a utility program that lets you adjust your printer's settings.

✓ Run your printer's software. Hewlett-Packard includes a software disk with its 870Cse inkjet printer, for instance, that helps you diagnose and fine-tune your printer. The software, available at its Web site and pictured in Figure 9-2, features help pages for replacing print cartridges and changing print settings. It also troubleshoots your printer, offering suggestions when things go wrong. Finally, it aligns your printer whenever you replace the ink cartridges, carefully ensuring optimal quality.

✔ Turn off your printer when not using it. Inkjet printers, especially, should be turned off when not being used. The heat tends to dry the cartridges, shortening their life.

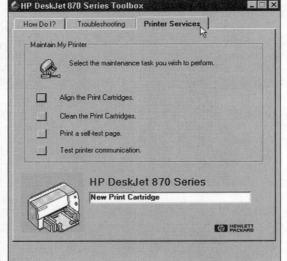

Figure 9-2:
Software designed for your printer model, like this from Hewlett-Packard, helps troubleshoot, adjust, and service your printer.

Don't unplug your inkjet printer to turn it off. Always use the on/off switch. The switch ensures that the cartridges have slid back to their "home" positions, keeping them from drying out or becoming clogged.

"How Do I Install a New Toner or Ink Cartridge?"

Printers need ink or toner to put on the page. When your pages start to look blotchy or faint, you probably need a new cartridge.

Various printers work differently, but here's the general rundown:

1. Turn off the printer and open its top.

Printers usually have a hood-release type of latch that lets their top pop up. You may need to remove the paper tray first.

If your laser printer has been turned on, let it cool off for 15 minutes. Laser printers get hot enough inside to brand a pig. The parts that seem hot *are* hot, and they can hurt your fingers.

2. **Pull out the old cartridge.**

The cartridge usually slides straight out. While the cartridge is out, wipe away any dust or dirt you see inside the printer. The printer's manual tells you the most appropriate places to clean. A little rubbing alcohol on a soft rag usually works well. Check your printer's manual to make sure that alcohol won't damage any parts inside.

Color printers come with two cartridges. One holds black ink; the other holds color ink. They're usually labeled to avoid confusion. If you're in doubt, the smaller cartridge probably holds the black ink. Some older inkjet printers come with just one cartridge housing, requiring their owners to swap cartridges.

3. **Slide in the new cartridge.**

Before sliding in a new cartridge for a laser printer, gently rock it back and forth to evenly distribute the toner that lurks inside. Don't turn the cartridge upside down or completely on one end.

Some toner cartridges have a protective plastic strip you must remove before you install the cartridge. Better check the instruction book on this one.

4. **When the new cartridge snaps in place, close the printer's top and turn it back on.**

You may need to put the paper cartridge back on the printer.

5. **Run your printer's software, if it has any.**

Some inkjet printers, for example, come with software that aligns the cartridge. It prints several coded designs and then asks you to examine them and choose the best-looking ones. The printer then knows the best way to print.

✔ You should check your printer's manual for mention of any "fuser pads" or "corona wires" that need to be changed at the same time.

✔ New toner cartridges are sometimes blotchy for the first few pages, so don't print any résumés right off the bat.

✔ If you run into trouble, take the printer to the repair shop. The printer probably needs a good cleaning anyway.

"Can I Save Money By Refilling My Cartridges?"

Some people say that recycling is a great way to save money and protect the environment. Other people say that a botched refill can ruin a printer. There's no clear-cut answer.

Let your own experience be your guide. If you do decide to refill your printer's cartridge, however, don't try to do it yourself. Let the repair shop handle the job. A qualified repairperson is a better judge of whether your cartridge should be refilled.

Inkjet cartridges can be refilled as well. Check the backs of computer magazines for mail-order outfits that sell the kits. Make sure that you're using the specially formulated inkjet cartridge ink, though.

"Can I Upgrade My Laser Printer?"

Like computers, laser printers often have secret compartments where you can add gizmos. Here's the rundown:

Cartridges: Some printers work like the old Atari computer game systems: You can stick different cartridges in them to make them do different things. You can add different fonts, for example, or add PostScript if you're serious about printing high-quality stuff.

Memory: Text doesn't take much oomph to print. But if you start adding graphics to a page — pictures, fancy borders, or pie charts — the printer will need lots of memory to handle it all. Some printers let you stick little memory modules inside them so that they can print fancier pages faster.

The memory that goes inside your printer usually isn't the same kind of memory that goes inside your computer. You can't swap them back and forth. (You can't grab any of the memory off your video card, either.)

Unfortunately, you have to buy most of these *add-on* gizmos from the printer's company. They're rarely interchangeable among different brands of printers.

"My laser printer smells funny"

Laser printers contribute to the Earth's ozone layer. Unfortunately, laser printers release the ozone right next to your desk and not 12 to 15 miles into the Earth's atmosphere.

Laser printers come with an ozone filter to absorb the dangerous gas before it reaches your nostrils. The filter can wear out, however. Check your printer's manual to see how often you need to replace your filter. Sometimes you can replace the old one yourself; other printers make you head for a repair shop.

"Why Is My Printer Cable So Short?"

It's short because parallel ports are wimpy. They lack the tongue muscles to spit data over a long distance, so the cables are usually only six feet long. Expensive cables may add a few feet, but generally your printer needs to sit pretty close to your computer. (See the nearby Technical Stuff sidebar on the IEEE 1284 specification if you're not only adventurous but if your printer also needs to be farther than six feet away.)

IEEE 1284 and other scary printer words

The BIOS of many computers lets you configure the printer port to ECP (Extended Capabilities Port), EPP (Enhanced Parallel Port), AT-style, and PS/2-style (see Chapter 3).

Choose ECP or EPP if your system supports it. (That information is in its manual.) But for the quickest and most trouble-free printer communications, check to see whether your computer supports the newer IEEE 1284 parallel-port specification. That protocol works with all the previous modes, so you shouldn't get into trouble.

Also, IEEE 1284 calls for a new printer cable, a miniature 26-pin Centronics-style connector referred to as a *Type C connector*. Traditional parallel cables can't be longer than 6 feet, but the new Type C connectors and braid-shielded cable allow for lengths of around 30 feet.

Of course, the cables cost lots more. But your printer and computer can talk much more quickly, meaning that you spend less time waiting for the printer to spit out fancy graphics.

How Can Two Computers Share One Printer?

Most folks solve the problem of having two computers and one printer with an *A/B switch box*. The printer plugs into the box's printer port. One computer plugs into the box's *A* port, and the other computer plugs into its *B* port.

When you want to print from one computer, flip the switch to A. When you want to print from the other computer, flip the switch to B.

It's a pretty simple arrangement, actually. The only problem occurs when you forget to switch the A/B switch box to your computer. Everybody does it. Some folks even brag about forgetting to switch the box.

When people brag about forgetting to switch their boxes, gently remind them that those old mechanical A/B switches were designed before today's sensitive (and expensive) laser printers. To avoid damage, turn off your printer before flipping the switch. Better yet, get one of the newer switch boxes, described in the next Tip.

The newer A/B switch boxes can automatically detect which printer is trying to print and route the incoming page to the appropriate printer. Although these boxes cost more, they can prevent lots of crankiness and avert potential damage.

A *network* — an expensive, high-class version of an A/B switch — connects bunches of computers with cards and cables. If you're using a network in Windows, you can print to any active printer that's listed on the network. You still have to get up and walk over to get your printout, but hopefully the network's printer isn't too far away.

What's the Best Paper for a Color Inkjet Printer?

The latest and greatest variety of printer, the inexpensive and powerful color inkjet, can spit out some awfully pretty color pictures, provided you use the right paper. On ordinary office paper, the paper's fibers soak up the ink a little bit, letting it bleed and blur. On specially designed (and especially expensive) color inkjet paper, the colors stay put, creating a sharp image.

Check the labels on paper before shopping, and be sure to get some of each kind.

Using a digital camera? Buy the best-quality paper to print your photographs, and print while in the highest-quality mode. Visit your printer's Web site as well, to make sure that you're using the latest drivers for your printer model. In fact, consider buying a dedicated printer for your camera. Some of the latest models print color photographs with panache.

"How Do I Install a New Printer?"

IQ level: 70

Tools you need: One hand and a screwdriver

Cost: Anywhere from $150 to $2,500

Stuff to watch out for: When shopping for a laser printer, compare printouts from several different printers. Laser printers use several different printing mechanisms, each with its own advantages and disadvantages. For example, one printer may be better for dark graphics but lousy for letters. Other printers may be just the opposite.

Be sure to compare the output from several inkjet printers before making a final decision. No matter what printer you choose, you may have to buy a printer cable; printers rarely include a printer cable. Just ask the salesperson for an IBM-compatible printer cable. All printer cables for PCs do the same thing (unless you have a serial printer, which I describe at the end of this chapter).

To install a printer, follow these steps:

1. **Turn off your computer.**

   Turning off your computer is a good idea when installing anything but software. Be sure to save your work and exit any programs before turning the computer off, however.

2. **Remove the new printer from the box.**

   Remove any stray bits of Styrofoam, tape, or plastic baggies. Check inside the box for any stray bits of stuffing. Grab all the manuals and disks; they can get lost amid all the packaging material.

3. **Find the printer cable, your computer's printer port, and the port on the back of your printer.**

   The printer port looks the same on a PC, an ancient XT, an antique AT, an old 386, a Pentium, or any other type of IBM-compatible computer. Look for the big port with 25 *holes* in it, as shown in Figure 9-3. (The big port with 25 *pins* is a serial port.)

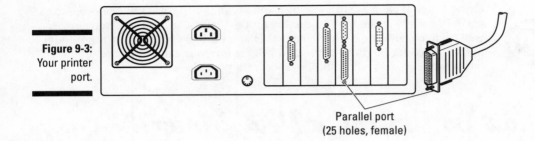

Figure 9-3:
Your printer
port.

Parallel port
(25 holes, female)

4. **Plug the cable into the printer and computer.**

   Plug the side of the cable that looks like a robot's mouth into the printer, and plug the other side into your computer's printer port.

   Different printers accept paper in different ways. Check the printer's manual for this one.

   Using a dot-matrix or inkjet printer? You probably need to slide in a ribbon or ink cartridges so that the printer has some ink to smear on the pages.

5. **Run any software that comes with the printer.**

   Many of today's printers come with special drivers and fancy programs. Be sure to install any of the software that comes with your printer.

Some printers come with a built-in *self-test* program. You run the self-test program by pushing buttons on the printer's control panel. The program squirts out a piece of paper showing alphabetical rows of letters. The test merely shows that the printer works by itself. The test doesn't prove that the printer is correctly hooked up to the computer. Your printer's software, described earlier in this chapter, helps align your inkjet printer's cartridges. Finally, Chapter 17 shows how to tell Windows about your new printer. Windows prints a test page to make sure that everything's connected to the computer correctly.

Part III
The Stuff Hiding Inside Your PC

The 5th Wave By Rich Tennant

"OOPS — HERE'S THE PROBLEM. SOMETHING'S CAUSING SHORTS IN THE MAINFRAME."

In this part . . .

You're probably pretty familiar with the stuff that lives outside your PC. You've shuffled the pieces around on your desk, pausing occasionally when a cable pops off the back of your PC.

This part of the book, however, describes the stuff you've never touched. Here, you find out about the unseen parts of your computer — the pieces that lurk deep inside its case, making ominous humming noises.

This part of the book uncovers what's beneath your PC's cover.

Chapter 10

The Motherboard (And Its CPU, BIOS, and Even a Battery)

*I*f your computer is one big omelet, then your motherboard is the great mass of egg that holds together all the mushrooms, cheese, and occasional bits of sausage.

That's why replacing your computer's motherboard is such a colossal bother. You need to pick everything off your motherboard before you can remove it. You can't overlook a single bit of sausage.

Replacing a motherboard isn't a job for weekend chefs. The task is best left for the technocooks at the computer shop.

If you're *sure* that you want to replace your motherboard, you can find the recipe at the end of this chapter. A few easier projects are sprinkled in along the way, however. In fact, the first section explains how to replace something that nobody expects computers to have: a battery.

Finally, if you're thinking about replacing your motherboard, it's probably time to think about getting a whole new computer. Compare prices and features thoroughly before putting down the cash. A new computer may not be such a bad deal, considering the time, trouble, and expense of replacing the motherboard.

A lot of effort for a little time

Because the old PC and XT computers from the 1980s didn't come with batteries, they couldn't remember the date.

So, some time-conscious owners opened 'em up and put special clock cards inside. Those cards have batteries that keep the clocks ticking. (Until the battery dies, of course, but I'll get to that later.)

However, those old computers are too dumb to look at that card for the current time and date. Computers need a special program to tell them where to look. Without that program, the clock card is useless.

If you buy an old PC or XT at a garage sale, make the people root through their boxes of old floppy

disks until they find that little program. It's usually called SETCLOCK or something equally clock-oriented.

Savvy PC and XT users copy the special program to their hard drive and put the program's name and location on a line in their AUTOEXEC.BAT files. Then each time they turn on their computers, that program runs and fetches the time and date.

That AUTOEXEC.BAT file stuff is wrapped up in Chapter 16. Oh, and you can install clock cards just like any other card, which I describe in Chapter 15.

"My Computer Is Losing Track of Time!"

Just like a cheap wristwatch, your computer relies on a battery to keep track of the date and time. That constant flow of electricity lets the computer remember the current time and date, even when it's unplugged from the wall. When the battery prepares to retire (after anywhere from one to ten years), the computer's clock begins slowing down. At first, it's merely annoying. Eventually, it drives you batty.

It gets worse. Computers also rely on that battery to remember what parts have been stuffed inside. Some computers forget the type of hard drive they've been using all these years. Frightened, those computers send out a scary message like this:

```
Invalid Configuration Information
Hard Disk Failure
```

This message is often your computer's friendly way of telling you that it needs a new battery.

"I can't find my computer's battery!"

Don't bother looking for a battery in most XTs and old PCs — they don't always come with one. That's why they often beg you to type in the current time and date every time they're turned on.

Some people ignore the computer when it asks them to type the current time and date. So their computers simply tack the date January 1, 1980, on every file they create that day. That makes it rough when you're looking for a file you created yesterday, though, because they *all* look nearly 20 years old.

If your computer knows the correct date when you turn it on, however, it's harboring a battery inside somewhere. But where? Computer batteries rarely *look* like batteries.

Computer batteries usually hail from one of these tribes:

✔ Many computers use a huge watch battery about the size of a quarter that pops into a little socket on the motherboard.

✔ The most elusive batteries hide inside a chip that looks nothing at all like a battery. The chip says *Dallas* and has a little picture of an alarm clock on it. (This chip is supposed to last about ten years.) When the chip dies, ask your local computer store for a *Dallas Real Time* chip. If the store's clerk stares at you funny, call Resource 800, at 1-800-430-7030. The company also sells the chips on its Web site, at www.resource800.com/, ranging from $25 to $30.

✔ Dallas clock chips often fail when used with computers powered by under-size power supplies. If your computer's power supply is less than 250 watts and you're adding lots of peripherals or 32MB of RAM or more, the chip may fail. Be sure to upgrade your power supply to more than 250 watts when your computer uses one of these chips.

✔ Some "backroom-assembled" computers use AA batteries in a little plastic pack that's taped to the power supply — that big, silver thing in the computer's back corner. Wires from the plastic pack connect to little pins on the motherboard. Those AA batteries last about three years. Pick 'em up at the nearest drug store.

✔ Other computers use a little cube-shaped battery, which is also taped to the power supply. (Some skip the tape in favor of Velcro.) Like the AA cells, these guys have wires leading to pins on the motherboard. A cube-shaped battery's life span is about three years. Call Resource 800, at 1-800-430-7030, or head to the company's Web site, at www.resource800.com/, to order your replacement.

✔ Older computers often use little battery cylinders about the size of a cigar butt. Call 1-800-430-7030 or visit www.resource800.com for those hard-to-find batteries. Battery cylinders live between little prongs on the motherboard, like the one shown in Figure 10-1.

A newer computer's batteries usually live close to where the keyboard or CPU plugs into the motherboard.

Figure 10-1: Many batteries, approximately the size of a quarter, slide into a round socket on the motherboard.

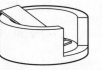
Empty battery socket

Socket with battery installed

"How do I install a new battery?"

IQ level: 80

Tools you need: Screwdriver, flashlight, and prying fingers

Cost: Anywhere from $5 to $25

Stuff to watch out for: If your computer's battery looks especially unworldly, try Radio Shack. A salesperson there can often special-order odd-size batteries from a wide variety of planets.

Some manufacturers were especially vile and *soldered* the computer's battery to the motherboard. Solder is like molten lead, so just give up. Although you can melt the solder with a *soldering iron,* doing so can be both scary and dangerous for beginners because it's easy to damage the computer. Take this one to the repair shop unless you've soldered something before and enjoyed the experience. Melting solder even smells evil.

Don't forget what your computer is supposed to remember

When you remove the battery, your computer forgets lots of information about itself. If your battery is dead, your computer has already forgotten, so this little tip comes too late.

To ignore this, press Enter

Even computers with a working clock occasionally query you for the time and date. Your computer picks up the current time and date from its internal clock, just like normal. But then your computer displays the date and time onscreen and asks you whether it's really okay.

Just press Enter to confirm that yes, indeed, the computer already knows the right time and date. This bit of weirdness pops up whenever a computer can't find an AUTOEXEC.BAT file. With that file missing, the computer gets suspicious and asks you whether it really knows the time and date.

Your computer is most likely to question its internal clock when you boot from floppy disks that don't have an AUTOEXEC.BAT file. Are you a little sketchy on what an AUTOEXEC.BAT file is supposed to do? Troop to Chapter 16 for a refresher.

If your battery is still grasping at life, however, head for Chapter 18. In that chapter, you find out how to access your computer's bizarre-sounding CMOS and find out the type number of your hard drive. While you're there, print all your CMOS information and stash it in the emergency folder. It usually comes in handy.

After you install the new battery, you may need to tell your computer the hard drive type number. If you didn't write down that information beforehand, you have to page through dusty manuals and search for the right number to type. Yuck.

To install a battery, follow these steps:

1. **Turn off your computer, unplug it, and remove its case.**

   This merry little chore is covered on the Cheat Sheet in the front of this book.

2. **Find and remove the computer's old battery.**

   Don't know what the battery looks like? Head for the "I can't find my computer's battery!" section, earlier in this chapter.

   Be sure to draw a picture of the old battery's position. Each end has a + or – sign. The signs need to face the same way on the new battery as they did on the old battery. Using a Dallas chip? Look to see which direction the letters on the old chip are facing.

   AA batteries simply snap out of their plastic case, just like in a small radio. The batteries shaped like a cigar butt slip out of their little prong sockets, but this process can take some pressure. Change the batteries every year so that they don't leak toxic goo on your computer's innards.

Don't force anything; some batteries may be *soldered* in, which means that you should stop immediately and take the computer to the shop.

If you have a Dallas clock chip, pry it out gently. If you don't have a chip-puller tool (and who does, anyway?), grab the chip between your thumb and forefinger and pull straight up with a gentle rocking motion. The chip is pretty big, so it's easy to grab. Keep track of which direction the chip faces; the new one needs to face the same way.

3. **Take the old battery to the computer store and buy a replacement battery.**

   The best place I've found for finding computer batteries (and detailed information about computer batteries) is Resource 800, at 1-800-430-7030 or www.resource800.com/.

4. **Place the new battery where the old one lived.**

   Make sure that the + and – ends of the new battery face the same direction as they did on the old battery. When installing a chip, make sure that it rests in the socket facing the same direction as the old one did.

If you accidentally yank any wires from their pins on the motherboard, all is not lost. Look for the pin with the number 1 written closest to it. *The red wire always connects to Pin 1.* Computer technicians have that statement on their bumper stickers. After you've connected the red wire, the other wires usually fall into place logically.

5. **Put the computer's case back on and plug the computer back in.**

   The battery problem should be solved, although the computer won't be grateful. When first turned on, your computer will probably send out a horrible-sounding error message about your *incorrect CMOS*.

   You usually need to tell your computer's CMOS what type of hard drive you have. (You remembered to write down that information before you started, didn't you?) You can find that CMOS stuff hashed out in Chapter 18.

"Will Replacing My Old CPU with a Hot, New CPU Speed It Up?"

Will your old CPU become some speed demon with the newest-technology replacement CPU? Well, that's a definite *sometimes.* Owners of a 486 probably shouldn't bother. They still need to add more RAM, a bigger hard drive, a faster video card, a faster CD-ROM drive, new software, a USB port card, and more to bring it up to steam. And by the time they've done that, they've reached the cost of a new computer — which automatically comes with a warranty and a package of the newest software.

Bus speeds, clock speeds, clock multipliers, and other motherboard lore

In the early years of computing, motherboards and CPUs worked hand in hand. Whenever a new CPU hit the scene, a new motherboard design arrived to run as fast as the new CPU. As CPUs began to run faster and faster, however, motherboards simply couldn't keep up the speed.

The solution? Intel released "clock doubled" CPUs. They could "think" twice as fast, but communicated with the motherboard and its components at half that speed. That situation sped up the computer's performance, worked on slower motherboards, and satisfied the consumer.

Today's chips still run faster with internal calculations, but they run slower when communicating with the motherboard.

There's more. Motherboard manufacturers no longer create a new motherboard for every CPU. They create a single motherboard with switches to handle a variety of CPUs. By flipping the switches or moving jumpers, you adjust the proper speeds for the motherboard and CPU to communicate without mumbling.

Still other motherboards let you make changes for CPUs in the CMOS area.

Now, bear with me — here are some ugly computer terms:

Clock speed: This term refers to the speed at which the CPU can think internally — not necessarily how fast it communicates with the motherboard. (CPUs are rated by their internal speed because that sounds faster. Even though a 300 MHz CPU may be talking to the motherboard at 66 MHz, the CPU's box will call it a 300 MHz CPU.)

Bus speed: Here's the speed of your motherboard.

Clock multiplier: Multiply this number by your motherboard's bus speed to determine what CPU is appropriate. For instance, installing a 400 MHz CPU on a motherboard with a 100 MHz bus speed requires a click multiplier of 4.0. Flip the motherboard's clock multiplier switches to 4, and all systems are go.

The moral of the story, now that you know your terms? Check your motherboard's manual to see its *bus speed* and *clock multiplier* settings. Then you'll know how fast of a CPU it can handle. Can't find the manual? Head for the motherboard manufacturer's Web site. Many keep copies there.

In fact, the speed of a PC is often determined as much by its peripherals — its video card, hard drive, memory, and other parts — than by its CPU speed. Don't expect miracles by installing a hotshot CPU in a computer with aging components. Those slow parts will still slow your computer's overall performance.

In short, replacing a slow Pentium with a faster chip can sometimes speed up your computer. But the CPU alone isn't the only thing powering your computer. You might not even notice the speed difference.

✔ First, bring the computer up to at least 32MB of RAM; sometimes, that step alone will speed up your system faster than replacing the old CPU.

Also, make sure that you're buying the right chip for the right motherboard. Not all upgrades work on all motherboards. You can't simply pop out the old chip and pop in a faster one. Try calling the technical-support people at the company selling the replacement chip to see whether their wares will work on your brand of motherboard. (You may also find the same information on the company's Web site, if it has one.) You can find more information about replacement CPUs in Chapter 3.

✔ Pentium-level chips usually run at higher temperatures than their predecessors. So, they have it written into their contract that they get a cooling fan. This tiny fan — just like the one on the power supply — clips onto the chip and blows air on it to keep it comfortable. When you install the chip, be sure to plug the fan's power cord into one of your power supply's unused cables.

If you buy a new computer, salvage your old computer's video card and monitor. Attach them to your *new* computer. Ever since Windows 98 arrived, computers have been able to spread their work across two monitors, doubling your screen space.

"How Do I Install a Faster or Upgraded CPU?"

IQ level: 100 to 120

Tools you need: Chip puller, screwdriver, and strong fingers

Cost: Varies widely

Stuff to watch out for: This one seems deceptively simple — it looks like you just yank out the old chip and push in the new one. But you may encounter several problems. Start by reading the section on CPUs in Chapter 3. Then read this chapter's short sidebar about bus speeds, clock speeds, and clock multipliers. Then sigh.

Then and only then, make sure that you buy the right style and speed of replacement CPU for your particular computer's motherboard. Computer motherboards have used several different-size CPU sockets over the years, as discussed in Chapter 3. Also, a motherboard's *chip set* sets its bus speed — which limits how fast of a CPU it can accept. Some motherboards simply can't handle a faster CPU.

The fastest and easiest answer? Check your computer's manual or inspect the motherboard to find out its manufacturer. Then visit that motherboard manufacturer's Web site to see which CPUs your motherboard will accept.

Next, remember that the replacement CPU fits into the socket only *one* way. The *marked* corner (known as Pin 1) on the upgrade CPU chip needs to match with the marked corner of the socket. The marked corner has either a notch, a dot, an extra hole, or something even harder to spot. Figure 10-2 shows a socket with a notch in one corner and a missing hole. The corner of the CPU with the missing pin corresponds to that corner of the socket.

Figure 10-2: The notched corner of a chip, known as Pin 1, plugs into the marked corner of its socket.

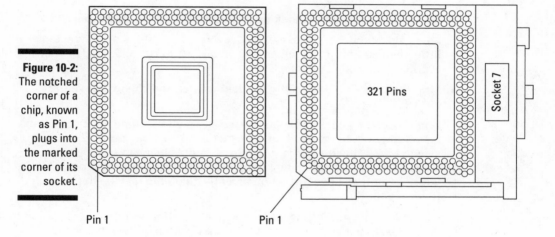

Pin 1   Pin 1

Third, not every chip works with every BIOS, particularly older ones. (Luckily, some CPUs come with installation software that inspects your computer and says thumbs up or down.)

If your BIOS is incompatible, you can often update it — a process described toward the end of this chapter.

Finally, make sure that you record your computer's CMOS information before you start poking around inside the case. (Chapter 18 covers CMOS navigation, and it's easier than it sounds.) Oh, and don't forget to back up all the important stuff on your hard drive — but that's something you should be doing all the time, anyway.

To install a new CPU, follow these steps:

1. Turn off the PC, unplug it, and remove its cover.

The Cheat Sheet in the front of this book explains how to do this step.

2. Find the CPU's socket and make sure that you bought the right upgrade chip.

First, find your CPU. It's almost always the biggest, black, square chip on the motherboard. The chip's number is usually printed somewhere along its top in somewhat confusing fashion. Sometimes you can't see the CPU's top because of its *heat sink,* a large metal thing with fins designed to cool down the chip.

Check to make sure that the upgrade chip in your hand is the one that is supposed to replace your specific type of CPU. Installing the wrong chip may permanently damage your computer, blow the replacement CPU, leave you looking foolish, or all three.

3. Set the motherboard's clock multiplier to match the incoming CPU.

Some motherboards make you flip a switch, and others make you move little jumpers around. Some let you change this crucial setting in your CMOS, described in Chapter 18.

4. Find the new CPU's specially marked corner and then remove the old CPU.

Don't touch any chip until you release any pent-up static electricity. Tap on a doorknob, file cabinet, or bare metal part of your desk. *Then* it's safe to touch sensitive computer chips. People living in static-prone areas should buy a grounding strap at their local computer store. Also, if your computer's been turned on recently, that chip may be hot enough to burn your fingers.

One corner of your CPU is marked with a little dot or notch, as shown in Figure 10-2. That corner doesn't have a pin, either. Remember which direction that marked corner faces; you need to install the new CPU upgrade chip so that it faces the same way.

The CPU upgrade kit for older computers should have come with a special chip-removal tool and instructions on how the tool works. Be careful when prying the chip out of the socket — don't mistakenly try to pry the *socket* off the motherboard. With newer computers, the chip sits in a ZIF socket, as shown in Figure 10-3: Just lift the lever and the chip practically drops out.

The CPU may be buried beneath other parts. Be prepared to remove some cards, a hard drive, or your power supply in order to reach the CPU.

Some AMD 386DX CPUs are fastened directly to the motherboard, with no socket. Unfortunately, you can't upgrade these chips, so return your upgrade chip to the dealer for a refund. (Or, if you don't like surprises, check the fine print in your computer's manual before trying to upgrade the processor.)

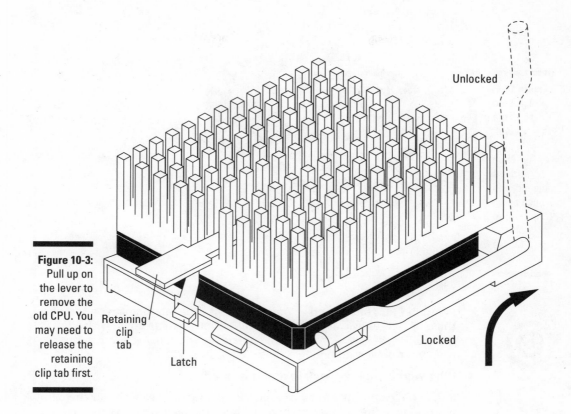

Unlocked

Locked

Figure 10-3:
Pull up on
the lever to
remove the
old CPU. You
may need to
release the
retaining
clip tab first.

Retaining
clip
tab

Latch

5. Press the upgrade chip into its socket.

The new chip's marked corner rests over the socket in the same direction as the old chip's marked corner, as you noted in Step 3.

Have you lined up the marked corner of the chip with the marked corner of the socket? Now make sure that all the little pins are lined up over all the little holes. Then push down the lever to hold the CPU in place, as shown in Figure 10-4.

No lever on your socket? Then carefully push the chip down into the socket. It may require some pressure, but don't bend your motherboard. If your motherboard bends more than slightly, stop and let the dealer or a repair shop finish the job.

Unless you have a ZIF socket with a handy little lever, pushing that little chip into the socket can take more pressure than you think. Be very careful not to crack your motherboard while pushing down.

Sometimes, slipping a magazine beneath the motherboard can keep it from bending as you push the chip into the socket.

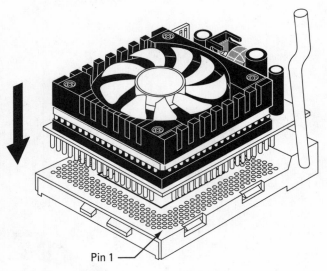

Figure 10-4:
Insert the CPU into the socket with their notched corners aligned, and push down the lever to hold the CPU in place.

Pin 1

Pentium CPUs often need a *cooling fan* — a little fan that sits on top of the chip and blows air to keep it cool. Although some come with a fan attached, others make you buy a fan and attach it, using spare wires from your power supply.

6. Plug your computer back in and turn it on.

If the chip came with software, run the software to see whether the chip is working. If the chip isn't working, check to make sure that the chip is firmly seated in its socket and is facing the right way.

7. Close your computer's case.

If everything seems to work fine, go ahead and close up your computer's case. You've finished the operation. Whew!

If the computer doesn't recognize your hard drive, check your computer's CMOS setting, as described in Chapter 18. Enter the type of hard drive your computer uses, save the settings, and reboot your computer.

Check the upgrade chip's manual — you may need to stick a *heat sink* on top of the new chip. The heat sink — which looks like a pin cushion — sticks on top of the chip and absorbs heat, keeping the chip from overheating.

"Can I Put a New Motherboard into My Old Computer?"

Yes, but let's start with the first problem: size. Motherboards come in a wide variety of sizes. Chances are, your new motherboard may not fit in your current computer's case. But that's not the biggest problem.

See, even if you could jam a new motherboard inside a 486, you would have to buy all new memory — the old memory chips won't fit. You need a new power supply because the old one's not powerful enough. Toss a new keyboard on the bill, too. Plus, you probably want newer, faster, bigger disk drives. Today's CD-ROM drives are probably ten times as fast as your old one.

The plain fact is that a completely new computer costs about the same as all that upgrading. Plus, a new computer has a better warranty. And some dealers toss in a free copy of the latest version of Windows and other software.

Sure, you can upgrade your old motherboard. However, be sure to add the cost of the additional parts that you won't be able to recycle from your old motherboard. As I mention earlier in this chapter, buying a new computer is usually a better deal.

A few companies went off the deep end when it came to the *standard* motherboard size. Some Compaq computers use weird-size motherboards, which makes replacement difficult. You probably have to go to a Compaq dealer for one of those.

Things to Look for When Shopping for a CPU and Motherboard

Shopping for a new motherboard can be as confusing as installing one. Here's a rundown on some of the terminology you'll encounter, what the heck it's supposed to mean, and whether you should care about it.

Brand: Just as cars come from different makers, a variety of companies make motherboards. Don't shop for price alone, because different companies make different-quality motherboards.

Socket: Your CPU fits into this socket, and, unfortunately, sockets vary according to your CPU type. Choose your CPU, find out which socket it requires, as described in Chapter 3, and then choose a motherboard with that particular socket. While you're at it, head to your CPU maker's Web page; it often carries lists of recommended motherboards.

Bus or clock speeds: Motherboards typically support more than one type of CPU, so they must be adjusted to run at different speeds. The latest ones top out at 200 MHz for the AMD Athlon; most Socket 7 motherboards are adjustable for speeds of 66, 75, 83, 95, and 100.

Voltage: CPUs are designed to run at a certain voltage. If the motherboard can't dish out this voltage, it might damage the CPU. Head to the Web pages of both the CPU and the motherboard to see whether they're a good match. Or, consider buying your motherboard with the CPU already installed. If the package has a warranty, it's probably a good match.

Size: Most motherboards now come in two sizes — "Baby AT" and ATX. The small, square ones are Baby AT; the small, rectangular ones are ATX. If in doubt, bring your old one in and see whether the replacement is the same size.

Flash BIOS: Look for a motherboard with a software-upgradeable BIOS, often known as a flash BIOS. It lets you update your motherboard to accept the latest parts and to repair any possible bugs.

Built-in controllers: Although all motherboards come with built-in controllers for your drives, look for one that comes with controllers for your parallel, serial, and USB ports. *Caution:* If it comes with controllers for your sound and video, make sure that those "built-in" circuits can be disabled. You may want to upgrade from those by plugging in the latest, greatest sound or video card.

Expansion slots: You want at least two 16-bit slots for your older ISA cards, three PCI slots for newer goodies, and an AGP slot for the latest in speedy video cards.

Memory: Motherboards come with slots for sliding in memory chips. Make sure that the chip handles at *least* 256MB of RAM. (Power users should look for space for 512MB of RAM.) Motherboards also have cache memory for the CPU's use. Look for 512K cache memory.

If in doubt, get more power than you need. You don't want to go through this hassle again.

You find more of this stuff hashed out in Chapter 3.

"Uh, should I really install the motherboard myself?"

Don't replace your motherboard unless you're used to fiddling around inside your computer.

Replacing the motherboard is a tedious, laborious chore. You need to remove every wire that plugs into the old motherboard and then plug the wires into your new motherboard. And those wires probably plug into different places!

You have to pull every card and every bit of memory off your old motherboard. Then you have to stick all that stuff back on the new one, in exactly the right spots.

Besides, motherboards are fragile things. When bent too far, motherboards break. Oh, you won't see the break because it's just one of those little wires etched along the bottom that breaks.

And the motherboard won't *always* be broken. It may work fine when you first turn the computer on. But when the motherboard heats up in about an hour, it can expand slightly, which aggravates the break. That brings on the worst kind of computer problem — a glitch that happens only once in a while, especially when no one's around to believe you.

Don't mess with your motherboard unless you've messed around with all the other parts in your computer first and feel like you've gotten the hang of it.

"How do I install a new motherboard?"

IQ level: 120

Tools you need: Big Phillips screwdriver, little flathead screwdriver, tweezers or needlenose pliers, two hands, and *lots* of patience

Cost: Anywhere from $100 to $1,000

Stuff to watch out for: Give yourself plenty of time. You need to remove just about everything inside your computer and then put it all back after the new motherboard is inside. Give yourself plenty of working space, too. You need room to spread out.

If you're dealing with an older computer, consider buying a new case along with the new motherboard. That way, you can be sure that they match up.

Finally, you are dealing with many of your computer's parts here. If you're stuck on the memory step, for example, head for Chapter 11 for memory information. All the card stuff is in Chapter 15. Need more info on CPUs? Chapter 3 contains both the details and general-purpose information on anything else. Just check this book's table of contents to see where your confusing part is discussed.

Good luck. (It's not too late to take this one to the shop, you know. Or just buy a new computer; that may be cheaper.)

To install a new motherboard, follow these steps:

1. **Back up your hard drive and buy the new motherboard.**

   The first step in computer repair is always to back up your hard drive.

   The new motherboard doesn't have to be the same, identical size as your old one. In fact, your new motherboard will probably be smaller. However, the motherboard's little screw holes must be in the same place as the old one, or else it may not fit into the case.

2. **Write down your computer's CMOS information.**

   Your new motherboard won't know the same things as your old one. So write down the *type* of hard drive your computer uses. (You can find that information by probing into your computer's CMOS, as I describe in Chapter 18.) Make sure that you know the *density* of your floppy drives, too. (Chances are, they're high-density, 1.44MB drives.)

3. **Unpack the new board.**

   Remove the new board from the wrapper and look for anything grossly wrong: shattered plastic, broken wires, gouges, melted ice cream, or anything loose and dangling. Now's the time to take it back if something's wrong.

   I can't say this enough — don't touch your motherboard until you release any stray static electricity. Touch a doorknob, file cabinet, or bare metal part of your desk. Even then, handle the board by its edges.

   Those innocent-looking silver dots on one side of your motherboard are actually savage metal pokers. If they brush across your hand, they leave bizarre yet oddly fashionable scratches.

   Look for any DIP switches and jumpers; you may need to flick them later. (That DIPpy stuff's all described in Chapter 18.)

4. **Turn off your PC, unplug it, and remove its case.**

   All this stuff is described in the Cheat Sheet in the front of this book.

5. **Unplug any wires that connect to the motherboard.**

   Don't touch anything inside your computer until you release your pent-up static electricity. Tap on a doorknob, file cabinet, or bare metal part of your desk.

   Bunches of little wires plug into little pins or sockets on the motherboard. While unplugging each one, write down any numbers, words, or letters you see next to the spot it was removed from on the motherboard. Those words or letters will help you plug those wires into the right spots on the new motherboard.

   Put a piece of masking tape on the end of any wires unplugged from the motherboard. Take note of anything written on the plug where the wire came from, and write that on the masking tape for later identification.

Make sure that you unplug these wires:

- **Power supply:** The power supply consists of two big, multiwired cables that plug into big sockets.

- **Lights:** Unplug the wires leading to the lights along the front of your computer's case. Most computers have a hard drive light and power light; some fancier computers have more.

- **Switches:** The wires from your reset button end up on your motherboard somewhere. Usually, the reset button wire goes next to where the lights plug in.

6. Remove all the cards and cables.

The cables from your printer, mouse, monitor, and other goodies all plug into the ends of cards. You need to remove each cable. Then you need to remove all the cards, which are held in place with a single screw at the back of the case. After you remove the screws, each card should pull straight up and out.

Keep track of which card lived in which slot. The cards probably don't need to be reinserted in the same order, but hey, why take chances?

7. Unplug your keyboard.

The keyboard plugs in through a hole in the back of the case. Pull the keyboard plug straight out without turning it.

8. Remove all the memory chips.

Chapter 11 covers all of this memory stuff. In that chapter, you find out what type of memory to look for and how to grab it.

You also discover whether you can stick that memory on your new motherboard. (The answer is rarely good news.)

Either way, save those chips in plastic sandwich bags. Some stores let you trade in old chips for a discount on new chips.

9. Put memory chips on the new motherboard.

If you were able to salvage any memory from your old motherboard, stick it on your new one. Add as many new memory chips as you can afford. Don't know how? Chapter 11 has detailed instructions for putting memory into its rightful place.

10. Adjust the motherboard's proper voltage and clock speed multiplier for its particular CPU.

First, set the motherboard's proper voltage. A CPU uses two voltages: a core voltage and an In/Out voltage. Check your motherboard's manual for its voltage settings. You probably need to move jumpers to match the motherboard's voltage with the intended CPU.

The manual also says how to set the motherboard's multiplier to match your computer's clock speed. It's usually 2.5, 3, 4, 4.5, 5.5, or something similar. This step usually involves moving jumpers as well.

11. **Insert the new CPU.**

    CPUs shaped like crackers push into a flat little socket on the motherboard. CPUs mounted on cards push into a large slot. Some sockets come with levers known as *ZIF (Zero Insertion Force):* Lift the lever, insert the CPU, and push the lever down to secure the chip. (This topic is covered in the "How do I install a faster or upgraded CPU?" section, earlier in this chapter.)

12. **Look at how your old board is mounted.**

    Usually, four to eight screws hold the thing in place. Remember where the screws are so that you can screw the new ones in the same place.

13. **Remove the old motherboard.**

    Unscrew the screws holding the old motherboard in place. Then gently grasp the board's edge and pull it straight out of the computer. You may need to move the board slightly back and forth until it comes free.

14. **Remove the plastic standoffs.**

    The screws keep the motherboard from moving around. But little plastic *spacers* keep the motherboard from actually touching the bottom of the case.

    You can remove the spacers by pinching their tops and pushing them down into the holes, as shown in Figure 10-5.

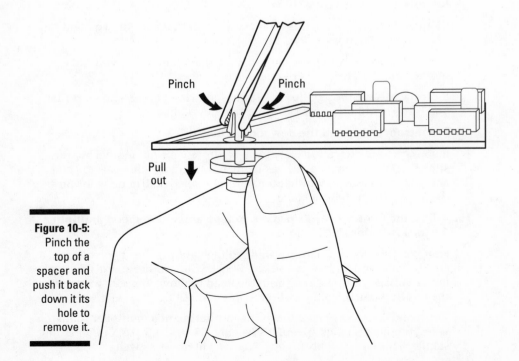

Pinch   Pinch

Pull
out

Figure 10-5:
Pinch the
top of a
spacer and
push it back
down it its
hole to
remove it.

15. Put the little plastic standoffs on the new board.

Then push those little plastic standoffs into the new motherboard. Push them up into the holes from the bottom.

16. Slide in the new board and tighten the screws.

Slide in the new motherboard just like you slid out the old one. Look for the keyboard cable hole — the keyboard plug on the new motherboard needs to go right next to it.

You may have to fiddle with the motherboard for a while until the little plastic spacers all line up in their little holes. When the board is in firm and all the holes line up, screw it down. Don't screw it in *too* hard because it may crack.

17. Replace the wires.

Is the motherboard in? Then hook all those little wires from the lights and switches to their spots on the new motherboard. If you're lucky, the wires are marked. If you're not lucky, you have to flip through the new motherboard's manual.

The red wire always connects to Pin 1. The two black wires always go next to each other on the power supply's two cables.

18. Replace cards and cables.

Put all the cards back in their slots, as described in Chapter 15. Make sure that you don't drop any screws inside the case; if you lose one, curse loudly. Then find the screw before going any further. If a screw lodges itself in the wrong place, it could ruin your motherboard. (Screw extraction tips live in Chapter 2.)

Did you buy a fast new AGP video card to go with your new motherboard? Then push it into your motherboard's new AGP slot.

Plug in all your card's cables: the printer, mouse, monitor, and any other odds and ends that need to plug back into the right card.

19. Plug in the keyboard.

The keyboard plugs into its hole in the back of the case.

20. Plug in the PC and turn it on.

This is the big test. Does it turn on? Do you see words on the monitor?

21. Put the cover back on.

If everything works, put the cover back on and breathe a sigh of relief. If the PC is not working, several things could be wrong:

- Make sure that all the cards and memory are sitting firmly in their sockets.

- Have you set the motherboard's voltage and clocking settings correctly for the new CPU?

- You may need to adjust the computer's new CMOS settings, as described in Chapter 18.

- Some of your cards may not be compatible with your new motherboard, unfortunately.

- Through the process of trial and error (and some flipping around from chapter to chapter in this book), you can probably find the culprit. As a last resort, take the whole thing to the computer shop. Because you've already installed the motherboard, the shop may charge you less money.

"What's This BIOS Business?"

Sometimes, you can stick a new toy in your older computer, fire it up, and start playing.

Other times, the computer balks. If, for example, a computer was built in 1993, it's not going to know how to handle the new technology stuff that came out five years later.

For example, you can install a huge new hard drive into a two-year old computer. But because that computer wasn't around when that high-capacity hard drive was created, it won't be able to use the drive. That two-year-old computer's *BIOS* — the built-in instructions for handling computer parts — is living in the dark ages of computer time.

Many of the newest computers sport a *flash BIOS*. That's a fancy word meaning that you don't need to buy new BIOS chips. You upgrade the BIOS by simply running a software program. Upgrading a flash BIOS is so easy that lots of nerds are up in arms about it. Head for your computer maker's Web page and look for the flash BIOS download for your particular computer.

- A flash BIOS upgrade sometimes fixes problems and bugs in old BIOS software. However, the upgrade can introduce new problems as well. Unless you're having problems with your old BIOS, don't automatically upgrade to the latest BIOS by using the flash BIOS program.

- A new BIOS won't make your computer run any faster. The BIOS is just a Band-Aid that lets an older computer use some newer parts. New motherboards always come with the newest BIOS chips as part of the package deal.

- The decrepit BIOS in some older computers can't handle Windows, VGA cards, OverDrive CPUs, the year 2000, or other new stuff. Luckily, those BIOS chips are easy to replace. You can pluck the old chips off the motherboard like ticks from a hound dog. Then the new chips plug right into their place.

✔ The problem comes with *finding* those replacement BIOS chips. Try bugging the dealer who sold you your computer. Show the dealer the receipt listing the specific brand of motherboard you bought many moons ago. The dealer may have some newer BIOS chips in the back room, mixed in with the snack foods.

✔ If you picked up your PC at a garage sale, check the backs of the thickest computer magazines, where the small ads live. Chances are that you can find somebody selling ROM BIOS upgrades. At last look, www.unicore.com sold BIOS upgrades for many computers.

✔ Own a Pentium III? Then call up your BIOS and check to make sure that your Pentium III serial number is listed as disabled. If it's enabled, switch it back to disabled, save the settings, and reboot your computer.

✔ Your computer probably has several *types* of BIOS chips. For example, a video BIOS chip probably lives on your video card to make sure that the pictures are showing up on the screen. But when you hear the word *BIOS* dropped in casual conversation, the reference is to the BIOS on your motherboard.

Eventually, you'll hear the two words *CMOS* and *BIOS* in the same sentence. Here's the difference: Your BIOS is a piece of hardware that contains a form for you to fill out about your computer's components. When you turn on your computer, the BIOS reads the form, performs grunt-level tests to make sure that everything's working, and then hands over the reins to Windows. Your CMOS is the memory containing the settings you've entered into your BIOS' form. A little battery preserves those settings.

"How Do I Replace My BIOS?"

IQ level: 80

Tools you need: One hand and a chip puller

Cost: Anywhere from $35 to $100

Stuff to watch out for: Check to see whether your computer has a *flash BIOS*. If so, you can simply update the BIOS by running a software program that's often available on the computer manufacturer's Web page.

Most of this section is for people with older computers that aren't working anymore after the year 2000. They need to replace their older, dated BIOS with something that can handle the new year.

Like all other chips, BIOS chips don't like static. Be sure to touch something metal — your computer's case or a filing cabinet — before picking up the chip.

Make sure that the little legs on the chip are aligned in a neat little row. Straighten out any bent legs.

Oh, and make sure that you can take your new BIOS chips back if they don't work. BIOS chips can be finicky in different types of computers, and they may refuse to work.

To replace the BIOS on an old computer, follow these steps:

1. **Turn off your computer, unplug it, and remove its case.**

   If you're new at this game, head for the Cheat Sheet in the front of this book. And don't forget to touch your computer's case to rid yourself of static before touching any of your computer's sensitive internal organs.

2. **Find your old BIOS chips.**

   They're usually the chips with the word *BIOS* on a stick-on label. You may find anywhere from one to five chips. (You may find a keyboard BIOS chip as well.)

   If you have more than one BIOS chip, look for distinguishing numbers on them: BIOS-1, BIOS-2, BIOS-3, or something similar. Write down which chip goes in which socket and the direction each chip faces. The new BIOS chips must go in exactly the same place.

3. **Remove the old BIOS chips.**

   Some of your cards or other computer paraphernalia may be thoughtlessly hovering in the way. You have to remove that stuff before you can reach the chips.

   To make it easy to pry out the old chips, some BIOS retailers toss in a chip puller — a weird, tweezers-looking thing. Don't carry a chip puller around? Try this trick: Using a small screwdriver, gently pry up one end of the chip, and then pry up the other end. By carefully lifting up each side a little bit at a time, you can gently lift the chip out of its socket.

   Or, look for one of those L-shaped metal things that cover up the slots in the back of your computer. These *expansion slot covers* also work to pry out chips.

   Don't try to pry the chip up from just one side. Doing so can bend or break its tiny little pins. Instead, pry up one side a fraction of an inch and then pry up the other side. By alternating and using gentle pressure, you can remove the chip undamaged.

4. **Insert the new BIOS chips.**

   Find your notes and make sure that you know which chip goes into which socket and the direction the chip should face. Can't find your notes? Then make sure that the *notched* end of each chip faces the *notched* or *marked* end of its socket.

Next, make sure that the little pins on the chip are straight. A pair of needlenose pliers can work here. Or, you can push them against a flat desktop to make sure that they're all in a straight line.

Put the first row of little pins into its row of holes and make sure that the rows line up perfectly. Next, line up the other row of pins over its row of holes and push down until the pins are lined up, too. Finally, give the chip a firm push with your thumb until it rests in the socket.

5. **Replace any cards or other items that had blocked your view.**

6. **Replace the computer's cover, plug the computer back in, and turn it on.**

Your computer should notice its new BIOS chips right away. When you turn on your computer, you can see the chips' new copyright dates on the screen's first or second paragraph.

Doesn't work? Then unplug the computer, take off the case, and make sure that you pushed those chips all the way into their sockets. Also, make sure that all those little pins are in their sockets. If one hangs out, like in Figure 10-6, things can get pretty goofy.

Figure 10-6:
If a single
pin misses
the hole, the
chip doesn't
work.

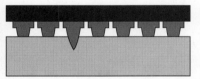

Chapter 11

Memory Stuff You Wish You Could Forget

· ·

In This Chapter

▶ Understanding Windows memory messages

▶ Dealing with parity errors

▶ Finding your computer's current memory

▶ Telling your computer about its memory

▶ Buying the right memory for your computer

▶ Installing or upgrading memory

· ·

Some parts of your computer are great fun: joysticks, compact disc players, sound cards, and cool games like Disney's age-old Stunt Island, where you can fly a duck around the tops of New York City skyscrapers.

Unfortunately, one part of your computer can send you screaming in the other direction: your computer's memory, especially when you don't have enough of it. Figuring out your computer's memory can be either the simplest or the most devastatingly complicated part of IBM-compatible computing.

And whether it's simple or complicated, memory is boring, no doubt about it. In fact, this chapter starts out with awful memory by-products called *parity errors* and closes with migraine-inspired details on pushing memory chips onto your motherboard.

If you don't want to be bothered with boring memory details, just let the folks at the computer shop handle your memory problems. They know which chips to use and whether your computer's existing chips can coexist with the newcomers.

"My PC Keeps Saying 'Parity Error' or Something Equally Weird"

That parity stuff means that your computer is not getting along well with its memory, and this isn't good.

If you just installed some new memory, perhaps the computer is merely confused. Run your computer's setup program or adjust the CMOS settings, tasks that are described in Chapter 18. Make sure that your computer recognizes your handiwork — its new memory.

If the message persists, though, your best bet is to take your computer to the shop. One of your memory chips is squawking, and the technowizards in the shop can track down the culprit much faster than you can.

Before giving up completely, though, give your computer's memory modules a little push. *Memory modules* are little strips of plastic that have chips hanging off the sides. Turn off your computer, take off its case, and give those strips a little push to make sure that they're in there tight.

Also, before touching any of your chips, touch a plain metal surface to discharge any static electricity. One stray spark — even the kind you can't see or feel — can annoy your chips something fierce.

"Windows Keeps Saying 'Not Enough Memory' or 'Insufficient Memory'"

Windows uses memory the way baked potatoes use butter: The more you have, the better they taste.

If you don't have enough butter, the potato just sits there and tastes dry. But if you don't have enough memory, Windows reminds you of it constantly, as shown in Figure 11-1. In fact, a Windows 95 system will just barely run well until it has at least 16MB of memory (also referred to as *RAM*). And if you're running several programs at once, playing large games, or running heavy-duty graphics programs, count on doubling that amount.

Windows 98 runs best with at least 64MB of RAM, and I'm getting best results with more than 128MB.

Figure 11-1:
When Windows runs out of memory, it sends this uncomfort-able-sounding message.

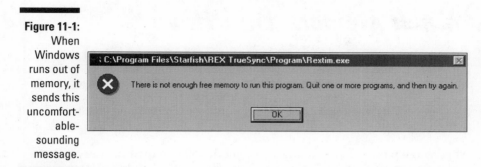

You can make Windows stop complaining in two ways. One way is to buy more memory. The other way is to make sure that your computer knows how to use the memory it already has.

- ✔ Adding memory can be pretty easy. Just buy more memory chips and stick the chips in the empty sockets inside your computer (after reading the installation instructions at the end of this chapter, that is).

- ✔ Unfortunately, some computers are maxed out; that is, their motherboards don't know how to talk to any more memory, even if you won zillions of memory chips from *Reader's Digest*. You simply have to buy a newer, flashier computer that has a capacity for more memory. Or, if you're feeling really ambitious, ogle the directions for installing a new motherboard in Chapter 10.

- ✔ The trickiest scenario is when a computer's slots are all full, but the computer can still handle more memory. The answer? Pluck the lower capacity memory chips — the 16MB chips, for example — and replace them with 32MB chips. The problem comes when you add up the actual total: Because you're subtracting 16MB chips from your system and replacing them with 32MB chips, you're actually only adding 16MB of additional memory. Sniff.

- ✔ Windows uses your hard drive for memory, too, in a method called "virtual memory." When you run several programs simultaneously, Windows stores the unused programs on a portion of your hard drive. If your hard drive is nearly full, however, Windows doesn't have enough memory to create its virtual memory area. The moral? Always leave some empty space on your hard drive. How much? Basically, 2.5 times the amount of your memory. So, if you have 32MB of memory, keep at least 80MB of space free for Windows to play with.

"How Much Memory Do I Have?"

For the most part, you don't need to know how much memory your computer has. If you don't have enough memory, your computer slows down when you run large programs, or it tells you through a rude message.

If you're curious, though, watch your computer's screen when you first turn it on for the day.

When you flip the On switch, most computers tally up their memory faster than a grocer can add up double coupons. The computer tests all the memory it finds so that it knows how much room is available for tallying up numbers.

Keep an eye on the screen for the total. That's how much memory your computer has found to play with. (It is possible, through wrong motherboard DIP settings and wrong CMOS settings, for the wrong amount of memory to be shown during bootup. Read on for more information.)

The second easiest way to discover your computer's memory is to look at the receipt to see how much memory you bought. Of course, it's more reassuring to have the *computer* tell you.

Users of Windows 95 or Windows 98 can simply right-click the My Computer icon and choose Properties from the menu that drops down. The Properties window displays the amount of memory, as shown in Figure 11-2.

My computer can't count RAM right!

My laptop has 128MB of Random-Access Memory (RAM), and it counts to 130048K each morning. Why doesn't the computer count to 128000K? Well, a megabyte is *really* 1024K, although people tend to round down to 1000K, or 1MB.

That means that 128MB *really* equals 131072K. But that still doesn't equal 130048K. What happened? It boils down to boring computer engineering history, which I don't elaborate on here. But some wacky engineers devoted the first 640K of your memory to an early operating system named DOS and gave DOS an extra 384K of memory to play with.

Add that extra 1024K of DOS memory to the 130048K displayed on the screen, and you find 131072K, or 128MB. Whew!

These weird memory terms all get their due in Table 11-1, which is a little way down the road in this chapter.

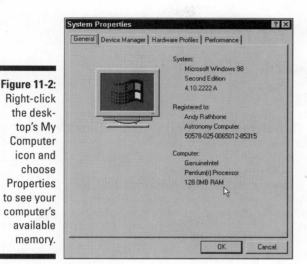

Figure 11-2:
Right-click
the desk-
top's My
Computer
icon and
choose
Properties
to see your
computer's
available
memory.

"I Installed a Bunch of Memory, but My Computer Doesn't Know It's There!"

There are several reasons your computer may not find new memory.

First, the memory may not be seated correctly in its sockets. Give it another push — after making sure that the memory modules are facing the correct way, of course.

Second, are you sure that you bought the correct type? Memory comes in different sizes, configurations, capacities, and speeds. If just one of these is wrong, your computer might barf on the memory.

✔ When you first turn on your computer after installing memory, your computer should recognize it immediately. It may beep and bring up its setup screen, allowing you to verify that it's recognized the correct amount of memory you've inserted. If all is correct, save the settings and you're done.

✔ Some older PCs aren't smart enough to know that you've spent a great deal of time and money to stick little memory-chip things inside them. To wise 'em up, you probably need to flip a *DIP* switch on the mother-board. (I'm not making this up, as you find out in Chapter 18's DIP switch section.) Some computers may make you fiddle with their *jumpers,* which Chapter 18 also covers.

"Why Can't I Move Memory off My Old Motherboard and Stick It on My New One?"

Here's a bit of bad news. You can't take memory off your old motherboard and expect it to fit on your new motherboard. As motherboards have evolved through the years, they've outgrown several different types of memory.

If you're replacing a bad motherboard with one from the same era, the memory may fit. But when buying a new motherboard, expect to buy all new memory along with it. The newer memory will be faster to keep up with the speedy new motherboard.

Plus, the packaging has changed on memory chips over the years. The memory chips on your old motherboard are probably a different size from the ones you need for your new motherboard.

That means your old chips just won't fit — like an 8-track tape won't fit in a CD player.

- ✔ You can usually tell whether your memory chips will work by just looking at them.

- ✔ Most memory today comes on small, thin cards called *SIMMs* or *DIMMs*. The 30-pin SIMMs measure about 3½ inches long; 72-pin SIMMs measure about 4½ inches long. DIMMs measure about 5¼ inches long and usually have chips on both sides. Make sure that you're buying the right replacement. Older motherboards used chips called *DIPs* or *SIPs*. A DIP, SIMM, and DIMM are pictured in Figure 11-3.

- ✔ Still using SIMMs? They must be replaced in pairs, and it's probably best to buy them in pairs of 32MB chips. DIMMs, by contrast, can be replaced singly.

- ✔ If you can't reuse your old chips, save 'em anyway. Some computer stores let you trade 'em in for a discount on the type of chips that *will* work.

- ✔ Other dealers sell converters that let one type of chip plug into another type of socket. This trick works only if your older memory chips can run quickly enough for your fast, new motherboard.

- ✔ Some men use their obsolete chips to make hip costume jewelry for their wives. Their wives, subsequently, serve their husbands 8-track tapes for dinner.

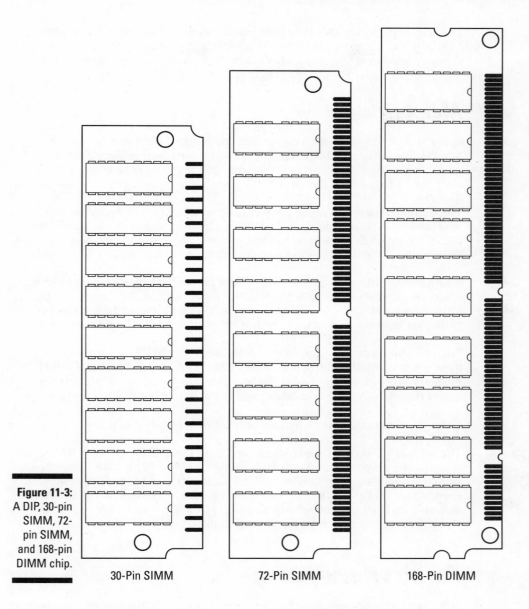

Figure 11-3:
A DIP, 30-pin
SIMM, 72-
pin SIMM,
and 168-pin
DIMM chip.

30-Pin SIMM   72-Pin SIMM   168-Pin DIMM

"Geez, What Memory Should I Buy?"

Everybody knows that they need *more* memory to make their computers run
better. But what *kind* of memory? Like living rooms, motherboards are all
arranged differently. Some motherboards can hold great gobs of memory.
Other motherboards can barely squeak by with a sliver.

The only way to know for sure how much memory your motherboard can hold is to dig out the manual and look for the following key words. (The memory section in Chapter 3 offers some background information as well.)

Memory type

Older computers came with memory chips plugged right into the motherboards, like in Figure 11-3. Each chip, called a *DIP (Dual In-line Package)* chip, plugs into its own little socket. DIP chips are the oldest type of memory and the hardest to find and install.

The second generation of memory chips are *SIMMs (Single In-line Memory Modules)*, also shown in Figure 11-3. They plug into long slots on the motherboard. Count your memory slots, put your old chips in a plastic bag, and take them with you to the store to make sure that you're buying the right types.

Another odd old beast, called a *SIP (Single In-line Package)*, plugs into little rows. The sockets have little holes rather than a slot to accommodate the little feet on the chips. Replacements are difficult to locate these days, providing yet another reason to scrap the entire computer if it still uses SIPs.

The push for increasing amounts of RAM has brought the latest type of memory: the *DIMM (Dual In-line Memory Module)*, also shown in Figure 11-3. Pushed onto a long, 168-pin circuit, these memory modules work best on newer Pentiums, which take advantage of the better technology.

Older Pentiums, however, often insist on SIMMs installed in pairs.

The term EDO SIMM applies to Extended Data Out (EDO) dynamic RAM chips mounted on Single In-line Memory Modules (SIMMs). EDO SIMMs have been installed on most computers since 1994. Computers made recently use speedy SDRAM DIMMs, which means Synchronous Dynamic RAM (SDRAM) mounted on Dual In-line Memory Modules (DIMMs). Yawn. Make sure that you're buying the right type for your system.

Parity or non-parity

This problem cropped up in the early 1990s, although it may come in handy if you're shopping for SIMMs. A SIMM usually comes with nine DIPs (although some come with three). Of those nine DIPs, the computer uses only eight for storing information. The last chip is used for *parity checking* — a computerized way of making sure that the other chips aren't messing up.

Some manufacturers say that DIP chips don't screw up very often — if at all. So they pull the ninth chip off the SIMM to save some cash in construction costs.

Other manufacturers say that there's no sense in building a computer you can't rely on, so they keep the parity chip enabled. In fact, they design their motherboards so that the memory has to have its parity enabled.

✔ Parity chips cost more to manufacture because they have an extra chip. Some manufacturers get sneaky by pricing the two types of chips the same, but here's the catch: They're usually selling slower-parity chips at the same price as faster, non-parity chips. (Memory speed comes up in the next section.)

✔ Make your own decision about parity. The price difference is usually less than 10 percent.

Higher-end PCs substitute a newer technology named *ECC (Error Correction Code)* to check for memory problems. They've outgrown the parity problem.

Memory speed for SIMMs

Buy chips that are the same speed or faster than your current memory chips. Buying faster chips won't make your computer run faster. Motherboards run at their own, internal limit (although some motherboards run at several different rates depending on their adjustable settings, as discussed in Chapter 10).

Also, don't buy chips that are slower than your current crop of chips, even though they *are* cheaper.

Chip speed is measured in *nanoseconds*. Smaller numbers mean faster chips: A 60-nanosecond chip is faster than a 70-nanosecond chip.

Dunno how fast your current chips can scoot? Look at the string of numbers written across the roof of the chips on your SIMM. The numbers usually end with a hyphen and are followed by another number or two. Table 11-1 shows what that magic number after the hyphen means.

Table 11-1	The Numbers after the Hyphen Display Your Chip's Speed	
The Number	*The Speed of the Chip*	*Computers That Like the Chip*
–6 or –60	60 nanoseconds	Most Pentiums and its varieties
–7 or –70	70 nanoseconds	Most 386s, 486s, and some Pentiums

(continued)

Table 11-1 (continued)

The Number	The Speed of the Chip	Computers That Like the Chip
−8 or −80	80 nanoseconds	Most 386s, 486s, and some Pentiums
−10	100 nanoseconds	Most ATs or 286s
−12	120 nanoseconds	Most ATs or 286s
−15	150 nanoseconds	XTs and PCs
−20	200 nanoseconds	Very old PCs

Memory capacity

Here's where things get even weirder. For example, your old motherboard may say that it can handle 64MB of memory. Your computer has only 16MB, and you're rubbing your hands in anticipation of an easy, plug-in-the-chip upgrade to bring your computer up to its 64MB maximum.

When you open your computer, you see that all your SIMM sockets are full of chips, just like in Figure 11-4. How can you fit more memory in there? Where's the crowbar?

✔ The problem is the capacity of the SIMMs that are sitting in those sockets. Those little strips can hold memory in the amounts of 1MB, 2MB, 4MB, 8MB, 16MB, or more.

✔ In this case, those eight SIMMs must each be holding only 2MB of memory. Eight sockets of 2MB SIMMs total 16MB of RAM.

✔ To upgrade that computer to 64MB of memory, you need to yank out all those 2MB SIMMs and put the higher-capacity 8MB SIMMs in their place.

✔ Yes, that means that those old 2MB SIMMs are useless to you. Some dealers let you trade in old chips for a discount on your new chips. Other dealers make you store your old chips in the garage until you forget about them.

✔ Actually, there's finally a better way: a SIMM expander. These little circuit boards plug into a SIMM socket and protrude above the other SIMMs. The expanders then let you plug two additional SIMMs into their own SIMM sockets (see Figure 11-5).

✔ In the preceding case, you would have to pull only two 2MB SIMMs, plug in a SIMM expander, and plug both the 2MB SIMMs into the SIMM expander's socket. That leaves you with an empty SIMM socket to insert more RAM — and you don't have to waste any of your existing memory.

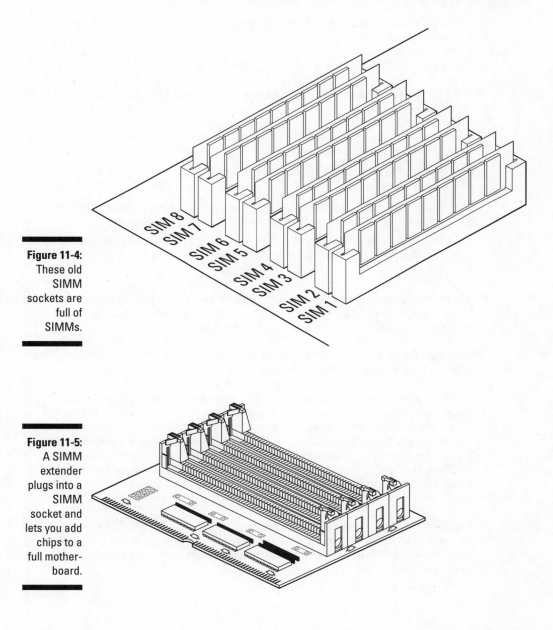

Figure 11-4: These old SIMM sockets are full of SIMMs.

Figure 11-5: A SIMM extender plugs into a SIMM socket and lets you add chips to a full motherboard.

"How Do I Install More Memory?"

IQ level: 100

Tools you need: Your motherboard's manual, screwdriver, and chip puller (optional)

Cost: Around $3 or $4 per megabyte, although the price constantly changes

Stuff to watch out for: Memory has more rules than Mrs. Jackson during her shift on lunch duty:

- ✔ First, be sure to buy memory that fits in your motherboard's sockets. Several different sizes exist.
- ✔ Second, buy memory that's the right speed so that your computer can use it without tripping.
- ✔ Third, buy memory that's the right capacity. Different motherboards have different limits on how much RAM they can handle.
- ✔ Finally, many of those picky old Pentium computers require SIMMs to be installed in pairs. The newer ones use DIMMs, which can be installed singly.

These four details are covered more fully in the "Geez, What Memory Should I Buy?" section, earlier in this chapter. And be sure that you pull out your motherboard's manual to see what rules to follow.

Actually, installing the memory is the easy part. The hard part is figuring out which chips to buy and where to put them.

If this stuff sounds confusing, feel free to pass this job over to the computer shop, especially if you don't have a manual for your motherboard. The folks in the back room can upgrade memory chips in just a few minutes. Or, if you can find a sympathetic computer salesperson, write down your computer's current memory configuration: the number of slots, the types of memory (SIMMs, DIMMs, DIPs, and so on), and which types of memory are in your slots. (Or, just count the total number of slots, put all the chips in a plastic bag, show them to the clerk, and say that you want to upgrade.)

Finally, some companies (IBM included) use some oddball chip sizes. If any of these instructions starts sounding weird or something is the wrong size, take the whole thing to the shop. You didn't really want to be a computer nerd, did you?

To install new memory chips, follow these steps:

1. **Turn off the computer, unplug it, and remove the case.**

   These steps get the full treatment on the Cheat Sheet in the front of this book.

2. **Figure out what memory your computer uses.**

   Dig out your motherboard's manual to see what sort of memory it's craving. Check for the memory's *type* (motherboards use DIPs, SIMMs, DIMMs, or SIPs), *speed* (measured in nanoseconds, or ns), and *capacity* (the memory size, listed in kilobytes [K] or megabytes [MB]).

   The most amiable motherboards can handle several different capacities and chip speeds.

3. **Figure out whether there's room for more memory.**

   Sockets for SIMMs or DIMMs are in little rows, usually in a corner of your motherboard. Spot any empty ones? If so, you're in luck!

   You can add as much memory as you want, under two conditions. First, don't add more memory than your motherboard can handle. (You can find its limit listed in the manual.) Second, your computer organizes those little sockets into *banks*. Some motherboards — especially Pentiums that use SIMMs — say that two sockets make a bank. Other motherboards say that four sockets make a bank. Still others use DIMMs that use a single socket as a bank.

   Regardless, motherboards either make you fill up a bank of SIMMs completely or leave the bank empty. You can't leave a bank half full, or else the motherboard will belch. (DIMMs don't have this bank problem.)

   Also, you can't mix amounts of memory in a bank. For example, you can't put a 16MB SIMM and a 32MB SIMM in a single bank. You have to use either all 16MB SIMMs or all 32MB SIMMs.

   If you don't see any empty sockets, your memory upgrade gets a little more complicated. Check your motherboard's manual to see whether it's maxed out. Your motherboard may already be stuffed to the brim and simply can't handle any more RAM.

   If the manual says that the motherboard *can* handle more memory but the sockets are all full, you have to yank out some of the old chips and replace them with higher-capacity chips. If you must remove existing SIMMs, be careful not to break the plastic clips that are on some SIMM sockets.

   If your sockets are full but your computer can handle more RAM, buy a SIMM extender, as described in the "Memory capacity" section, earlier in this chapter. That section shows how to add more memory to a maxed-out motherboard.

4. Buy the right type of new memory chips.

By now, you should know whether you need to buy DIPs, SIMMs, DIMMs, or SIPs. And your pocketbook (and the motherboard's limit) decides what capacity of chips you buy.

Make sure that you buy the right *speed* of chips. There's really only one rule: Don't buy chips that are *slower* than your current ones.

Don't know the speed of your current chips? Head to the "Geez, What Memory Should I Buy?" section, earlier in this chapter, for pointers.

5. Install the new memory chips.

Make sure that you ground yourself by touching something metallic before picking up any of the chips, or else you could destroy them with static electricity.

If you're working in a dry area with lots of static around, take off your shoes. Working barefoot can help prevent static buildup. If you have your own office, feel free to take off all your clothes. Compute naked!

Check your motherboard's manual to make sure that you're filling up the correct sockets and rows.

SIMMs and DIMMs: Look for the notched end or bottom of the SIMM or DIMM. The notches let the chip fit into its socket in only one way. Position the SIMM over the socket and push the SIMM down into place. When the chip is in as far as it goes, tilt it slowly until the little metal tabs snap into place. The whole procedure should look like the three steps shown in Figure 11-6.

Most DIMMs and some older SIMMs, like the one shown in Figure 11-7, just push straight down and lock in place. Other SIMMs, like the one shown in Figure 11-6, need to be tilted while they're being inserted. Some SIMMs need to be tilted *after* being inserted. If you're careful, you'll figure out which way the chips fit.

DIPs: Make sure that the little pins on the chips are straight. A pair of needlenose pliers can help flatten the pins. Or, you can push the chips against a flat desktop to make sure that the pins are in a straight line.

Make sure that the notched end of the DIP is over the notched or marked edge of the socket. Then put the first row of little pins into its row of holes, making sure that the pins line up perfectly.

Next, line up the other row of pins over its row of holes. Then push down until the pins line up, too.

Finally, give the chip a slow, firm push with your thumb until it rests in the socket. Repeat the process until you've filled up the row.

The process is shown in Figure 11-8.

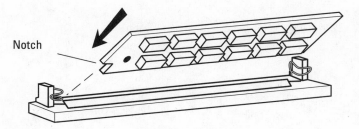

Notch

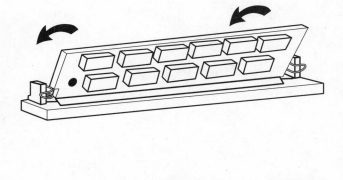

Figure 11-6:
Some
SIMMs are
pushed in at
an angle
and then
straightened
out, like this;
other
SIMMs are
pushed
straight in
and then
pushed
down at an
angle.

SIPs: Make sure that the *notched* or *marked* end of the SIP is aligned with the *marked* side of the socket. Then carefully push the SIP's little legs into the holes until the SIP is firmly in place.

As with the other SIPs, make sure that you fill up the sockets *one bank at a time.*

6. **Double-check your work.**

Make sure that all the DIP chips face the right way and make sure that all the legs are in the holes. Also, check the legs to be sure that none of them is bent underneath or hanging over the sides.

Check your motherboard's manual to make sure that you've filled up the banks in the right order.

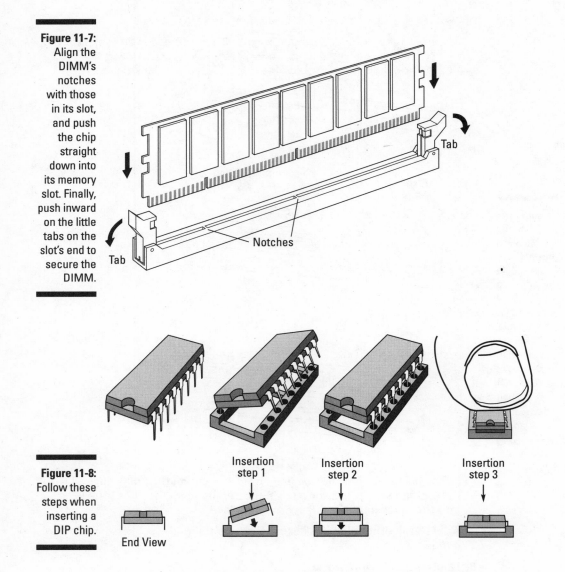

Figure 11-7: Align the DIMM's notches with those in its slot, and push the chip straight down into its memory slot. Finally, push inward on the little tabs on the slot's end to secure the DIMM.

Tab

Tab

Notches

Figure 11-8: Follow these steps when inserting a DIP chip.

End View

Insertion step 1

Insertion step 2

Insertion step 3

7. Flip appropriate DIP switches or jumpers on the motherboard.

Some older computers don't automatically recognize the chips that you agonizingly inserted. The computer requires you to flip a DIP switch or move a jumper to tell it how much memory you've added.

Which do you do? Check your motherboard's manual. The manual is the only place you can find these secrets.

Unsure about how a jumper or DIP switch works? Jump to Chapter 18.

8. **Replace the case, plug in the computer, and turn it on.**

   Your computer should greet you with an error message about memory mismatch or something weird. The message sounds scary, but it's good news! Your computer found the memory chips that you stuck inside it.

   Your computer is grateful, but it's also a little wary. Your computer wants to show you the amount of memory it found and ask you to confirm that yes, indeed, you did put that much memory inside it.

   All this stuff happens in your computer's CMOS area or on the setup screen. And all that stuff's tucked away in Chapter 18. (It's not nearly as hard as it sounds, either. In fact, some computers will already have the change listed in the CMOS or setup program; just exit the program, and everything will be fine.)

   XT computers don't have a setup program or a CMOS area, so XTs just take your word on how much new memory you've installed, based on the DIP switches and jumpers you moved around.

   If your computer still doesn't recognize your new memory chips, turn it off and push those chips into their sockets a little more firmly. That may do the trick.

9. **Put the case back on.**

   Whew. You did it. Boot up your computer and see how much better Windows runs.

Chapter 12

Floppy Drives

. . . .

. . . .

Put floppy drives on the Endangered Species list. For years, they thrived because people had no alternative. When somebody wanted to store some information, install a program, or move data to another computer, they popped a floppy disk into their floppy drive.

But when CD drives appeared, floppies couldn't compete. CDs not only hold hundreds of floppies worth of information but they also let people listen to Santana on their computers.

Today, the latest CD drives write to discs as well as read from them. Plus, DVD drives let people watch *The Matrix* during their lunch hours. Floppies simply can't keep up.

Although floppies are slowly turning into the 8-track of the computer world, they're not dead yet. This chapter shows how to repair or replace those aging computer parts.

"My Computer Barfs on My Friend's Disks!"

A floppy disk may work fine in your friend's computer but not in your computer. Rather than read the disk, your computer barfs a weird error message onto the screen.

For example, my friend Wally could store stuff on his disks with no problem. Unfortunately, no other computers in the office could read his disks.

That's because Wally's disk drives were slightly out of alignment with the computers in the rest of the world. A few PC repair shops can tune up a disk drive if its disks don't work in other machines, but the alignment almost always costs more than a brand-new drive. Wally didn't buy a new drive, so everybody just avoided his computer. (We still ate lunch with Wally, though.)

Alignment problems aren't the only causes of disk weirdness, however. Some other causes for disk barfs include

- ✔ If you have the older, *low-density* drives (the ones that read only 360K or 720K floppies), your computer will barf on a friend's newer, *high-density* floppies (the ones that hold 1.2MB or 1.44MB of data). The older drives simply can't decipher that newer, fancier format. Those older, low-density drives came preinstalled on computers in the 1980s and very early 1990s.

- ✔ Also, IBM-compatible computers and Macintosh computers don't like each other. (Their owners often squabble, too, but that's a different story.) PCs and older Macs often can't read disks used by the other because each sticks stuff on a floppy disk using a different *format*.

- ✔ The latest crop of Macintosh computers are much friendlier. They can automatically tell when an IBM disk has been stuck in their mouths, and they can read the information from the disk without causing a fuss. (Slow and expensive software called SoftWindows allows some Macs to run an IBM PC's Windows programs, too.)

"When I Put In a New Disk, It Says 'Invalid' Something or Other"

Several gremlins can cause this Invalid stuff. The number one culprit is an *unformatted disk*.

Your computer can't always use floppy disks right out of the box. Unless the box specifically says "formatted," your computer needs to format the floppies first. A new floppy disk is like an empty wall: When a computer formats the disk, it sticks little electronic shelves on the wall so that it can store data on them.

Windows users can right-click the My Computer icon and choose Format from the pop-up menu.

Windows 3.11 users can format a disk in drive A by choosing Disk from the File Manager menu and clicking the OK button in the Format Disk box.

Who cares why a 1.2MB disk holds more than a 360K disk?

Computers measure stuff by the metric system, which works out great for nearly everybody except Americans, who prefer the precise measurements found on yardsticks.

Computers measure the amount of data they can store in either *kilobytes (K)* or *megabytes (MB)*. One megabyte is much more than one kilobyte. It's *1,000* times as much. Actually, it's exactly 1,024 times as much, although everybody rounds it down to 1,000 during standard cocktail-hour talk.

So, a 1.44MB disk can hold *twice* as much as a 720K disk. And a 1.2MB disk can hold *four* times as much as a 360K disk.

The disks that can hold 1.44MB or 1.2MB of data are called *high-density* disks. The others, the 360K and 720K disks, are called *low-density* disks, although some manufacturers call them *double-density* to confuse the issue.

Finally, some bizarre hybrid disks hold 2.88MB, and they're called *extended-density* disks. Chances are, you'll never encounter one. I certainly haven't.

Regardless of your operating system, the computer lets you choose a *volume label*. That's a fancy computer word that translates roughly to *name*. So, type **Tina** or **Lars** or **Ulrich** or whatever name you prefer and then press Enter. (Or, just press Enter to forget about the volume label. Instead, write a name on the disk's sticker where you can see it.)

Don't ever format drive C (or any other drive with a letter higher than A or B). Those drives are rarely floppy disks; they're probably hard disks, and formatting wipes a hard disk clean. You need to format a hard disk only once, after it's first installed. Then you never format it again.

If your disk is properly formatted, you may get an Invalid message for several other reasons:

- ✔ You get an Invalid message if you try to use a high-density disk in a low-density drive.

- ✔ Sometimes, a floppy disk simply goes bad. If this happens to all your disks, your floppy drive may be acting up. If it happens on an occasional floppy, just toss that floppy and use another.

- ✔ If you see the Invalid message and you're not using your floppy drive or a CD-ROM drive, you're in for some serious disk trouble. Your hard drive might be failing, and you should make a backup copy of its contents *immediately*. (See Chapter 13 for hard drive information.)

✔ If your computer has trouble reading its own disks, it may have forgotten what kind of disk drive it owns. To remind it, head for its CMOS area or setup screen to make sure that it lists the right type of drive. (Better head for Chapter 18 before heading down this road.)

✔ Finally, your drive's controller may be on vacation. Turn off your computer, take off the case, and look for a flat ribbon cable snaking out of your drive. Push one end of the cable snugly into the drive and where the other end plugs into either your motherboard or a card. What are *controllers?* They're explained later in this chapter, near the section "How Do I Install a New Floppy Drive?"

"My Computer Says That My Sector Isn't Found or My FAT Is Bad!"

This is particularly discouraging news.

If you see a message to this effect while using a floppy disk, try your best to copy the floppy's contents to another floppy or to your hard drive. If you're lucky, you may be able to salvage some of its contents.

If you're not lucky and you *really* need that data back, head to the software store's utilities aisle and buy a *disk rescue program.* For example, both Norton Utilities and First Aid (CyberMedia) can usually rescue some data off a disk that's gone bad. Some computer shops can also retrieve data from malfunctioning disks. Without one of these special programs, however, there's not much you can do.

If the error message pops up while you're trying to read something off your hard drive, try saving your current work and then push your computer's reset button. Sometimes that fixes it.

If the message keeps popping up, though, you'd better start saving money for a new hard drive. First, though, give one of the rescue programs a shot at it. They're cheaper than a new hard drive, and they often grab information from a disk that you thought was a goner.

✔ Computers toss information onto disks in little areas called *sectors.* When a sector goes bad, it's like a shelf collapsing in the garage: Everything spills onto the floor and gets mixed up.

✔ During manufacturing, almost all hard drives pick up a few bad sectors. The bad areas are retired, and the drive shifts incoming data to other areas. When the computer uses the drive, it appears to be free of bad sectors. If a sector dies while the drive's installed, Windows puts warning signs next to its bad spots so that it doesn't store any information on them.

What's an extended-density disk?

One breed of floppy disk, dubbed *extended-density,* can hold 2.88MB of data. That's twice as much as the former storage champs, the high-density disks. (If you're curious about high-density disks, check out the earlier sidebar "Who cares why a 1.2MB disk holds more than a 360K disk?")

These disks are still 3½ inches wide, just like the older guys, but they have the letters *ED* stamped on a corner. They're rare; hardly anybody uses them. Actually, I've never seen one, but everybody insists that they're out there somewhere.

If you want to use the extended-density disks, you need to buy a special, more expensive disk drive. (I've never seen one of those, either.) This type of disk and drive have been slow to catch on. But, hey, Hollywood snobs booed *Citizen Kane* during the Academy Awards in 1941.

Chances are, the format has now died with the introduction of newer storage mediums like the Zip drives described in Chapter 13.

✔ Your *file allocation table,* dubbed *FAT,* is your computer's index to what stuff it has stuffed in what sectors. When your FAT goes bad, your computer suddenly forgets where it put *everything*. A bad FAT is even grosser than it sounds.

✔ If you don't have a rescue program and don't feel like buying one, try running the disk tools that come with Windows. Described in Chapter 17, these freebies can often fix a misbehaving disk, which means that you don't have to buy utility software.

"How Do I Install a New Floppy Drive?"

IQ level: 80

Tools you need: One hand and a screwdriver

Cost: Around $50

Stuff to watch out for: If you're adding a second floppy drive, better check under your computer's hood to see whether there's room to slide one inside. That magic spot is called a *bay*. Sometimes a second hard disk, CD-ROM drive, Zip drive, DVD drive, or tape backup drive can hog all the available bays.

Twisted cable tales

Some floppies don't get along with their ribbon cables. It boils down to whether the ribbon cable has a little twist near its end. Some do and some don't. You need to set the drive's *DS (Drive Select) switches* accordingly.

Where are those DS switches? They're little switches or jumpers on the side of the floppy drive, as shown in the following figure. The drive's manual can tell you what to start flipping.

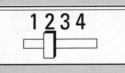

✔ If your ribbon cable has a *twist* in its middle, like the one shown in Figure 12-3, later in this chapter, set both your drives' switches to *DS2*. (Most likely, they already came set that way.)

✔ If there's *no* twist in the ribbon cable, set drive A to DS1 and drive B to DS2. (If your switches start at DS0, then set drive A to DS0 and drive B to DS1. Hey, I didn't design this stuff. . . .)

✔ If your drives already work fine, ignore all this stuff. Finally, for the lowdown on jumper flippin', head for Chapter 18.

Your new floppy drive probably needs rails or mounting brackets before it can fit inside your PC. Some drives come with the rails or mounting brackets right in the box; many don't. If you're *replacing* a drive, you can swipe its old rails. If you're adding a second drive and need rails or brackets, they cost a couple bucks at the computer store. If the store doesn't carry them, you need to contact the computer's manufacturer; chances are, generic rails don't fit on their computers.

To add or replace a floppy drive, follow these steps:

1. **Turn off the computer, unplug it, and remove the case.**

   These chores are covered on the Cheat Sheet in the front of this book.

2. **Remove the cables from the old drive.**

   Found the old drive? Floppy drives have two cables plugged into them:

   Ribbon cable: The flat ribbon cable connects the drive either to a special socket built right onto the motherboard of newer computers or to a controller card (on older computers). Look to see which kind you have so that you can replace it if it falls off.

   If you're replacing the drive, grab its ribbon cable by the plug and pull it straight off the drive, as shown in Figure 12-1. The cable should slide off pretty easily.

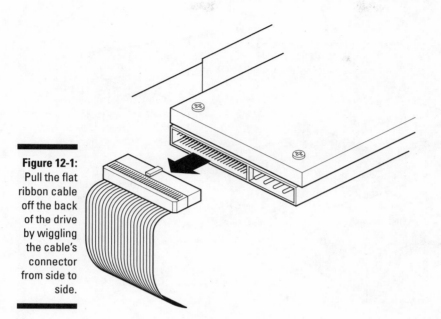

Figure 12-1: Pull the flat ribbon cable off the back of the drive by wiggling the cable's connector from side to side.

Power cable: The other cable is made of four wires that head to the power supply. Like the ribbon cable, the power cable pulls straight off the drive's connector, although it usually takes *lots* more pulling. Don't pull on the wires themselves; pull on the cable's plastic connector. Sometimes a gentle back-and-forth jiggle can loosen it.

Drives can use one of two power-supply plugs, pictured with their sockets in Figure 12-2.

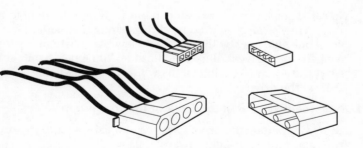

Figure 12-2: Power supply cables come in two sizes. Each size plugs into its own socket.

Adding a second floppy drive? Then look at the flat ribbon cable connected to drive A. Do you see a second, vacant connector on it, as shown in Figure 12-3? (Most cables come with two connectors.) If not, head back to the store for a new ribbon cable with two connectors. Got the new cable? Then jump to Step 5.

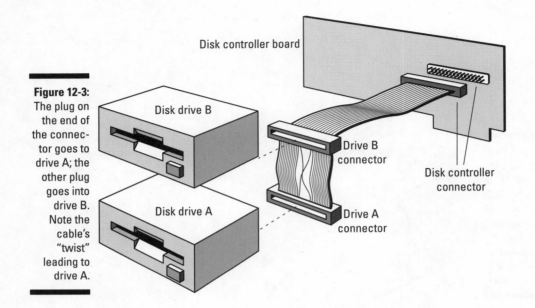

Disk controller board

Disk drive B

Drive B connector

Disk controller connector

Disk drive A

Drive A connector

Figure 12-3: The plug on the end of the connector goes to drive A; the other plug goes into drive B. Note the cable's "twist" leading to drive A.

3. **Remove the mounting screws holding the old drive in place.**

   Drives fit inside your computer in two main ways:

   Rails: Some drives let you screw little rails onto their sides. The rails hold the drive in place as it slides into the computer. Finally, two screws along the front keep the drive from sliding back out. To remove the drive, just unscrew the screws.

   Choose short screws to attach rails to the drive. If you use long ones, they may damage the drive.

   No rails: Some drives also slide in but without rails to hold them in place. They're also secured by screws along their sides. The screws along one side may be hidden from view by a particularly long card or even another drive mounted on its side. You have to pull out the card to get at the screws, cursing all the while. Note that using long screws may damage the drive.

4. **Slide the drive out of the front of the computer.**

   After you remove the drive's screws and cables, grab the drive from the front and slide it straight toward you.

5. **Slide the new drive in where the old one came out.**

   Slide your new drive into the spot where the old drive lived. You may need to remove the rails from the old drive and screw them onto the new drive.

   Adding a second drive? Find an available bay either above or below the other drive and slide the second drive in.

6. Attach the two cables to the drive.

Sometimes it's easier to attach the cables if you slide the drive back out a little bit first.

Ribbon cable: The plug on the *end* of the ribbon cable attaches to drive A; the plug in the ribbon cable's *middle* goes to drive B, as shown in Figure 12-3. A little barrier inside the ribbon cable usually makes sure that it can plug in only one way: the right way.

Sometimes the ribbon cable can fit either way. Horrors! Look closely for little numbers printed near the connecting tab on the drive. One edge of the tab has low numbers; the other side has larger numbers in the 30s. The colored edge of the ribbon connector always faces toward the low numbers. It should look like the one shown in Figure 12-4.

The connector on some 3½-inch drives doesn't look like the one shown in Figure 12-4. Instead, the connector has a bunch of little pins, like the one shown in Figure 12-5. You may have to head back to the computer store for an adapter if one wasn't included in the drive's box.

Power supply: The power supply cable fits into the drive's socket in only one way. Even so, check carefully to make sure that you're not forcing the two together the wrong way.

If you're adding a second drive, look at all the cables coming out of the power supply and grab one that's not being used. All used up? Then head back to the store and ask for a *Y adapter* for your power supply's drive cable.

7. Screw the new drive in place.

If the drive's inserted right, its holes line up with the holes in the computer's case. Got it? Then put the screws back in the right holes. You may need to slide the drive a little farther in or out until the holes line up.

Make sure that you use a screw of the right length to keep from damaging the disk drive.

8. Test the drive.

Plug in your computer, turn it on, put a disk in the drive, and see whether the drive works. Okay? Then turn it off, unplug it, and replace the cover. You're done!

However, if the drive doesn't work, turn off the computer, unplug it, and try a couple of things before pounding the walls. First, are the cables lined up right? Plugged in firmly? Check the connection where the ribbon cable plugs into the controller card or the motherboard. Sometimes all that jiggling around can pull it loose.

If you did anything more than simply replace a dead drive, you probably need to tell your computer about your accomplishment. Some computers aren't smart enough to figure out what kind of drive you installed. Here's what you do:

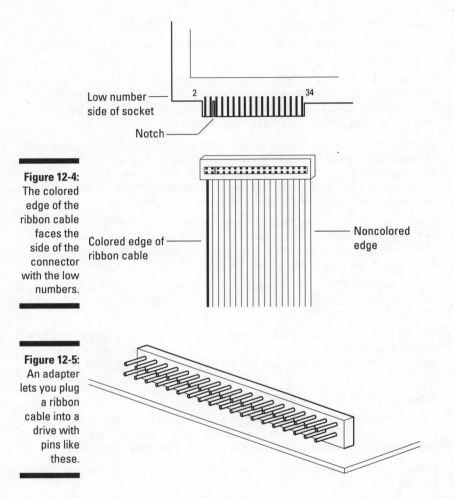

Low number side of socket

2   34

Notch

Figure 12-4:
The colored edge of the ribbon cable faces the side of the connector with the low numbers.

Colored edge of ribbon cable

Noncolored edge

Figure 12-5:
An adapter lets you plug a ribbon cable into a drive with pins like these.

If you added a second drive, you may need to change your computer's CMOS or setup screen so that it knows what happened. (That's covered in Chapter 18, too.)

If you're installing one of those new combo drives (the ones with a 5¼-inch drive and a 3½-inch drive in one little unit), you need to fiddle with the drive's jumpers. That's how the computer knows which one will be drive A and which will be drive B. The drive's manual should explain which way to jump.

Chapter 13

Hard Drives, CD and DVD Drives, Zip Drives, and Other Storage Devices

· ·

In This Chapter

▶ Defragmenting a hard drive

▶ Fixing disk errors

▶ Understanding types of hard drives

▶ Installing a hard drive

▶ Installing a CD-ROM or DVD drive

▶ Exploring backup drives

▶ Installing a tape backup drive

▶ Installing a removable storage drive

· ·

*P*eople pile their junk into closets, garages, and kitchen drawers. Computers stuff it all on a hard drive buried deep in its bowels.

Hard drives suffer from the same problems as their household counterparts, however. They're rarely large enough to hold everything.

Every version of Windows is larger. Programs continue to expand. The Internet keeps dishing out stuff that's fun to store. Can anybody bear to delete all his or her e-mail?

To deal with the information explosion, some people upgrade to a larger hard drive. Others add a second hard drive. Tape backup units and Zip drives are other possible solutions. Still others spring for those read/write CD drives that let you store information — and music — on cheap compact discs.

This chapter shows how to do it all.

"Does My Hard Drive Need to Be Defragmented?"

When your computer first copies a bunch of files on the hard drive, it pours them onto the hard drive's internal spinning disks in one long strip. When you delete some of those files, the computer runs over and clears off the spots where those files lived.

That leaves holes in what used to be a long strip. When you start adding new files, the computer starts filling up the holes. If a file's too big to fit in one hole, the computer breaks up the file, sticking bits and pieces wherever it can find room.

After a while, a single file can have its parts spread out all over your hard drive. Although your computer still can find everything, it takes more time because the hard drive has to move around much more to grab all the parts.

To stop this *fragmentation,* a concerned computer nerd released a defragmentation program. The program picks up all the information on your hard drive and pours it all back down in one long strip, putting all the files' parts next to each other.

"The Defragment program stops working!"

Windows doesn't like to defragment a drive while programs are running. Because programs often write information to the hard drive, Windows has to stop defragmenting and start all over from the beginning, to be sure that it's doing things right.

If Windows gets bored with all this stopping and starting and it refuses to defragment your drive, follow these steps:

Click the Start button, choose Shut down, and select the Restart option. Then, as your computer starts back up, hold down the Ctrl or F8 key. A Windows screen pops up, offering you several options. Choose Safe Mode.

Windows then loads itself using its bare-bones setup, bypassing those troublesome background programs. When Windows is through loading, turn off your screen saver (found in the Control Panel's Display area) and run the defragmentation program on your disk drives.

When you're done defragmenting the hard drive, shut down Windows and restart it again, this time allowing it to run in normal mode. Your computer's hard drive should then run much faster.

To speed things up, Windows 98 users can defragment a disk drive — either a hard drive or a floppy drive — by following these steps:

1. **Right-click your slow drive and choose Properties, as shown in Figure 13-1.**

   Right-click the drive from either My Computer or Windows Explorer. Windows tells you the drive's capacity and how much space you have left on your drive.

2. **Choose Tools from the menu.**

3. **Click the Defragment Now button.**

   Windows peeks at your drive and lets you know whether your disk is defragmented. Follow the program's onscreen advice; unless you use your computer constantly, you probably won't have to defragment your drive very often.

   Some people tell their computers to defragment their drives during the evening or lunch hour when they're not working on them. Windows has problems defragmenting a drive in the background while you're working, and it often slows things down.

   If your hard drive still runs slowly even after you defragment it, the drive may be too full. Better consider buying a larger hard disk or running the Windows 98 Disk Cleanup program.

   Compact discs don't have a defragmentation problem because computers only *read* information from them. Because they're not constantly erasing and adding new information to the discs, the information on the discs is never broken into pieces.

   Defragmenting a drive can take several minutes, especially if you haven't done it for a while. In fact, on some slow drives, the process may take up to an hour. The more often you defragment a drive, however, the less time it takes.

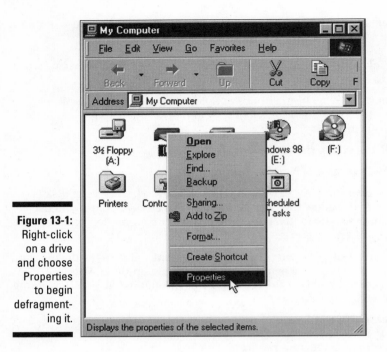

Figure 13-1:
Right-click
on a drive
and choose
Properties
to begin
defragment-
ing it.

Cleaning up the house with Windows 98

Windows 98 comes with a computerized equiv-alent of Drano for plugged-up hard drives. When your hard drive is getting too full, you can labo-riously pick and choose which files to delete. Or you can run Disk Cleanup, a cute little program hidden in the System Tools area (which is hidden in the Accessories area, which is hidden in the Programs area, which you can find by clicking on the Start button).

Disk Cleanup lets you quickly delete any useless temporary files left over from the Internet and crashed programs. The program also automati-cally empties your Recycle Bin.

In addition, Disk Cleanup lets you pare down the size of Windows by removing components you don't need. Dump desktop themes, for instance, to save 30MB. Your screen saver and wallpaper won't look as pretty, but Windows will run better. Not using the Internet? A purge in that area saves you 13MB of space. While you're at it, you can also delete programs you no longer use.

"How Can I Check for Disk Errors?"

Ever lost your train of thought after somebody snuck up and tapped you on the shoulder? The same thing can happen to your computer.

If the power goes out or a program crashes while a computer's working, the computer loses its train of thought. Your computer forgets to write down where it put stuff on the hard drive. (That's why you should always close your programs before turning off your computer.)

These lost trains of thought result in *disk errors,* and Windows fixes them pretty easily when you follow these instructions. In fact, Windows 98 can often sense when it has crashed and can automatically fix any resulting errors. If your computer's running strangely, checking for disk errors is often the first step toward a quick fix:

1. **Right-click your drive's icon and choose Properties (refer to Figure 13-1).**

   Open My Computer or Windows Explorer and right-click the drive's icon.

2. **Choose the Tools tab from the top of the Properties page.**

3. **Click the Check Now button.**

   A new window pops up, full of options.

4. **Choose Thorough from the Type Of test box, and click the Automatically Fix Errors box to put a check mark inside it.**

5. **Click the Start button.**

   Windows examines your disk drive, looking for suspicious areas and fixing the ones it can. A large hard drive can take a long time; floppy drives don't take nearly as long.

   When Windows finishes the process, the proud little program leaves a window on the screen summing up the number of errors it found and fixed.

Depending on the way your drive's error-patching program is set up, your computer may gather any unused file scraps and store them in files like FILE000.CHK, FILE001.CHK, FILE002.CHK — you get the point. Feel free to delete those files. They contain nothing worthwhile, as you quickly discover if you try to open them with your word processor.

"Does My Computer Have a Controller Card?"

Used by older computers, a *controller card* plugs into one of the slots inside your computer. Long, flat cables run from the controller card over to your disk drives, as illustrated in Figure 13-2. (The connectors on newer-style drives use little pins and sockets, as shown later in this chapter, in Figure 13-3.)

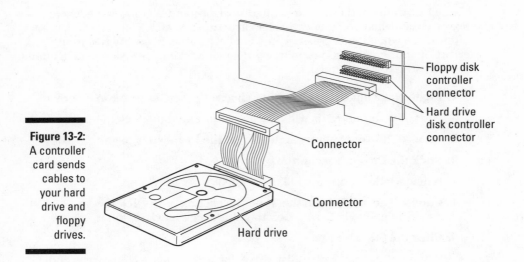

Floppy disk controller connector

Hard drive disk controller connector

Connector

Connector

Hard drive

Figure 13-2: A controller card sends cables to your hard drive and floppy drives.

When your computer wants some information, it tells the controller card. The controller card grabs the right information from the drive through the cable and shoots it back to the computer.

✔ Newer computers don't use controller cards. Instead, the drive's cables plug right into connections on the motherboard. That frees up more slots for other important computer devices, like TV tuners.

✔ If your current hard drive plugs straight into your motherboard, your floppy drives probably do the same thing. They usually plug in near the power supply — in the right-rear corner of your computer. (That's the same location where the tuba players sit in an orchestra pit.)

✔ If your older motherboard *doesn't* have those special sockets, buy an EIDE controller card. They're cheap little things that plug into a slot and give you a place to plug in the drive's cables.

"Should I Buy an IDE, EIDE, UDMA, or SCSI Drive?"

With so many little letters bouncing around these days, it's difficult to avoid a table. So check out Table 13-1 for the scoop.

Table 13-1	**Hard Times with This Many Hard Drive Types**		
This Drive	**Also Known As**	**Is Best for This**	**Techie Talk**
IDE	Intelligent Drive Electronics or Integrated Drive Electronics	A key advancement in hard drive technology, this fast and cheap standard for hard drives quickly chased the older types of drive out of the barroom. Most computers now use some form of IDE technology for their drives.	Older hard drives used the controlling information stored on expensive cards. IDE drives skip the cards and incorporate their "brains" right into the hard drive itself, leading to a new era in performance and price.
EIDE	UIDE, AT-2, Fast ATA, Ultra ATA	Yesterday's wonder warriors, these Enhanced IDE drives have been honed for speed.	EIDE drives use the same technology as an IDE drive but allow for faster access times and larger storage space.
UDMA	Ultra Direct Memory Access	The current darling, these are the fastest and largest variety of IDE hard drives.	UDMA comes in two varieties: UDMA/33 and the newer and fastest UDMA/66. The computer's motherboard must support UDMA; luckily, most Pentium motherboards support UDMA/33, and an increasing number support UDMA/66.

(continued)

Table 13-1 (continued)

This Drive	Also Known As	Is Best for This	Techie Talk
SCSI ("scuzzy")	Small Computer Systems Interface, Fast Wide SCSI, Ultra SCSI, SCSI-1, SCSI-2, SCSI-3	The second most popular hard drives, these are favored by power users and network administrators. However, they're expensive and a bit on the technical side, limiting their use by home or small-business owners.	After they are installed, SCSI drives can "chain" as many as seven other devices per channel.

Some rich folks prefer SCSI drives because those drives are quick, hold gobs of data, and can be strung together for enormous amounts of file space. If you're installing a new drive today, however, the choice is pretty clear: Pick up a UDMA drive.

These UDMA drives are the latest generation of a long string of drives using IDE technology. They don't need fancy controller cards, as described in the preceding section. They're the fastest type of drive around. And they're usually the easiest drives to install because most of them come with their own installation software. Good news!

If you're replacing your old-technology hard drive with any type of big, new EIDE drive, you need to replace your old controller card also. Luckily, a controller card for an EIDE drive is relatively inexpensive, especially when compared to a SCSI drive.

IDE-technology drives turn up their noses at older-technology drives. If you want to add an IDE-style drive as a second hard drive, your *first* hard drive must be the same type. If you've been using an older-style ST506 drive, you have to ditch it.

- ✔ If you're using older-style drives, don't feel too bad about ditching them for the IDE-style drives. IDE technology is faster and more reliable than its predecessors. Plus, most newer computers come with special sockets designed specifically for the IDE drives' cables.

- ✔ If you're adding a second IDE-style drive to a new computer, you probably don't need to buy a new controller card.

- ✔ Some folks are excited about SCSI-style hard drives. Theoretically, you can plug a SCSI card into your computer and "chain" up to seven other computer toys, including hard drives, CD-ROM drives, scanners, and tape backup drives. Unfortunately, SCSI drives are more difficult to set up, more expensive, and prone to conflicting standards. Plus, the number of chainable devices depends on the capabilities of the SCSI card.

✔ Dunno what all those terms for older hard drive words mean? Check out Table 13-2.

Table 13-2	What Do All Those Hard Drive Words Mean?	
This Word	*Means This*	*So Look for This*
Capacity	The amount of data the hard drive can store	The more gigabytes (GB), the better. If you're buying a new drive, look for something with 15 gigabytes or more. In fact, buy the biggest drive you can afford. Remember: When the drive is formatted, it loses about 5 percent of its capacity.
Access or seek time	How long your drive takes to locate stored files, measured in milliseconds (ms)	The smaller the number, the better. You want speed, and 9 ms is considered pretty speedy. (CD-ROM drives are considerably slower.)
Data transfer rate	How fast your computer can grab information from files after it finds them	The higher the number, the better. Don't place too much stock in it, though; it has become a meaningless statistic bandied about by vendors.
Cache	The ability to remember frequently accessed information	The bigger, the better. Because memory chips are faster than hard drives, these chips remember frequently acquired pieces of information. If the computer needs the information again, it can grab it from the cache, saving some time.

"My CD-ROM Drive Doesn't Work When I Leave Windows 98!"

Believe it or not, Windows still belongs to that evolutionary era in which the old world of DOS is transforming into the new world of Windows. That means some areas remain in transition.

See, Windows can automatically recognize most CD-ROM drives on sight. DOS, by contrast, needs a special piece of software called a *driver,* which tells DOS that the drive is there and translates all the talking back and forth.

To avoid using up precious memory, Windows doesn't bother loading that DOS driver for the CD-ROM drive. After all, it doesn't need it. But that means that when you move to DOS — either by using the Restart the Computer in MS-DOS mode command or by running a DOS program — the driver probably won't be there to tell the computer about its CD-ROM drive.

The fix? Well, it's a bit technical, so don't bother reading this except during a last resort.

In Windows 98, you can usually open the CONFIG.SYS file and remove the word REM from a line reading DEVICE=CDROM.SYS /D:OEMCD001 or something similar; yours may differ. Then, when you reboot your computer, the DOS driver for your CD-ROM drive will be loaded. Be sure to put that REM word back when you're through with the CD-ROM in DOS mode so that Windows will have its memory back. (Chapter 18 explains CONFIG.SYS files.)

The solution? You need to locate the CD-ROM's driver and put it in your computer's AUTOEXEC.BAT and CONFIG.SYS files. Usually, a CD-ROM drive's installation program can do this automatically. But if it's giving you problems, head for Chapter 16.

"How Do I Get the Drive Lights to Turn On and Off?"

If your hard drive's light comes on when you use the drive but never turns off, check out the installation section, coming up in the section "How Do I Install or Replace an IDE-Type Hard Drive?" Somebody may have fastened the flat ribbon cable connector upside down when pushing it onto the disk drive.

Also, some disk drives mount inside your computer where they're never seen. That means that you can't see the light regardless of whether it's on or off.

If the hard drive light on the front of your computer never comes on, you need to push the light's little wires onto a *jumper* that lives on your hard drive or controller card. (I discuss jumper pushing in Chapter 18.)

Some hard drives even have a little jumper that lets you choose one of two options: You can keep the little light on all the time, or you can have it turn on when the hard drive's actually fetching data. (Traditionalists stick with the fetching-data option.)

"How Do I Back Up My Hard Drive?"

Nothing lasts forever, not even that trusty old hard drive. That's why it's important to keep a copy — a backup version — of your hard drive for safe-keeping. Table 13-3 shows some of the most popular backup methods and their pros and cons.

Table 13-3	Ways to Back Up a Hard Drive	
Method	*Pros*	*Cons*
Backup program and floppy disks	Cheap, comes with Windows 98	This method worked fine 10 years ago, when people used about 20 floppies to back up a 20MB disks hard disks. Now, with 20GB hard disks in use, it would require about 200 floppies.
Backup program and tape drive	Relatively inexpensive, slow	Although easy to install and boasting a large capacity, it's slow. Still, it can back up your hard drive automatically while you're sleeping — meaning that you'll do it more often. If you're choosing tape, choose the more expensive, high-quality systems. They're more reliable.
Removable-cartridge disk drive, like the Iomega ZipPlus drive or SyQuest SparQ	Relatively inexpensive, fast, and portable	Unfortunately, they're not practical for today's huge drives because you need too many of them. Plus, you need to sit in front of the computer, constantly swapping in a fresh cartridge until the backup is complete.
Read/write CD-ROM drive	Relatively inexpensive, with the price dropping daily	These CD-ROM drives let you write information to blank compact discs. The discs cost only a dollar or two apiece and hold 600MB of information. Unfortunately, they're slow and require you to sit at the computer, feeding it dozens of disks until you've backed up your 20GB hard drive.

(continued)

Table 13-3 *(continued)*

Method	Pros	Cons
Optical drive	For business users	These drives write information to special discs, like read/write CD-ROM drives. They're too expensive for consumers, however, and are usually used in business settings.

✔ Although the best backup method changes over the years according to capacity, cost, and the size of the hard drive, tape backups seem to be making a comeback.

✔ Don't skimp on your backup system. If it's not accurate, it's a waste of time. And if it's not convenient, you'll never use it.

"How Do I Install or Replace an IDE-Type Hard Drive?"

IQ level: 100

Tools you need: One hand, a screwdriver, and a system disk

Cost: Roughly $100 to $300

Stuff to watch out for: If you're replacing your current hard drive, make sure that you have a system disk on hand. Don't have one nearby? Race to Chapter 2 for instructions. You may need some of the programs on that disk.

IDE-technology drives (IDE, EIDE, and UDMA) don't work with the older-style ST506 (MFM or RLL) drives. If you have one of those oldsters, pull it out and try to sell it. That old drive was probably going to die soon, anyway.

If you're adding a *second* IDE or EIDE drive to accompany your first IDE or EIDE drive, you have to tell your computer which drive you want to be drive C. (Drive C is the one that the computer looks at first and boots from.) That drive's the *master,* and the second drive is the *slave.* You need to move a little jumper on the second drive to make that drive work as the slave (see Figure 13-3).

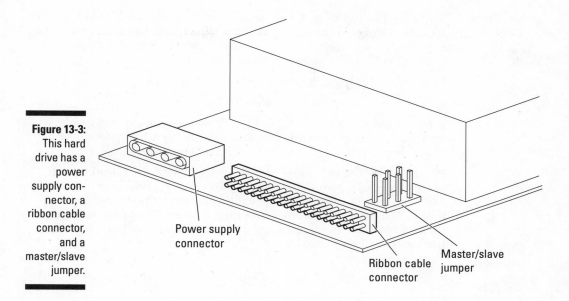

Figure 13-3:
This hard drive has a power supply connector, a ribbon cable connector, and a master/slave jumper.

Power supply connector

Ribbon cable connector

Master/slave jumper

Some hard drives also ask you to move a jumper, depending on whether you're using one hard drive or two. Others automatically set themselves up for one hard drive if they're set up as the master. You may have to check the drive's manual on this one.

You may need rails to mount your hard drive inside your computer. Some drives come with mounting rails; others don't. If you're replacing an old drive, you can often unscrew its old rails and swipe them. Otherwise, you may need to head back to the store to buy some. (They're usually pretty cheap.)

Hard drive capacity quickly outpaced computers. The BIOS on pre-1994 computers couldn't handle hard drives larger than 504MB. The next generation of BIOS chips could work with hard drives up to 8.4GB, but Windows 95 choked on drives larger than 2MB. Later versions of Windows 95 fixed the problem, as did a newly updated BIOS. You still may need to upgrade your BIOS before installing any drive larger than 8.4GB. In fact, some BIOS chips can't handle drives larger than 32MB. The solution? Ask your computer manufacturer or head to its Web page to see your computer's current size limitations.

The following steps show you how to install an IDE-technology hard drive:

1. **Back up your hard drive, turn off the computer, unplug it, and remove the case.**

   Be sure to back up your hard drive before playing with it. You don't want to lose any of your data. You can find instructions for removing the computer's cover on the Cheat Sheet in the front of this book.

If you live in a static-electricity prone environment, buy a grounding strap that wraps around your wrist and attaches to the computer. If you don't have static electricity in your area, remember to touch your computer's case before touching its innards.

2. **Remove cables from the old drive.**

   Hard drives have one or two cables plugged into them.

   Ribbon cable: The ribbon cable leads from the hard drive to its controller on the motherboard or a card. The ribbon cables pull straight off the drive pretty easily. Leave the other end connected.

   Power cable: The other cable is made of four wires that head for the power supply. Power cables come in two sizes, as shown in Figure 13-4. Like the ribbon cable, the power cable pulls straight off the drive's socket; it usually takes *lots* more pulling, though. Don't pull on the wires themselves; pull on the cable's plastic connector. Sometimes a gentle back-and-forth jiggle can loosen it.

Figure 13-4:
Your hard drive uses one of these two sizes for the power cable.

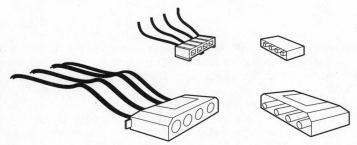

   Adding a second IDE drive: If you're adding a second IDE drive, check out the flat ribbon cable connected to the first drive. Do you see a second, vacant plug on it, like the one shown in Figure 13-2? If not, head back to the store for a new ribbon cable. It needs to have *two* drive connectors. (Most already do, luckily.) You second-drive installers can jump ahead to Step 5.

3. **Remove the mounting screws holding the drive in place.**

   Some drives are held in place by two screws in front. Other drives are held in place by screws in their sides. The screws on one side may be hidden from view by a particularly long card or even by another drive mounted on its side. That means that you have to pull out the card or remove the obstructing drive just to get at the screws!

4. Slide the old drive out the computer's front.

After you remove the old drive's cables and screws, you can slide the old drive out of the front of the computer. Give it a gentle tug.

Drives that mount on their sides slide out toward the computer's center; be sure not to gouge your motherboard while pulling out the drive.

Replacing a controller card: Are you pulling out your old-style drive to replace it with an IDE-technology drive? Then pull out your old controller card as well. You can see a picture of one in Figure 13-2. Look for the card where all the ribbon cables end up. Found it? Pull all the ribbon cables off, including the ones heading for your floppy drives. See that tiny screw holding the controller card in place? Remove the screw and pull the card straight up out of its slot. (For more card details, head for Chapter 15.)

5. Slide the new drive in where the old one came out.

Your new IDE-technology drive should slide in place right where the old one came out. Doesn't fit? If the new drive's smaller than the old one, you need to add rails or mounting brackets to make it fit.

When handling drives, be careful not to damage their exposed circuitry by bumping them into other parts of your computer. Also, be sure to touch your computer's metal case to get rid of any static electricity before picking up your drive.

Adding a second IDE drive? Slide it into a vacant bay, which usually is next to the first drive. Check your computer's manual; you may be able to mount the drive on its side in a special spot inside your computer.

6. Add the new controller card if necessary.

Are you replacing an older-style drive with an EIDE or IDE drive? Then you need a new controller card to go with it.

Handling the card by its edges, push it down into the slot where the old controller card sat. Then fasten it down with the screw. (You can find more card-installation tips in Chapter 15.) Check the controller's manual; you need to push ribbon cables onto the controller's connectors for your floppy disks and hard disk.

7. Attach two cables to the hard drive.

Try sliding the drive out a little bit to connect the two cables more easily.

Ribbon cable: The plug on the ribbon cable should push onto little pins on the end of the drive. The other end of the cable goes either to the controller card or to a socket on the motherboard.

If you're installing a second hard drive, the ribbon cable should have a spare connector on it. (If not, head back to the store.) It doesn't matter which connector goes onto which drive; the computer looks at the drives' master/slave jumpers, described in the next few paragraphs, to figure out which one is drive C.

Power supply: The power supply cable fits into the drive's socket only one way. Even so, check the ends to make sure that you're not forcing it in the wrong way. Check out Figure 13-4 to make sure that you've found the right power cable socket.

Power supply cables come with both large and small connectors. The connectors are supposed to fit only one way, but the small ones often fit either way. The trick? Look for the number 1 somewhere near the drive's little socket. The power supply connector's red wire fastens onto the number 1 prong.

Adding a second IDE drive: If this is your second drive, look for its master/slave jumper. Make this second drive the slave drive. You can see the jumpers in Figure 13-3. The drive's manual tells you where to put the jumper. (Chapter 18 tells you how to move around the jumpers.)

Note that some hard drives also ask you to move a jumper depending on whether you're using one hard drive or two. Others automatically set themselves up for one hard drive if they're set up as the master. You may have to check the drive's manual on this one.

IDE-technology drives usually come configured as master drives. If you're installing just a single IDE or EIDE drive in your computer, you usually don't need to mess with any jumpers.

What's a CD-ROM read/write drive?

The older CD-ROM drives could simply read information from a CD, which made them great for storing large amounts of information as well as letting computer users listen to Santana CDs at work.

The latest CD-ROMs, however, can read *and* write information to CDs. They can still read information and play music. When you toss a blank CD (costing less than $2) into the drive, however, you can write information on it for later use.

Best yet, when you toss a more expensive CD (around $20) into the drive, you can not only write information on the CD but also erase the information and write more information. The CDs are reusable, so they're great for backing up important projects on your hard drive.

Musicians like the technology — called *CD-R/W,* or *CD-recordable* — because they can record their own music CDs. Others like to store huge multimedia presentations on the CDs. The price of these drives has dropped below $200, and they're getting faster and faster.

Keep your eye on these gizmos; they're hot enough to be standard equipment on many new PCs.

8. **Replace the screws.**

   Cables attached? Master/slave jumper set? Then fasten the drive in place with those little screws. Make sure that they are short screws to prevent damage to the inside of the hard drive.

9. **Replace the cover, plug in the computer, and turn it on.**

   Chances are, your computer's BIOS will recognize the drive right off the bat.

10. **Run the drive's bundled installation software.**

    Look for a floppy disk inside the hard drive's box. Insert the floppy and run the drive's installation software. It formats the drive to prepare it to accept data, and then it lets you separate the drive into partitions, assigning different drive letters to different areas of the drive.

    If it doesn't work, start by double-checking all your cables. On tight? Upside down? In the right place? Is the drive partitioned right? Formatted correctly? If you installed a second disk drive, twice as many things could have gone wrong.

If your two IDE drives just won't work right, try switching the master/slave relationship. Sometimes IDE drives from different manufacturers just don't like to work with each other, no matter who's in charge. You may have to exchange one IDE drive for one that's the same brand as the other.

If you have to turn your computer on several times in the morning before the hard drive starts working, you may need a new power supply. The power supply may not provide enough power to bring the drive up to speed quickly enough. You can find power supplies dissected in Chapter 14. (Or, if your drive is old, it may simply be worn out.)

"How Do I Install a CD-ROM?"

IQ level: 90

Tools you need: One hand and a screwdriver

Cost: Anywhere from $50 to $200

Stuff to watch out for: Compact disc players (CD-ROM drives) come in two types: *internal* and *external.* The external ones are little boxes that take up room on your desk. The internal ones slide into the front of your computer like a floppy disk drive. They may also be IDE or SCSI.

Older varieties plugged into a card inside your computer. Newer ones plug directly on the motherboard.

A new breed of CD-ROM drive, called *CD read/write (CD-RW)* or *CD-recordable*, lets you write information to a disc, as well as read information from its drive. This drive now costs about twice as much as a regular CD-ROM drive, but the price is constantly dropping. It's installed in the same way as a normal CD-ROM drive.

Installing an external CD-ROM drive

Follow these steps to install an external CD-ROM drive:

1. **Turn off your computer, unplug it, and remove its case.**

   You can find complete instructions on the Cheat Sheet at the front of this book.

2. **Plug the CD-ROM drive's card into one of your available slots and screw it down.**

   Chapter 15 describes cards and how to stick them in the right place.

3. **Replace your computer's cover and plug in your PC.**

4. **Plug the CD-ROM drive's cable into the card.**

   You will find a thick cord in the box with the CD-ROM drive. One side of the cord plugs into the connector now peeking from the back of your PC; the other end fits into the back of the CD-ROM drive.

5. **Plug in the CD-ROM drive and turn it on.**

   External CD-ROM drives have a power cord that needs to be plugged into the wall. A second cord often plugs into your parallel port.

   Don't have enough power outlets? Head back to the computer store and buy a power strip. These gadgets let you plug six or more accessories into one outlet.

6. **Turn on your computer.**

   When Windows boots up, it may recognize the new CD-ROM drive right off the bat and automatically install it for you. If not — or if you aren't using Windows — move to Step 7.

7. **Install the CD-ROM's software.**

   If you're not using Windows 98, put the CD-ROM's installation disk in drive A and type **INSTALL** or **SETUP**, depending on what your manual says.

   For a few extra tips and tricks, head to the end of the following section, "Installing an internal CD-ROM drive."

Installing an internal CD-ROM drive

Follow these steps to install an internal CD-ROM drive:

1. **Turn off your computer, unplug it, and remove its case.**

   You can find complete instructions on the Cheat Sheet at the front of this book.

2. **If necessary, plug the CD-ROM drive's card into one of your available slots and screw it down.**

   No card? Don't worry. The latest CD-ROM drives plug straight into the motherboard, just like a hard drive.

3. **Slide the CD-ROM drive into the front of your computer.**

   You need a vacant drive bay, which is an opening where your disk drives normally live. The drive should slide in the front. For tips, check out Chapter 12. The CD-ROM drive slides in the same way as a floppy drive.

4. **Connect the cables.**

   We're talking three sets of cables here.

   First, connect the flat ribbon cable between the CD-ROM drive and the motherboard or its card you installed in Step 2. It should fit only one way.

   Second, rummage around the tentacles of wires leading from your power supply until you find a spare power connector. That plugs into your CD-ROM drive. Those drives usually use the small-size connector shown in Figure 13-4.

   Finally, connect the thin audio cables between the CD-ROM drive and the little jumpers on the sound card.

5. **Screw the drive in place.**

   Although some drives screw in from the sides, most fasten with two screws along the front.

6. **Replace your computer's cover, plug the computer in, and turn it on.**

   When Windows boots up, it may recognize the new CD-ROM drive and automatically install it for you. If not — or if you aren't using Windows 98 — move to Step 7.

7. **Run the CD-ROM drive software.**

   The software should take over the rest of the installation chores. If it tosses bits of weirdness, like *interrupts* or *drivers,* page on ahead to Chapters 16 and 18.

Most of today's CD-ROM drives plug directly into your motherboard. Others use SCSI ports and cards. If you already have a SCSI card in your computer, things can get either better or worse. Here's why:

The Good News: SCSI ports can chain a handful of other SCSI devices. That means that you can hook your CD-ROM drive into your chain. For example, if your sound card comes with a SCSI port, you don't need the CD-ROM drive's card. Just plug the CD-ROM drive's cable into the sound card's SCSI port, saving time and, more importantly, a slot.

The Bad News: Different brands of SCSI ports aren't always compatible with each other. Sometimes they work; sometimes they don't. Before investing in SCSI devices, call the manufacturers to be sure that the devices can all get along.

"How Do I Install a DVD Drive?"

IQ level: 90

Tools you need: A system floppy, a free drive bay, an extra power connector on your power supply, an IDE controller, a flat ribbon cable, and a decoder card

Cost: Anywhere from $150 to $300

Stuff to watch out for: DVD drives, described in Chapter 3, let you watch movies on your computer. Most of them read CDs as well. However, they require a decoder to translate the movies and a sound card to play back the sound.

1. **Turn off your computer, unplug it, and remove its case.**

   You can find complete instructions on the Cheat Sheet at the front of this book.

2. **Plug the DVD drive's decoder card into one of your available slots and screw it down.**

   Some of the fancier video cards come with decoders for DVD players, but don't count on it unless you're sure about it.

3. **Slide the DVD drive into the front of your computer.**

   You need a vacant *drive bay,* which is an opening where your disk drives normally live. The drive should slide in the front. For tips, check out Chapter 12. The DVD drive slides in the same way as a floppy drive.

4. **Connect the cables.**

   You might need to connect four cables.

   First, connect the flat ribbon cable between the DVD drive and its decoder card. It should fit only one way. If you already have a CD-ROM drive, use one of the empty connectors on its cable. No extras? You need a ribbon cable that can support two gadgets. Head back to the store.

Second, connect a thin wire between your sound card and your DVD decoder card. This step may not be necessary, depending on your particular model.

Third, check to see whether you need to connect your monitor. This means unplugging the monitor from your video card and connecting a small cable between the DVD card's video port and the video card's video port. Then connect the monitor's cable into the DVD card's VGA port. This stuff is much easier than it sounds.

Finally, connect one of the power supply's cables to the DVD drive.

5. **Screw the drive in place and set its jumpers.**

   Although some drives screw in from the sides, most fasten with two screws along the front.

   Using more than one drive on the cable? Set the jumpers for Master or Slave so that the computer knows which drive gets what letter. (Check out the earlier section about installing hard drives for more information about setting master/slave jumpers.)

6. **Replace your computer's cover, plug the computer in, and turn it on.**

   When Windows boots up, it may recognize the new CD-ROM drive and automatically install it for you.

7. **Run the CD-ROM drive software.**

   The software should take over the rest of the installation chores. If it tosses bits of weirdness, like interrupts or drivers, page on ahead to Chapters 16 and 18.

"How Do I Install a Tape Backup Unit?"

IQ level: 90

Tools you need: One hand and a screwdriver

Cost: Anywhere from $200 to $1,000 or more

Stuff to watch out for: The easiest tape backup units live in little boxes. You just plug a cable between the box and your ever-versatile parallel port. That's it! Just pop its installation floppy disk in your disk drive and you're through.

An internal backup unit is a little rougher to install, but not much. Just follow these steps:

1. **Turn off your computer, unplug it, and remove its cover.**

   The Cheat Sheet at the front of this book covers this step.

2. **Push the unit into a drive bay.**

   You need a free *drive bay* — one of those spots into which you can slide floppy disk drives. If you don't have one, you can remove drive B to make room. Be sure to tell your computer's CMOS that it doesn't have a drive B anymore, however, although Windows 98 can often detect this automatically. I explain the cautious task of informing your CMOS in Chapter 18.

3. **Fasten the unit down.**

   If the unit has rails on the sides, fasten it in place with two screws along the front. If it doesn't use rails, put two screws in each of its sides.

4. **Attach the cables.**

   Power cable: Find a spare power cable hanging out of your power supply. Don't have one? Head to the store for a Y adapter.

   Ribbon cable: The drive comes with its own ribbon cable. Unplug your floppy drive's old ribbon cable from your controller card and plug in the new backup unit's cable.

   See the extra connector on the backup unit's ribbon cable, about an inch away from where it's plugged into the card? Plug your floppy drive's cable into that new little connector. Then plug the end of the backup unit's new ribbon cable into the backup drive.

   The cables fit only one way, but look at the ribbon's colored edge: That's the side that plugs into Pin 1.

5. **Replace the computer's cover, plug in the computer, and turn it on.**

   That should do the trick. Now you have to run the tape backup unit's installation software.

Whew. No more feeding 40 backup disks to the computer every week. Don't you wish that you'd bought this a year ago when you first bought your computer?

If any of these steps leaves you scratching your head, flip to Chapter 12. You install tape backup drives almost exactly like floppy drives.

"So What's an External Storage Drive, Anyway?"

Floppy disks just aren't big enough these days, so several manufacturers decided to build a better disk. Of course, none of them gets along with each other, but each has its pros and cons.

Some fit inside a *disk drive bay* — the place where your floppy disk drives and internal CD-ROM drives sit. Others connect through a cable attaching to your parallel port. Still others require a SCSI card.

The Iomega ZipPlus holds up to 100MB of information. It's certainly not the fastest or cheapest, and it doesn't hold as much information as some of the competition. But because you can simply plug it into a parallel port of any PC, it's very transportable — making it great for carrying information back and forth from work. You'll find plenty of others using it, too, because more than 10 million units have been sold.

Many other external storage drives fill the shelves right now, but for a beginning user, the Iomega ZipPlus is still a good bet, despite its age. Most external storage drives install the same way as the ZipPlus, so I use that as an example.

The ZipPlus replaces the older Zip drive, but it can still read and write information stored by the older drive.

"How Do I Install a ZipPlus Drive?"

IQ level: 90

Tools you need: One hand and a screwdriver

Cost: Around $150 to $200

Stuff to watch out for: Although Windows took its time getting used to these little cartridges, Iomega ZipPlus and Windows seem to have patched up their differences.

ZipPlus drives come in two types: One type simply plugs into your parallel port, and the other requires a SCSI drive. The parallel-port model is slower and may be a little cheaper; the SCSI-drive model costs more and works faster.

To install a ZipPlus drive, follow these steps:

1. **Shut down your PC, unplug your printer cable, and identify the connectors on the back of your ZipPlus drive. SCSI-model users, move to Step 3.**

   ZipPlus drives come with two connectors. Parallel drives have one 25-pin male connector for the cable that connects to your PC and one 25-pin female connector for your printer's cable to plug into.

   SCSI drives have two identical-looking 25-pin female connectors.

2. **Connect the ZipPlus drive's cable between your computer's printer port and the parallel drive's connector. Go to Step 5.**

3. **Plug the ZipPlus SCSI card into a vacant slot as described in Chapter 15 and connect the drive to the card.**

4. **Connect the cable from the ZipPlus drive to your PC's external SCSI connector. You may need to set the drive's SCSI ID number by flipping its little rotary switch (usually with a small screwdriver.)**

   This step tells your SCSI adapter to recognize the new device.

5. **Plug the Zip drive's AC power connector into a wall socket and plug its power cord into the Zip drive.**

6. **Double-check all your connections and turn your computer back on.**

   Some Zip drives have a power switch; most remain on all the time.

7. **Install the Zip drive's installation software.**

   Run the drive's setup software from within Windows or DOS and place the Tools disk in the drive to complete the process.

Chapter 14

Power Supplies

You can't see it, but you can sure hear it: Your computer's power supply sits inside one corner of your computer and whirs away.

This chapter covers that restless little beast that sucks up electricity all day long. When the power supply stops grabbing power, this chapter tells you how to grab the power supply and replace it with a new one.

"My Computer Makes a Whining Noise"

Some power supplies wail like a Volkswagen from the early '60s. Other power supplies purr quietly like a BMW.

The noise comes from the fan inside the power supply that blows air across the power supply's innards. The fan cools off the inside of your computer at the same time.

As for the racket? Well, many power supplies are just noisy little beasts. There's just no getting around the racket.

- ✔ If your power supply is absolutely *too* noisy, consider replacing it. Today's power supplies are often a little quieter than the rumblers released five or more years ago.

- ✔ If your power supply doesn't make any noise, you're in even *worse* trouble. Hold your hand near the fan hole in the back. If you don't feel any air blowing out, the fan has died and your computer is getting hotter by the second. Buy a new power supply — and quickly. Your computer can overheat like a car in the desert and suddenly die without warning.

Don't try taking apart your power supply to quiet down the fan or make repairs. Power supplies soak up electricity and can zap you, even when they're unplugged. Never mess around inside a power supply.

"Nothing Happens When I Turn On My PC"

Nothing? No little lights go on along the front? No purr from the fan whirring merrily? If you're sure that your computer is plugged in, then your power supply probably died during the night. It's time for a replacement. (And it's a relatively easy process, too.)

"My Computer Forgets the Date, Even After I Changed the Batteries!"

Drinking fountains never work the same way. Some fountains make you bend down really low and press your cheek against the gross, crusty metal part to get any driblets of water. Other fountains squirt up and hit you in the forehead.

Power supplies, however, are specifically designed to provide a steady stream of electricity at just the right voltage. If the power level strays from the norm, even by just a few volts, it can interfere with your computer's lifestyle.

Is it your hard drive, or is it your power supply?

Sometimes it's hard to differentiate between a noisy power supply fan and a noisy hard drive. Both have a constantly running motor, so both are susceptible to the burned-out bearing syndrome.

To tell whether the noise is from your power supply or your hard drive, turn off your computer, unplug it, and open the case. Then pull the power supply's cable out from the back of your hard drive. Plug your computer back in and turn it on. Because the hard drive isn't getting power, it doesn't turn on with the rest of your computer. If you hear a noise, it's your power supply.

If you don't hear a noise, it's your hard drive. Unfortunately, hard drives cost much more to replace, as I discuss in Chapter 13.

✔ Plug a lamp into your power outlet to make sure that the outlet *really* works. You may have a blown fuse or a flipped circuit breaker. That's much cheaper.

✔ A lightning bolt that barrels down your electric line can kill your power supply. The power supply has been designed to sacrifice itself for the good of the whole computer. Chances are that you can replace the power supply, and then everything will return to the pre-lightning state. Then again, it's never easy to wager confidently against lightning bolts.

✔ Power supplies are pretty easy to replace. Just grab a screwdriver and page ahead to the section "How Do I Install a New Power Supply?"

If your power supply is not dependable, replace it. Uh, how can you tell whether your power supply is dependable? The following list should help:

✔ If your computer constantly forgets the date and the hard drive type, even after you change the battery, the power supply is a likely suspect. Sometimes, the power supply doesn't deliver enough power to keep your computer's settings in place. Try a second replacement battery, though — they're cheaper.

✔ After you change the power supply (or battery), head for Chapter 18 to restore your computer's settings to the right place. Luckily, XT computers don't have these setting problems. Unfortunately, XTs have enough other problems to keep their owners busy.

✔ Your computer's power supply and its battery are two different things. The power supply gives your computer electricity when it's turned *on* so that it can accomplish computer-like chores. The computer's battery provides electricity when your computer is turned *off* so that it can remember what computer-like things have been installed.

✔ Have you had to replace any of your computer's disk drives lately? The power supply may be at fault, producing too much power. Being off just a few volts can burn up your computer's disk drives or make them work erratically.

✔ If you recently added a second hard drive or extra cards to a computer with an older power supply, consider upgrading your power supply. The old one may not be putting out enough watts to support all the extra gadgets. See the "What Power Supply Should I Buy?" section, later in this chapter.

"What's a UPS or Backup Power Supply?"

When your computer loses its power, *you* lose your work. Everything you haven't actually saved to a disk just sort of dribbles away.

If the power suddenly fails and the lights go out, your computer goes out, too. To protect against such scariness, some people use an *uninterrupted power supply,* often called a UPS.

The *UPS* is a big box that connects your computer and its power outlet. The big box constantly sucks up power and stores it, like a huge car battery. Then, if the power dies, the big box instantly turns itself on and provides uninterrupted power to your computer.

Then the big box provides you with a rewarding feeling of accomplishment for having bought and installed a UPS before the power died.

✔ The more money you spend on your UPS, the more time you can work in the dark. Common times range from ten minutes to a half-hour.

✔ For the most part, the UPS isn't designed to keep your computer running all day in the dark. The UPS just keeps your computer going when the power dies, which gives you a few extra minutes to save your work, turn off your computer, and drink some carrot juice until the lights go back on.

✔ Some uninterrupted power supplies also work as a *line conditioner,* which filters out any nasty voltage spikes or surges that may come through the power lines. A line conditioner can make your computer last longer.

✔ A UPS isn't cheap; it costs anywhere from $100 to $500, depending on its power. Still, a UPS can be an important investment if you live in an area prone to power outage problems.

"What Power Supply Should I Buy?"

If you expand your living room by knocking down a wall, you need more than a single 100-watt bulb to light everything up. Computers work in a similar way.

Like a light bulb, a computer's power supply is rated in watts. The more gizmos you've plugged into your computer, the more watts you need to feed them.

If you're using a 386, 486, or older Pentium, make sure that your power supply is rated at least 200 watts. Newer, faster computers, or computers with lots of peripherals should have a 250-watt power supply. A sticker on the power supply displays the wattage rating.

If you've been upgrading lots of computer parts lately — a new motherboard, a second hard drive, extra cards, or a tape backup drive — your next purchase should be a more powerful power supply.

"How Do I Install a New Power Supply?"

IQ level: 90

Tools you need: One hand and a screwdriver

Cost: Approximately $50

Stuff to watch out for: Power supplies can't be repaired; they're simply replaced. Throw the old power supply away.

Don't ever open your power supply or try to fix it yourself. The power supply stores powerful jolts of electricity, even when the computer is turned off and unplugged. Power supplies are safe, but only when they are not open.

Also, the shelves in the back room of the computer store are filled with different kinds of power supplies. To find the right replacement, bring in your old power supply and say, "I need another one of these." Or check with the place that sold you the computer. If you're upgrading your power supply to a higher wattage, tell the dealer, "I need a power supply like this but rated at a higher wattage."

To install a new power supply, perform the following steps:

1. **Turn off your PC, unplug it, and remove its cover.**

   If you've never gone fishing inside your computer, the Cheat Sheet in the front of this book covers how to remove your computer's cover.

2. **Unplug the power supply cables from the motherboard, the drives, and the power switch.**

Your power supply is that big, boxy, silver thing in your computer's corner. Bunches of cables run out of a hole in the power supply's side.

Each cable has one of several types of plugs on its end. The plugs are all shaped differently to keep them from plugging into the wrong place. Even so, put a strip of masking tape on the end of each plug and write down its destination. You and your computer will feel better that way.

Here's a rundown of the plugs, their shapes, and their destinations:

Motherboard: Power supplies come with either one or two rectangular-shaped plugs that fit into a single socket on the motherboard.

Older-style power supplies come with two "AT" power connectors. These two plugs nestle together into a single socket. Newer power supplies come with a single connector that plugs into a single socket.

Both the AT- and ATX-style of connectors and sockets are shown in Figure 14-1.

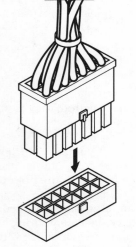 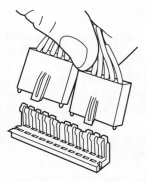

Figure 14-1: The newer, ATX power supplies sport a single plug and socket; the older, AT power supplies sport two plugs that nestle together into a single socket.

ATX socket and connector   AT socket and connectors

Drives: Disk drives, tape backup units, and other internal goodies get their power from two different sizes of plugs, as shown in Figure 14-2.

Switch: Some power supplies have an on/off switch built right onto the end of a cable. Other power supplies have a wire that connects to an on/off switch along the computer's front or side. Those power supplies have little connectors like the one shown in Figure 14-3. (An increasing number of power supplies don't connect directly to the computer's power switch. A small pair of wires lead from the motherboard to the power switch.)

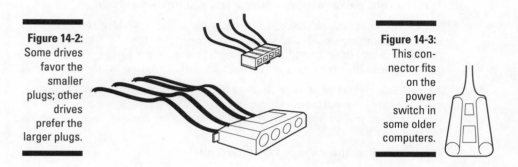

Figure 14-2: Some drives favor the smaller plugs; other drives prefer the larger plugs.

Figure 14-3: This connector fits on the power switch in some older computers.

The plugs fit into their sockets in only one way. The power switch tabs can be rough, though, so draw a picture of which colored wire connects to which tab.

Unless your computer is packed to the brim with goodies, you probably have a few stray cables left over. Those cables are thoughtfully supplied to power any future additions.

3. Remove the screws holding the power supply to the back of the computer's case.

Look on the back of your computer near the fan hole, and you see several screws. Some of these screws hold your power supply in place, but other screws hold your fan inside your power supply.

With the case off, you can usually tell which screws hold the power supply in place. Try loosening the screws slightly; that sometimes makes it easier to tell which screws are which.

The screws that hold the power supply in place are generally closer to the outside edge of the computer's rear. The screws that hold the fan are generally closer to the fan's edge. Don't loosen the fan's screws if you can help it.

You may need to remove extra plastic vents from the power supply; they help route air to your CPU to keep it cool and refreshed.

4. Lift out the power supply.

Does the power supply come out easily? If the power supply is cramped, you may need to loosen the floppy drives and pull them forward a bit. (I describe how to loosen floppy drives in Chapter 12 if you're not sure how the floppy drives are mounted.)

If the power supply still won't come out, make sure that you've removed all the screws. Some power supplies have extra screws around their base to hold them down.

Power supplies are pretty hardy beasts, so don't be afraid to pull hard.

5. **Take the old power supply to the store and buy a new one.**

That's the best way to make sure that you get the right-size replacement. If you're planning on adding some other computer toys — such as compact disc players or sound cards — or filling up your slots with more gadgets, consider buying a power supply with a higher wattage.

Some name-brand computer makers make you buy new power supplies directly from them. Head to the company's Web page to see how it describes its power supply, and whether it can be replaced with a more generic model.

6. **Make sure that the voltage is set correctly.**

Look on the back of the power supply, which is near the fan. A switch usually lets you toggle the power to either 120 volts or 220 volts. If you're in the United States, make sure that the switch is set to 120 volts. If your country uses 220 volts, flip the switch to the 220-volt setting.

If you're working on a computer in a country other than the United States, be sure that you toggle the voltage setting switch appropriately. Also make sure that you have the proper cord for 220 — look on the cord's little yellow tag for this rating.

7. **Put the new power supply where the old one sat.**

Sometimes it's easier to reconnect the cables before sliding the power supply in place.

8. **Reconnect all the cables to the motherboard, the drives, and the power switch.**

Grab any little pictures you drew and look at any masking tape labels you put on the old power supply's cables. (Forgot to label them? Well, it doesn't really matter which disk drive gets which plug.)

The two black wires on the two AT-style plugs almost always face each other when pushing them into their sockets. Make sure that they snap into place. Make sure that you hook up the power switch connectors according to your notes. You don't have any hard-and-fast rules to follow, and different computers vary in their construction.

9. **Replace the screws holding the power supply to the back of the computer's case.**

Do you have the cables back on? If so, screw the power supply back into place. Be sure that you tighten down any disk drives you may have loosened.

Also, check to make sure that you haven't knocked any other cables loose while moving around inside your computer.

10. **Reconnect the power cord.**

    Plug your computer back in; its power cord should push into the socket near the fan.

11. **Turn on the power and see whether it works.**

    Do you hear the fan whirring? Does the computer leap to life? If so, then all is well. If the fan is not spinning, though, something is wrong with the new power supply or your power outlet.

    Try plugging a lamp into the outlet to make *sure* that the outlet works. If the outlet works, take the power supply back. The computer store sold you a bad power supply.

12. **Turn off the computer and put the case back on.**

    Is everything working right? If it is, turn off the computer, put its case back on, and put a cool glass of iced tea in your hands. Congratulations!

Chapter 15

Stuff on Cards

• •

In This Chapter

▶ Making cards fit in slots

▶ Repairing cards that aren't working

▶ Understanding card varieties

▶ Installing new cards

• •

Most computer upgrades are a shoehorn process: trying to force an old computer to do something that it wasn't really designed to do.

Adding expansion cards, however, is a different story. These cards, described in Chapter 3, provide the 100-percent-approved way of upgrading your system. That means that this is going to be easy. So, relax. Smile! You're just playing with cards.

"My New Card Doesn't Fit in the Slot!"

Unlike other computer organs, expansion cards have remained remarkably uncomplicated over the years. In fact, most people need to worry about only one thing: card size.

For many years, cards came in two main sizes — 8-bit and 16-bit. Newer, 16-bit cards (as shown in Figure 15-1) slowly replaced the small 8-bit cards.

If you have a newer computer, chances are it has a combination of expansion slot types that include a couple of the 16-bit AT slots as well as a few of the new types. The newer slots and cards can be *PCI, AGP, VESA Local Bus,* or *EISA.* If these terms don't sound familiar, check out Chapter 3. There, you find descriptions and pictures of what the different breeds of cards look like, which cards are best, and how to tell which ones are inside your computer.

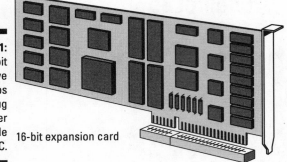

Figure 15-1:
The 16-bit
cards have
two tabs
that plug
into a longer
slot inside
your PC.

16-bit expansion card

How do you handle cards that bump cards in adjacent slots or are too long? Well, you can break or scrape off the troublesome parts that don't fit. But then the card doesn't work. Instead, move the cards to different slots, trying different positions until they all fit. It's like packing bags in the car trunk on the way home from the grocery store. You have to try different combinations before the trunk lid will close.

"My Card Doesn't Work!"

Not much can go wrong when you install a card. It usually just slips into the slot, like a knife sliding into its sheath.

Chances are, your nonfunctioning card *does* work; the computer just doesn't know it's attached. The card lies unnoticed, like a dribble of spaghetti sauce on the corner of a mouth.

✔ The latest versions of Windows come with Plug and Play technology that recognizes most newly inserted cards and immediately puts them to work. Check out Chapter 17 for more information on Windows and Plug and Play.

✔ Many cards also come with an installation program. The program tells the computer how to hold conversations with the card. This usually takes two steps:

   • The installation program may put a *driver* program onto your computer's hard disk.

   • The program may tell you to change a *jumper* or *DIP switch* on the card.

✔ All this stuff's covered in Chapter 18. (Windows users can find more information in Chapter 17.)

If one of your older cards stops working, turn off your computer, unplug it, remove the cover, and remove the card. Then take a plain old pencil eraser and rub it over the contacts on the part of the card that fits into the slot. This can remove any corrosion or buildup of crud. Also, try pushing the card more firmly into its slot. Sometimes, the cards creep up and out with age.

An older card sometimes stops working if its driver is disturbed. You need to check your AUTOEXEC.BAT or CONFIG.SYS file, as I describe in Chapter 16.

"What Kinds of Cards Can I Buy?"

Hundreds of cards fill the store shelves. But here's a look at the most popular. You probably have at least two or three of these cards inside your computer right now.

Video cards: These give your monitor a place to plug into. Every computer has a video card, except for the ones from the early '90s that came with the video circuitry built right into the motherboard. (In fact, you may need to disable that motherboard circuitry if you ever put a video card in a slot. Better check the motherboard's manual.)

A 3-D accelerated AGP video card displays images much faster than its boring predecessors. These AGP cards plug into a special AGP socket found on the motherboard of most newer computers. (AGP graphics cards are different than the graphics-enhancing features of MMX or 3D-Now, which are functions of your computer's CPU. Chapter 10 provides more details on that stuff.)

Start stocking up on those old video cards and monitors. Windows 98 lets you install several monitors to your computers. Toss a spare PCI video card and monitor into your computer and let Windows 98 double your desktop space. Add a TV tuner card and watch TV on one monitor, while watching the Internet on another! By adding cards and monitors, you can stretch your desktop to be as large as your precarious stack of monitors.

Sound cards: You need one of these to hear anything besides a "beep" from your computer. Without a sound card, you miss out on Internet radio stations, game sound effects, and the Windows helpful assortment of sounds.

You won't hear anything from a sound card unless you also bought speakers. Another alternative is to buy a *long* phono cord and run it from the sound card to your stereo's tape or auxiliary jack. The hard part then becomes trying not to trip over the cord.

Modems: Modem cards cause two main problems. First, you need to configure the modem cards for a COM port so that your computer has an electronic doorway to yell in and out of. (COM ports are covered in Chapter 17.)

Second, modem cards come with *two* phone jacks on them. Your phone line plugs into one, and you plug your telephone into the other. But those phone jacks are rarely marked. Which one goes where? Grab that manual or just try connecting the wires one way; if it doesn't work, try the opposite plug.

Interface cards: Add one of these, and you've added a new connector on the back of your PC. Now you can plug in your new CD-ROM drive, synthesizer, scanner, PC Card reader for the laptop, network, FireWire for digital camcorders, and a whole lot more. Any card that lets your computer send information to and from something outside — a video image, musical signal, or network setup — is an interface card.

TV tuner cards: After you install a TV tuner card, it displays television shows on your monitor — either filling the screen or inside a fully sizable window anywhere on your screen. Hook up your TV antenna or cable TV cord, and you're ready to watch *Seinfeld* reruns while you work!

Video capture cards: Hook up the camcorder to a video capture card and record movies directly onto your PC. Make digital Christmas cards by the open fire and mail them on floppy disks to your friends!

I/O cards: You know where your printer plugs into the back of your computer? It's probably plugging into the back of your I/O card. Chances are, there's a serial port above your printer port, too. (A mouse or modem usually plugs into that port.) I/O cards are a vanishing breed, however, because more computers include those ports directly on the motherboard.

- All types of cards plug in the same way. No special tricks. Some of them just plug into different places on the motherboard.

- Not all cards start working right away, though. You may have to flip some switches on them or move some jumpers around. That's covered in Chapter 18.

- After you buy the right card for your particular computer, the biggest problem you'll probably have with cards is finding room for them. Most computers come with six or eight slots. After you plug in your video card, sound card, internal modem, and network card, you'll realize how quickly those slots get used up.

When fastening a cable to the back of a card, look for little screws or clips on the cord's end. Some have big thumbscrews designed especially for clumsy people. (Thank goodness.) Others have tiny screws that frustrate the myopic. Either way, fasten the cord tightly onto the back of your computer. That keeps it from falling off whenever you adjust your computer's position on your desk.

"How Do I Install a New Card?"

IQ level: 90

Tools you need: One hand and a screwdriver

Cost: Anywhere from $70 to $300 and more

Stuff to watch out for: Cards are particularly susceptible to static electricity. Tap your computer's case to ground yourself before touching the card. If you live in a particularly dry, static-prone area, wear rubber gloves — the kind that doctors and dentists are wearing these days.

Be careful not to bend the cards while installing them. That can damage their circuitry.

Cards are pretty easy to install. They're self-contained little units. For example, they suck electricity right out of that little slot that they plug into. You rarely need to plug special power cables into them.

Cards are delicate. Handle them only by their edges. The oil from your fingers can damage their circuitry.

Also, those little silver dots on one side of the card are actually sharp metal pokers that can leave scratches across the back of your hand.

Different-sized cards need different-sized slots. You may need to rearrange some of your cards to accommodate different lengths and thicknesses.

To install a card, follow these steps:

1. **Turn off your computer, unplug it, and remove the cover.**

   Don't know how that cover comes off? Flip to the Cheat Sheet at the front of this book for the answers.

2. **Find the slot that is the right size for your card.**

   See the row of slots along the back wall of your computer, as shown in Figure 15-2? Your new card will plug into one of those slots. Don't confuse your computer's expansion slots — the ones where the cards plug in — with its memory slots, where the memory-chip-laden SIMMs plug in.

   Check out the pictures in Figure 15-1 so that you know whether you have an 8-bit or 16-bit card. Or just look at its bottom: Two tabs make it a 16-bit card; just one tab makes it an 8-bit card.

   Three tabs on the card? Then you're probably dealing with a VESA Local Bus card, which needs a VESA Local Bus slot. (You can find pictures of cards and their appropriate slots in Chapter 3.)

Memory slots

PCI Card slots

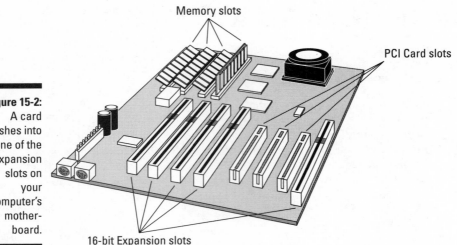

16-bit Expansion slots

You can stick an 8-bit card in a 16-bit slot, but rarely vice versa. You may have to shuffle your cards around until there's room for the new card.

If you have lots of room, keep your cards spaced as far apart as possible. That keeps them cooler.

3. Remove the slot's cover.

Unused slots have a little cover next to them to keep dust from flying in through the back of your computer. With a small screwdriver, remove the screw that holds the cover in place. Don't lose the screw! You need it to secure the card in place.

Dropped the screw in there "somewhere?" Head for Chapter 2 for tips on getting it back out. (You can't just leave it in there, or your computer will choke on it and possibly electrocute itself.)

Got the screw out? Keep it handy, and keep the little cover bracket, too.

4. Push the card into its slot.

Chapter 3 describes each type of card and contains a picture. Yes, there are lots of different types of cards. The good news is that you can't push the wrong type of card into the wrong slot. It simply won't fit. The tabs and notches on the card's bottom line up with the notches in the slot, so they only line up one way.

To spare yourself some possible aggravation, first check your card's manual to see whether you need to flip any of the card's switches or move any of its jumpers. Then you won't have to take the card back out if it's not working right.

Holding the card by its edges, position it over the slot. The edge with the shiny, metal bracket should face toward the *back* of your computer. Got it?

Push the card slowly into the slot. You may need to rock the card back and forth gently. When it pops in, you can feel it come to rest. Don't force it!

Don't let any card come into contact with any other card. That can cause electrical problems, and neither the card nor the computer will work.

5. **Secure the card in the slot with the screw.**

   Yep, all those expensive cards are held in place by a single screw. Make sure that you *use* a screw, however; don't just leave the card sitting there. Cards need to be grounded to the computer's case. Without a secure connection, they may not work.

6. **Plug the computer back in, turn it on, and see whether the Windows Plug and Play feature recognizes and installs the card.**

   Windows usually recognizes newly installed cards and sets them up to work correctly. If something goes wrong, head for Chapter 17 for quick-fix tips.

7. **If it works, carefully put the cover back on. You're done!**

If the card still doesn't work — or you're not using Windows — you probably have to run the card's installation software. Still doesn't work? Then try the following:

✔ Check the manual to make sure that the card's switches and jumpers are set right.

✔ You usually have to run the card's software and then reboot your computer before it will work. That's because the card puts a driver in one of your computer's special files. Your computer reads that file only when it's first turned on or when it's rebooted.

✔ Make sure that the card is seated securely in its slot and screwed in reasonably tight.

✔ Make sure that the card's in the right slot: 16-bit, PCI, or AGP. Older computers may have VESA, EISA, or a few other oddball types of cards described in Chapter 3.

✔ It can take some fiddling to get a card working right. The key is not to get frustrated.

✔ Nine times out of ten, the problem lies with the software. Although the card is sitting in the slot correctly, the software is conflicting with some other software or is not talking with the card.

✔ If the card still doesn't work, root around in its box for the manual. Most manuals list a technical support phone number you can call for help. Be sure to read the tail end of Chapter 4 before calling; it can save you lots of time.

Part IV
Telling Your Computer What You've Done

The 5th Wave   By Rich Tennant

"FRANKLY, I'M NOT SURE THIS IS THE WAY TO ENHANCE OUR COLOR GRAPHICS."

In this part . . .

Upgrading a computer is kind of like recording something on a VCR. The easy part is stuffing the videotape inside. The hard part is making the VCR automatically record the late show while you're snoozing, so that you can watch the show the next day and fast forward through all the commercials.

Computers present a similar situation. The easy part of upgrading your computer often turns out to be sticking in the new part. The hard part is making the computer recognize that new part and start putting it to work.

That's where this part of the book comes in. It helps avert that sinking sensation — that feeling you get when you've finally tightened the last screw, but the ungrateful computer *still* doesn't recognize your handiwork.

Hold on; you're almost there.

Chapter 16

That AUTOEXEC.BAT and CONFIG.SYS File Stuff

● ●

In This Chapter

▶ Understanding your CONFIG.SYS file

▶ Understanding your AUTOEXEC.BAT file

▶ Taking a look at paths

▶ Creating a PATH statement

▶ Adding a driver to a CONFIG.SYS file

▶ Changing your AUTOEXEC.BAT file

▶ Understanding what really happens when you turn on your computer

● ●

Great news: Windows users don't need to bother with this treacherous chapter because most versions of Windows don't really need the two files discussed here. Sure, Windows 95 and Windows 98 read the files. But for the most part, they don't use any of the information in them. Windows has simply outgrown them.

Why devote a chapter to these two files? Because they're complicated and, sooner or later, some renegade program will make a reference to those files. When that happens, it's time to turn here. Otherwise, feel free to ignore this chapter.

This chapter's here mainly for people who still use DOS, Windows 3.1, or an even earlier version of Windows.

Now, here's the story: When your computer wakes up in the morning, it reaches for its cup of coffee. However, a computer thinks that *everything* is either a file or piece of electronic circuitry, so its cup of coffee consists of two small files: AUTOEXEC.BAT and CONFIG.SYS.

You've probably seen those weird names in either a directory on your hard drive or a manual somewhere. Normally, you don't have to mess with these files, thank goodness. But when a program or manual tells you to modify your AUTOEXEC.BAT or CONFIG.SYS files, follow the numbered steps in this chapter.

DOS users should pick up *DOS For Dummies,* 3rd Edition, by Dan Gookin (IDG Books Worldwide, Inc.). That book is devoted to curing the problems DOS users encounter.

What's a CONFIG.SYS File?

A CONFIG.SYS file is simply a file filled with text. However, it's designed for your *computer* to look at, not you. That's why its contents look like the fine print on a bottle of multivitamins. For example, look at the nerdy verbiage in the older CONFIG.SYS file shown in Figure 16-1.

Figure 16-1: A CONFIG.SYS file from an old computer; yours may differ from this one.

```
DEVICE=C:\WINDOWS\HIMEM.SYS
DEVICE=C:\WINDOWS\EMM386.EXE NOEMS
DOS=HIGH,UMB

DEVICEHIGH=C:\UTIL\DEV\MDSCD FD.SYS /D:MSCD000 /N:1
DEVICEHIGH=D:\COMM\FAX\SATISFAX.SYS IOADDR=0310
DEVICEHIGH=D:\SOUND\PROAUDIO\MVSOUND.SYS D:3 Q:7

STACKS=9,256
FILES=80
BUFFERS=40
LASTDRIVE=Z
```

Why show a CONFIG.SYS file from an old computer? Because most newer computers — and the ones running the latest version of Windows — often have empty CONFIG.SYS files. They've become obsolete.

What is all that stuff that older computers used? Well, a CONFIG.SYS file traditionally contained the names of *drivers* — pieces of software that help your computer talk to mice, sound cards, extra chunks of memory, and other gadgets. The CONFIG.SYS file lists where all those drivers live on your hard drive; it's sort of like a phone book for computer parts.

Whenever you turn on or reboot your computer, it flips open its CONFIG.SYS file to see all the drivers listed in there. As it reads each driver's name, it finds that driver's software on the hard drive. It then reads the driver to learn how to carry on a conversation with whatever component the driver represents.

The computer immediately forgets about the drivers as soon as you turn it off. But when you turn it back on again, it heads straight back to the CONFIG.SYS file and calls those drivers back into action. Sure, it's repetitious. But computers never get bored.

✔ Newer computers already know where to look for drivers and other information that used to appear in a CONFIG.SYS file, so they just peek inside the file for any information describing old parts.

✔ If your computer can't find a part's driver, it probably won't be able to find the part, either. In fact, it won't even know that it's supposed to *look* for the part. And if it stumbles across the part accidentally, it won't know how to talk to the part, leading to arguments and general discomfort. Indeed, that's why many people have switched to Windows 95 and Windows 98, which calm most of this turbulence internally, without any discomfort to the user.

✔ When everything's working correctly, your computer reads its CONFIG.SYS file so quickly and automatically that you don't have to mess with the file — except when you need to toss in the name of an older part's driver.

✔ Some older computer parts come with installation programs that automatically place the names of their drivers into the CONFIG.SYS file. Other computer parts are lazy and make you list the drivers yourself.

✔ Your computer looks at the CONFIG.SYS file only when it's rebooted or turned on. That's why so many installation programs want to reboot your computer when they're through — it's how they force your computer to notice their changes.

✔ Not *all* computer parts force you to fiddle with a CONFIG.SYS file or a driver. Some make you fiddle with an AUTOEXEC.BAT file instead. (That's the file I describe next.) Some make you fiddle with both. Others don't make you fiddle with *anything:* The computer handles all the fiddling chores itself. The boxes that the parts come in rarely give much of a clue to what you should expect, unfortunately.

✔ The lines listed in a CONFIG.SYS file aren't commands you can type at the DOS prompt. Your computer will probably spit out an error message if you try. Your computer understands those lines only when they're packaged in the CONFIG.SYS file.

✔ Your computer is picky about the location of its CONFIG.SYS file. It looks for CONFIG.SYS only in your *root* directory — that `C:\>` directory. If you move the file to a directory like `C:\DOS>` or `C:\WINDOWS>` or any other directory with words in the name, your lazy computer won't be able to find it.

✔ A *directory* is what Windows calls a *folder.* The older, DOS operating system calls them directories, although folders are the same thing: portions of your hard drive where you store files.

> ✔ When you flip on the power switch, your computer always reads the CONFIG.SYS and AUTOEXEC.BAT files — even if you use Windows. (Even Windows 98 wants to know what a DOS program may want to see, in case you decided to run one from within its kingdom.)

What's an AUTOEXEC.BAT File?

Imagine that it's your first day on the job. You walk into a new, unfamiliar office and don't know where to start. Then you see a to-do list the boss tacked to the desk.

An AUTOEXEC.BAT file is a to-do list for your computer. It's a text file filled with computerized commands. (Users of the old DOS operating system used to type them by hand at the computer's C:\> prompt.) You can see a sample of an AUTOEXEC.BAT file in Figure 16-2.

Figure 16-2:
A typical
AUTO
EXEC.BAT
file. Yours
will probably
differ from
this one.

```
@IF ERRORLEVEL 1 PAUSE
@PATH C:\PROGRA~1\MICROS~5;C:\PROGRA~1\WIN98RK;%PATH%

REM[Header]
@ECHO OFF
```

Whenever you turn on or reboot your computer, it looks for a file named AUTOEXEC.BAT. If it finds one, it reads the file line-by-line and carries out all the instructions in the file. It AUTOmatically EXECutes all those commands when you first turn it on. (Get it?)

An AUTOEXEC.BAT file is a sneaky way to make computers do some of their start-up work automatically so that you don't have to boss them around for every little thing.

> ✔ An AUTOEXEC.BAT file contains a list of commands for the computer to run whenever it's turned on or rebooted. In fact, those are the only times the computer ever bothers reading the AUTOEXEC.BAT file.

> ✔ If the AUTOEXEC.BAT file ever changes, the computer won't notice until the next time it's rebooted. That's why the installation programs for most new computer parts insist on rebooting your computer. Rebooting forces your computer to notice the changes made by the installation program.

✔ Like the CONFIG.SYS file, the AUTOEXEC.BAT file lives in your computer's root directory, the directory you see when you type **DIR** at the C:\> prompt. Sure, you can put those two files anywhere on your hard drive you want. However, your computer won't find them unless they're in the root directory.

✔ Some computer parts want to stick some lines into your CONFIG.SYS file. Others prefer adding to the AUTOEXEC.BAT file. Some want to put a line in *both* files. Other, more easygoing parts don't use *any* drivers or programs, sparing you from bothering with this entire chapter.

✔ There's no surefire way to tell whether a certain computer part prefers to stake its mark in the CONFIG.SYS file or the AUTOEXEC.BAT file. It depends on the manufacturer and whoever invented the part. Only the manual knows for sure.

Keep a backup copy of your AUTOEXEC.BAT and CONFIG.SYS files on a floppy disk. If something goes wrong, you can copy them back over to your root directory. Feel free to keep a printout of them on hand, too. Just be sure to update your printout or floppy disk whenever the files change.

What's a Path?

Computers aren't terribly clever beasts. When you copy a file or program to your computer's hard drive, your computer doesn't always pay attention. Your computer can't automatically find the file or program later.

That's why a *path* comes in so handy. A path is a computer's road map — it shows where a particular file is located.

For example, perhaps your file COUGH.EXE is in your C:\SYMPTOMS subdirectory. After the C:\> prompt, you type **COUGH** and press Enter, like this:

```
C:\> COUGH
```

But your computer doesn't run COUGH. Instead, it gives off the following confused shout: Bad command or file name.

That's because the computer couldn't find COUGH. What your computer did was look in the directory it was in at the time — the C:\> directory — and it couldn't find COUGH, so it gave up.

However, if you add COUGH's *path,* the computer knows where to look for the file. To make the computer run COUGH, you type the subdirectory as well as the filename, like this:

```
C:\> C:\SYMPTOMS\COUGH
```

PATH=C:\WHO\CARES>

This path stuff is a bother. Why can't the computer just look everywhere on the hard drive and find files automatically? Well, because that can take a long time. If you have an old computer and an older hard drive, it can take a *very* long time.

DOS offers a compromise. It lets you put your most popular directories on a special list. When you type the name of a program at the C:\> prompt, the computer searches for the file in the current directory, just as it normally does. But if it doesn't find the program there, it also searches the directories you placed on the special list.

This special list is called the PATH statement, and it lives in the AUTOEXEC.BAT file. Your computer staggers through every directory listed in the PATH statement when searching for files.

Listing a program's directory on the PATH can make things easier. You can type a program's name from anywhere on your hard drive, and if its directory is on the path, your computer finds and runs the program.

In fact, that's part of the problem. Because it's so easy to find and run a program that's on the PATH, almost every installation program wants to put its directory on the PATH.

DOS bylaws decree that a PATH statement can be no longer than 127 characters. The solution? When your PATH gets too long, open up your AUTOEXEC.BAT file and give it a trim. You need to keep Windows and DOS in there, that's for sure. But you may be able to cut out some other, less frequently used directories. The PATH may list some directories you deleted years ago in a fit of hard-drive housekeeping.

The point? If all the programs and drivers in your CONFIG.SYS and AUTOEXEC.BAT files include paths, your computer will always be able to find them.

- ✔ If you see the words Bad command or file name while your computer is booting up, it's a sure sign that the computer couldn't find a file listed in your AUTOEXEC.BAT file.

- ✔ The problem probably occurred because the file's name or path is spelled wrong, no matter how subtly. Or it may be that you moved the file to a different place on your hard drive. If you did, your computer can't find it anymore — you have to update the file's path in your AUTOEXEC.BAT file to reflect its new location.

- ✔ When your computer can't find something in your CONFIG.SYS file, it's a little more specific about the problem: Your computer lists not only the name of the driver that it can't find but also the line number in your CONFIG.SYS file that's causing the problem.

How to Edit a CONFIG.SYS or AUTOEXEC.BAT File

Once in a while, some new program or gadget will send you a blast of rudeness. From out of the blue, its manual tells you to modify your CONFIG.SYS file or edit your AUTOEXEC.BAT file.

Some installation programs make all the changes automatically; others make *you* wear the file-changing hat. Luckily, Windows makes the process somewhat easier by tossing in a special program just for that task.

When you're forced to change your CONFIG.SYS or AUTOEXEC.BAT file, carefully follow these steps.

1. **Click the Start button, choose Run, type** sysedit **in the pop-up box, and click the OK button.**

   Windows comes with a secret program named Sysedit for handling AUTOEXEC.BAT and CONFIG.SYS chores. It's a simple editor that automatically finds and displays those files (along with a few other key Windows files). Best yet, it also allows you to edit those files, just as though they were sitting in the Windows Notepad program.

2. **Load the Sysedit program.**

   Click the Start button, choose Run, and type **sysedit** into the Open box. Click OK to open the program. Sysedit blasts up to the top of the screen quickly, as shown in Figure 16-3.

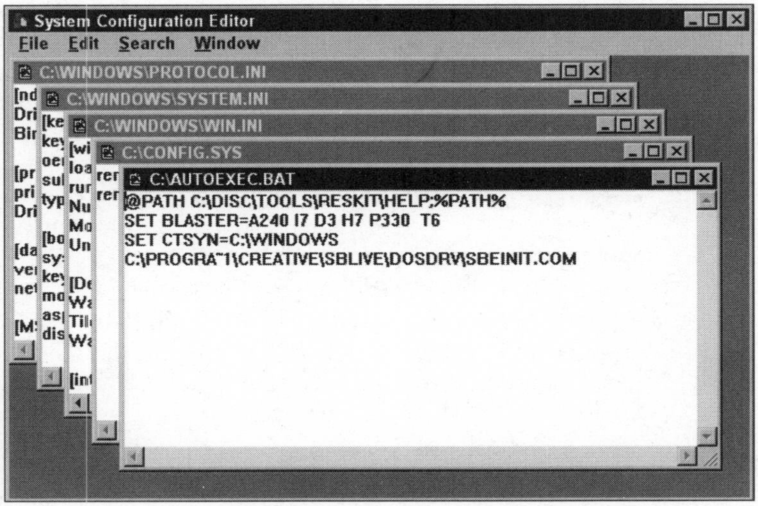

Figure 16-3: The Windows Sysedit program allows for quick editing of your AUTOEXEC.BAT and CONFIG.SYS files.

Although Sysedit brings up a handful of Windows techno-setting files, the CONFIG.SYS and AUTOEXEC.BAT files are the first two in Sysedit's stack of windows.

3. **Click in the window that needs to be changed.**

Click on either the CONFIG.SYS or AUTOEXEC.BAT window, and Sysedit brings that window to the top, ready for editing.

4. **Add the new line.**

Whether you're adding the new line to the CONFIG.SYS or AUTOEXEC.BAT file, put it at the very bottom of the file. Unless the manual says otherwise, that's probably the safest spot.

You can find that line listed in the new part's manual or whatever else is forcing you to do all this nonsensical stuff.

Be sure to include the file's path so that the computer can find the file. (Paths have their own section earlier in this chapter.) Check for typos, too. If you don't spell everything 100 percent correctly, your computer will grow a hair bun and give you cross looks.

Done typing the line? Press Enter.

5. **Save the file.**

Did you double-check your work? Then it's time to save the file. Just as in Notebook, choose Save from the File menu.

6. **Exit the program.**

Exit Sysedit like you would any other Windows program: Double-click on the little X in its upper-right corner.

7. **Exit Windows and restart the computer.**

Your computer reads its AUTOEXEC.BAT and CONFIG.SYS files only when it's rebooted. So click the Start button, choose Shut Down, and choose Restart from the menu. The screen clears, your computer gathers itself together, and you're ready for the big moment: It reads those AUTOEXEC.BAT and CONFIG.SYS files.

- After you change these files, watch your computer closely when it reboots. If the screen says something like `Bad or missing file name` or `Error in CONFIG.SYS line 13`, something's wrong. Jump back to Step 3 and check to see that you spelled everything right and that the program's path is correct.

- If you did everything correctly, your computer won't toss anything strange onto the screen — not even a thank-you message. Try using your new part or program; chances are, your computer will finally recognize it.

Boring boot sector balderdash

What's the computer looking for in the boot sector? Two files with important operating system information. Normally, the two files are invisible, so you don't have to bother with them, thank goodness.

One file, named IBMBIO.COM or IO.SYS depending on your version of DOS, helps DOS communicate with your computer's hardware. The other file, named either IBMDOS.COM or MSDOS.SYS,

holds computer-language answers to bare-bones DOS questions: What are files, what is memory, and other questions answered in *DOS For Dummies,* 3rd Edition, by Dan Gookin (IDG Books Worldwide, Inc.).

While you work in some programs, you may see these two files sitting on your hard drive. Don't delete them, or else your computer won't be able to get out of bed.

Sometimes you need to *change* a line, not add a new one. To be safe, find the line you need to change and type the word **REM** in front of it. For example, a program may want you to change an AUTOEXEC.BAT file line that looks like this:

```
PROMPT $p$g
```

To change the line, type the word **REM** in front of it and type the new, changed line directly beneath it, like this:

```
REM PROMPT $p$g
PROMPT $D$_$T$_$P$G
```

The REM stands for *remark.* Because remarks are designed for humans, DOS ignores any line starting with REM.

If something goes wrong with your change, delete the line that messed things up and remove the REM from the original line — the one that worked. Doing that brings things back to normal. Well, as normal as computers can be, anyway.

"What Are Those Weird Sounds When I Turn On My Computer?"

A computer jumps through the same hoops whenever you press its Reset button or flip its On switch. Here's a rundown of its same ol' runaround:

1. **You turn the switch on, and electricity starts flowing.**

   When you first turn on your computer, you hear the power supply's fan start to spin and your hard drive begin to whir. All the circuits inside your PC get a waking burst of electricity.

2. **The BIOS begins.**

   After the computer's CPU wakes up, it heads straight for its *BIOS* — basic, gut-level instructions stored inside special BIOS chips on the motherboard. (More BIOS babble bubbles up in Chapter 10.) By reading its BIOS, the computer knows how to talk to its floppy drives and other basic parts.

3. **The computer tests itself (POST).**

   After the computer figures out how to talk to its parts, it begins testing them with the *POST,* or *power-on self test.* I describe the POST more fully in Chapter 4. The POST looks for the equipment list stored in your computer's CMOS. The CMOS, which I cover in Chapter 18, contains a battery backed-up list of the parts inside your computer. The POST grabs the list and starts looking for everything that's listed.

   As the POST goes around kicking tires, it lets you know what's going on. For example, you see an onscreen tally as the POST counts your memory chips. You hear your floppy drives gnash their teeth as the POST gives 'em a quick spin. Your hard drive's little red light flashes as the POST peeks inside.

   If the POST finds something askew, it flings out a coded series of beeps (which Chapter 24 decodes) or flashes a cryptic error message (decryptified in Chapter 23). Or both. If everything's fine and dandy (most of the time), the computer gives one or two affirmative, head-nodding beeps and moves to Step 4.

4. **The computer looks for an operating system.**

   The computer first looks for an operating system on drive A. That's because *everybody* used to keep their system disks in drive A. (Hard drives weren't invented yet.) The computer is searching for the *boot sector.* If the computer finds a disk in drive A but there's no boot sector to be found, the computer stops dead, leaving this epitaph:

   ```
   Non-system disk or disk error
   Replace and strike any key when ready
   ```

   Odds are, you accidentally left a normal, everyday disk in drive A. The computer couldn't find its life-giving boot sector, so it gave up. Remove the disk, tap the spacebar, and the computer will continue.

   Don't *ever* leave floppy disks sitting in your disk drive. Many of the worst viruses copy themselves to floppy disks. When your computer first wakes up, it's at its most vulnerable state; the virus then infects your computer as it peeks into the floppy drive looking for its boot sector.

When your computer can't find a disk in drive A, it moves on to the hard drive, looking there for the boot sector.

5. **The computer looks for the CONFIG.SYS file.**

Next, the computer looks for a CONFIG.SYS file. Described earlier in this chapter, this file contains mostly drivers: bits of software that help a computer deal with things like compact disc players, memory managers, mice, video cards, and other gadgets attached to it.

6. **The computer runs the COMMAND.COM program.**

You may have noticed this file sitting on your hard drive or a floppy disk. It contains more basic DOS stuff — form-letter reactions to commands you type at a C:\> prompt, for example.

7. **The computer runs AUTOEXEC.BAT.**

The computer's had its fun; now it gives the user a chance to jump in. It reads each line in the AUTOEXEC.BAT file, covered earlier in this chapter. The computer treats each line as though the user typed the command at the DOS prompt.

Chapter 17

Fixing Squeaky Windows

● ●

In This Chapter

▶ Upgrading your computer for Windows 98

▶ Telling Windows 98 and Windows 95 about new hardware

▶ Adding a new printer

▶ Changing video modes

▶ Finding new drivers

▶ Troubleshooting Windows

▶ Using Windows System tools

▶ Keeping Windows up-to-date

▶ Optimizing Windows 98's performance

● ●

*1*t's an old joke by now. One of the great Windows 95 and Windows 98 features, dubbed *Plug and Play,* was supposed to instantly recognize any new
device you plugged into your computer. The pitch was that with Plug and
Play, Windows could set up computer parts so that they wouldn't squabble
with previously installed parts and the world would be a better place.

Unfortunately, Plug and Play can turn into Plug and Pray when something
goes wrong. In that case, you probably have to doff your hat and *personally*
introduce Windows to your new part, or else the two will never get along.

This chapter explains how to upgrade to Windows 98, if you're considering it.
It also helps you tell Windows about new hardware you've added to your
computer as well as make adjustments to the parts already installed.

Finally, this chapter tells you how to lift the hood and make a few adjustments so that Windows 98 can run at its greatest power.

Upgrading Your Computer to Run Windows 98

Just as an old Model T Ford can't pull a 46-foot sailboat, some computers can't run Windows 95 or Windows 98. Those oldsters just don't have enough oomph. But how much oomph is enough? Oomph Table 17-1 has the answers.

Table 17-1	Computers Need This Much Oomph to Run Windows 98	
Computer Requirements Politely Recommended by Microsoft	*What Your Computer Really Needs to Run Windows or Windows 98*	*Why?*
24MB of memory (RAM)	From 32MB to 64MB of memory or more	Windows 98 crawls across the screen with only 24MB; it can't handle much Internet Web surfing either, especially if you're running other programs simultaneously. Using Outlook, Internet Explorer, and Microsoft Word? You may even want to consider 128MB. When buying a computer, add as much memory as you can afford. More memory means fewer crashes.
260MB of hard disk space	At least 1GB	That 260MB can hold the major disk space parts of Windows 98 but little else. Add all parts of Windows, and you've reached more than 400MB. Don't forget to add in your files and other programs. Some Windows programs want more than 100MB of space just for themselves. Don't be afraid to buy a hard disk that's several gigabytes. My laptop has 5 gigabytes, and it's getting full.

Computer Requirements Politely Recommended by Microsoft	What Your Computer Really Needs to Run Windows or Windows 98	Why?
A 486DX/66 microprocessor	A speedy Pentium II with MMX	While at the store, compare Windows 98 running on different speeds of computers. The faster the computer, the less time you spend waiting for Windows 98 to do something exciting. Seriously consider a fast Pentium II with MMX technology. (MMX lets graphics run faster.)
A 3½-inch floppy drive	At least one high-density 3½-inch floppy drive	Although very few programs come packaged on high-density, 3½-inch disks anymore, you need that drive to reboot from its Windows system disk when things go wrong.
Color VGA card	Accelerated SuperVGA card, VL-Bus card for most 486s, AGP bus card for most Pentiums	Because Windows 98 tosses so many little boxes onscreen, you need to get an accelerated, high-resolution, SuperVGA card.
14,400 or higher-baud modem	56,000 baud modem, DSL, or cable modem (see Chapter 7)	You don't *need* a modem, but without one you can't dial up the online services that come packaged with Windows 98 and Windows 95, send e-mail, or water ski across the Internet using the Microsoft freebie Internet Explorer. (And isn't it time you joined the Internet revolution, anyway?)

(continued)

Table 17-1 *continued*

Computer Requirements Politely Recommended by Microsoft	What Your Computer Really Needs to Run Windows or Windows 98	Why?
CD-ROM or DVD-ROM drive	Same	Yep, Windows 98 is too huge to fit practically on floppy disks; they can triple the installation time. Besides, most programs come on CDs.
Miscellaneous	A 17-inch monitor or larger	The bigger your monitor, the bigger your desktop: Your windows won't overlap so much. Unfortunately, superlarge monitors are superexpensive. Luckily, Windows 98 lets you add several monitors to your computer, doubling or tripling your desktop.
Miscellaneous	Internet provider	Just like you need to pay the water company for water, you need to pay an Internet Service Provider to access the Internet.
Miscellaneous	Microsoft Mouse, Microsoft IntelliMouse, or compatible pointing device	Only hunt- and-peck typists can live without one. They're cheap and considered standard equipment by nearly everyone.
Miscellaneous	Sound card and speakers	Gamers need them to hear explosions, encyclopedia fanatics need them to hear foreign languages, Microsoft Word users need them to hear words pronounced, and CD-ROM drive users need them to hear their favorite music CDs. Oh, face it — they're fun.

Telling Windows 98 About New Hardware

When you wolf down a sandwich for lunch, you know what you ate. After all, you picked it out at the deli counter, chewed it, swallowed it, and wiped the bread crumbs away from the corner of your mouth.

But when you add a new part to your computer, it's turned off — Windows 98 is asleep. And when you turn the computer back on and Windows 98 returns to life, it may not notice the new part.

Here's the good news, however: If you simply tell Windows 98 to *look* for the new part, it can probably find it. In fact, Windows 98 not only spots the new part but also introduces itself and starts a warm and friendly working relationship by using the right settings. Ah, the beauty of modern Plug and Play convenience.

Here's how to tell Windows 98 to examine what you stuffed into its belly and make it put those new parts to work. If you've already used Windows 95, you're in luck — the steps are practically the same:

1. **Click the Windows 98 Start button in the screen's lower-left corner, choose Settings from the pop-up menu, and choose Control Panel.**

   The Control Panel's Add New Hardware icon, shown in Figure 17-1, handles the process of introducing Windows 98 to anything you recently attached to your computer.

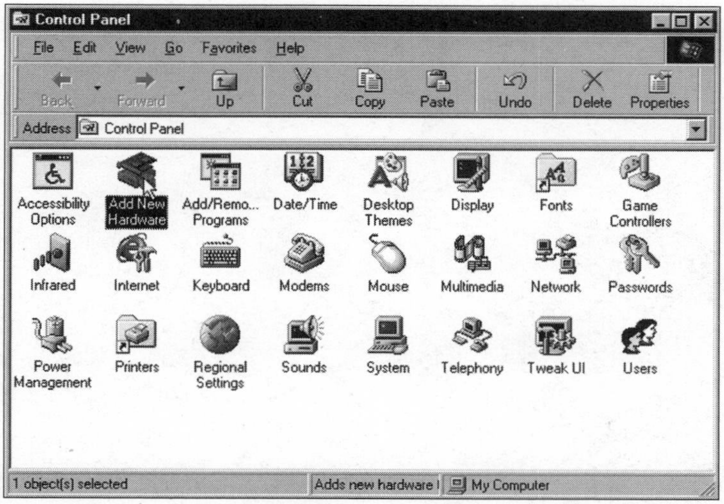

Figure 17-1: The Control Panel contains the Add New Hardware program, which introduces Windows 98 to new computer parts.

2. **Double-click the Control Panel's Add New Hardware icon.**

   The Windows 98 Add New Hardware Wizard, shown in Figure 17-2, pops out of a hat, ready to find the part you've stuffed inside your computer.

3. **If you've already installed your new part, make sure that you close all your currently running programs, and then click the Wizard's Next button.**

   Windows cautions that the screen may go blank as it searches for any recognizable incoming gear. Don't fret — this is normal.

4. **Click Next again.**

   Twiddle your thumbs as Windows 98 peers into the inner workings of your computer, looking for any new Plug and Play devices.

   If it finds any, it displays them in a list, as shown in Figure 17-3.

5. **From the list, click the name of the computer part you installed and then click the Next button.**

   Then click the Finish button and follow the instructions. Whew! You were able to take the easy way out. If Windows didn't find your newly installed part, however, proceed to Step 6.

6. **If Windows 98 *doesn't* find your new part, click the No button and then click the Next button, which presents a choice.**

   At this point, you can tell Windows to search for parts that aren't Plug and Play, or you can choose the part from a list.

   If you want Windows to do the work, click the Yes button. If you don't trust Windows — or your new part came with a disk marked Driver, click No.

Figure 17-2:
The Windows 98 Add New Hardware Wizard automatically installs most computer parts.

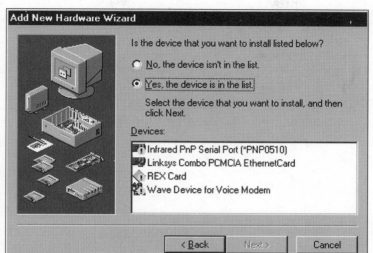

Figure 17-3:
Windows 98
lists any
new Plug
and Play
parts it
recognizes.

7. **If you click Yes and Windows finds the part, everything is just ducky. You can stop now. If you clicked No, move to Step 8.**

8. **Windows lists various types of computer parts; choose the one you've installed.**

   Usually, you have an inkling of what you installed: a new video card (Windows 98 calls them display adapters), a new modem, or perhaps a sound card or CD-ROM drive. If so, click that part's name from the box, and Windows 98 shows you a list of manufacturers.

   Click the manufacturer that made your particular part, and Windows 98 shows you a list of models made by that manufacturer. See yours listed? Click it, and Windows handles the labor from then on.

   If a disk marked Driver came in the box with your new part, put that disk in drive A and click the Have Disk button. Windows 98 grabs the driver from the disk, copies it to the hard drive, and, hopefully, begins talking to your computer's new part.

   If Windows 98 can't find your new device or can't make it work right, you need to contact the manufacturer of your new part and ask for a "Windows 98 driver." Chances are, you'll find the driver available for download on the manufacturer's Web site. Copy the driver to a folder, and use the Browse button to make Windows search for the driver in that folder rather than on the floppy disk.

✔ Adding a new modem? Then Windows 98 wants to know your current country and area code as well as whether you dial a special number (like 9 to reach an outside line or *70 to turn off call-waiting). If you want to change this stuff later, double-click the Control Panel's Modem icon — that brings you to the same page as the Add New Hardware icon does.

✔ Windows 98 is pretty good about identifying various gadgets that people have stuffed inside the computer, especially if you're installing a Plug and Play part.

✔ If you're not sure what type of part you've installed but you know the company that made it, choose Other devices from the Add New Hardware Wizard's Hardware types box. Then when Windows 98 lists a bunch of companies, click the company that made your part. Windows 98 lists all of that company's parts that it can recognize.

✔ Found an updated driver for a computer part? Head for the section "Fine-Tuning Windows 98 System Properties," at the end of this chapter, for the lowdown.

Adding a New Printer

Congratulations! Don't you love that "new printer" smell? If you're installing a new printer in Windows 98, head back to the "Telling Windows 98 about New Hardware" section, earlier in this chapter. Windows 98 treats printers like any other piece of hardware. (Or you can choose Printers from the Start button's Settings area. Or, for variety and spice, choose Printers from the Control Panel.)

"I Want More Colors and Higher Resolution!"

Most video cards can display more than one video *mode*. For example, some let you choose between seeing 16, 256, High Color (16 bit), or True Color (24 bit) varieties of color on the screen. Others let you change *resolutions* and pack more information on the screen.

Just as some people prefer different brands of toothpaste, some people prefer different video modes. To figure out which mode's right for you, try all the modes your card has to offer and stick with the one that you think looks best.

Adjusting Colors and Resolution in Windows 98

To change video modes in Windows 98, follow these steps:

1. **Right-click anywhere on your screen and choose P\u0332roperties from the pop-up menu that appears.**

   The Display Properties dialog box appears, as shown in Figure 17-4.

2. **Click the Settings tab.**

   The Settings menu lets you change the number of colors the screen can display as well as its resolution.

3. **To change your number of colors, click the Colors drop-down menu.**

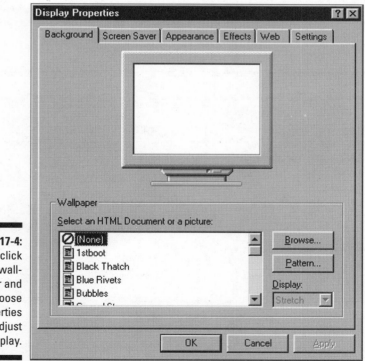

Figure 17-4:
Right-click
your wall-
paper and
choose
Properties
to adjust
your display.

4. **To change your video resolution, slide the Screen area bar from left to right.**

   Sliding to the right gives you more resolution, meaning that you can pack more information on the screen by making everything smaller. Sliding to the left gives you less, but everything on the screen is large and easy to read.

   Your video card has to work extra hard when it displays either lots of colors or lots of video resolution, so it rarely lets you display both at the same time. In other words, the more colors you choose, the less desktop area Windows 98 allows.

5. **Click the Apply button for a preview of the new look.**

   Like the new number of colors and the resolution? Move ahead to Step 6. Otherwise, head back to Step 3 and fiddle with the controls for a while.

6. **Click OK.**

   When you're satisfied with your selection, click OK to save your choices. If you changed the number of colors, Windows 98 probably wants to reboot your computer. (Luckily, it gives you the chance to save your work first.)

What are the differences among all those colors?

The 16 and 256 options aren't very confusing; they display everything on your screen in either 16 or 256 colors. Today's computer users don't bother with the primitive option of 16 colors. Internet users almost always see 256 colors; Web page owners convert their pictures and graphics to 256 colors for faster download times.

High Color (16 bit) can spit out 65,536 varieties of color on your screen, and True Color (24 bit) runs wild with 16,777,216 shades of color. Photos taken by digital cameras almost always look best when viewed with the most colors.

Owners of fast Pentiums with fast video cards will probably enjoy True Color; owners of slower computers should use fewer colors.

The moral? Experiment. Then choose the fewest number of colors that leaves your screen looking fresh and natural, which leaves your computer as speedy as possible.

Hooking up more than one monitor in Windows 98

Pentium users get a special treat in Windows 98. Because most of them have PCI video cards, they can hook up more than one monitor. Here's the trick: Either buy another video card and monitor, or salvage them from that old computer sitting in the garage.

Insert the video card into one of the computer's vacant slots, just like any other card, and plug the monitor's cord into the card's video port, which doubles the size of your Windows desktop. You can stretch or slide your windows over to the second monitor. In fact, you can add up to eight cards and monitors, if you have enough vacant slots (and enough room on your desk), creating a desktop that's big enough for Godzilla.

One monitor can constantly be collecting e-mail while another is displaying a TV show. A third can be searching Web pages. Gamers with lots of money put one monitor in front and two at the sides (which creates an airplane with a windshield and windows).

"Windows Doesn't Work Right!"

Start Windows in Safe mode by holding Ctrl or F8 just before Windows loads itself on the screen. (You may have to try this technique several times to catch the magic moment.)

Select Safe mode to load Windows with a bare-bones setup without extra drivers, start-up programs, or fancy graphics. If the computer works, reboot and call up the Safe mode menu again. This time, however, choose Step-by-step confirmation. This step loads one driver at a time. When your computer freezes up, look to see what driver caused the problems. Voilà! It won't fix itself, but you'll know what's gone wrong.

Still having problems? Then hold down F8 while rebooting, but choose Logged (bootlog.txt). Windows obliges by creating a file listing all the drivers it's loaded, right up to the moment when it freezes. It says whether the driver loaded and worked correctly or, more important, whether it failed.

By finding the driver that's messing things up, you can search for a solution (see the section in Chapter 4 about fixing your computer through the Internet). Or, you'll have something to describe to a technician over the phone, as a last resort.

Use the Windows Troubleshooter

Windows 95 and Windows 98 make an effort to be friendly by supplying software that tries to play doctor when things go wrong. By using one of these built-in Troubleshooter programs, you can sometimes make Windows do the dirty work of figuring out what's wrong and fixing it without charge. Follow these steps to put a wrench into the hands of Windows:

1. **Click the Windows Start menu and choose Help.**

   The Help dialog box appears.

2. **Select the Contents tab, click the Troubleshooting topic, and, in Windows 98, click the Troubleshooters icon.**

   The information shown in Figure 17-5 appears. (In Windows 95, double-click the Troubleshooting topic and move forward to Step 3.)

3. **Click on the problem that plagues you and follow the instructions.**

   For example, click the Print selection to see the window shown in Figure 17-6 that offers suggestions on fixing printers.

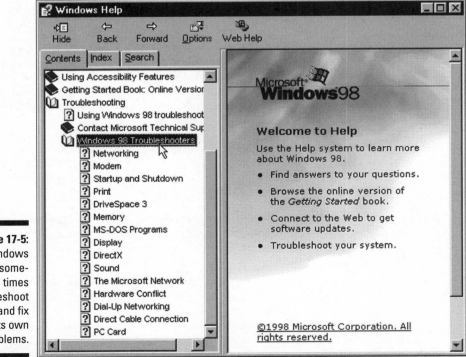

Figure 17-5: Windows can sometimes troubleshoot and fix its own problems.

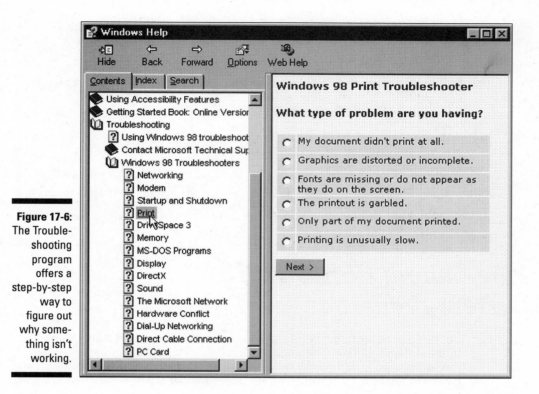

Figure 17-6:
The Trouble-shooting program offers a step-by-step way to figure out why something isn't working.

Windows offers a more advanced method of self-diagnosis through its System Properties area. Right-click My Computer and choose Properties from the pop-up menu. Then click the Device Manager tab to see a list of all your computer's parts.

A red X or a yellow exclamation point next to a computer part's name on the Device Manager list means that particular part isn't working right.

"My Driver's Too Old and Cruddy to Work Right!"

After you buy a new piece of hardware — a sound or video card, for example — it's not going to change as it sits inside your computer.

But its *driver* will change. Drivers, like any other piece of software, are subject to perpetual tinkering. As months pass, the manufacturers add bits of code here and there, making drivers faster and less likely to start arguments with other pieces of software.

Some companies release a new driver every two months. When a gadget doesn't work right or conflicts with some other part, your first step should be updating the gadget's driver.

In fact, that's usually the *second* thing you hear if you call the company's tech support line: "Are you using the latest driver?" (The first thing you usually hear is "All lines are busy right now.")

- ✔ All versions of Windows work best when you're using the latest driver for all your gadgets.

- ✔ Your best bet is to call up the gadget's manufacturer. Sometimes the manufacturer mails you a new driver for free. Other times the manufacturer directs you to its Web page or BBS. If you know how to use a modem, you can dial the Internet or BBS and download the latest driver.

Fine-Tuning Windows 98 System Properties

Unlike its predecessors, Windows 98 comes with a toolbox for tinkerers. When something's going wrong, your first step should be the System Properties dialog box. There, you can find a list of all the hardware that Windows 98 thinks is inside your computer and whether any of the hardware is acting up.

To get to the System Properties dialog box, right-click the My Computer icon and choose Properties from the pop-up menu. From there, you can manipulate Windows 98 in a wide variety of ways.

Changing drivers in Windows 98

Windows 98 works best with updated drivers, that's for sure. Finding the updated driver is the hard part; after you locate the driver, whether it's on the Internet or directly from a company, Windows 98 makes installing the driver easy:

1. **Right-click the My Computer icon and choose Properties from the pop-up menu.**

2. **Click the Device Manager tab.**

   The dialog box shown in Figure 17-7 appears, displaying all the goodies connected to your computer.

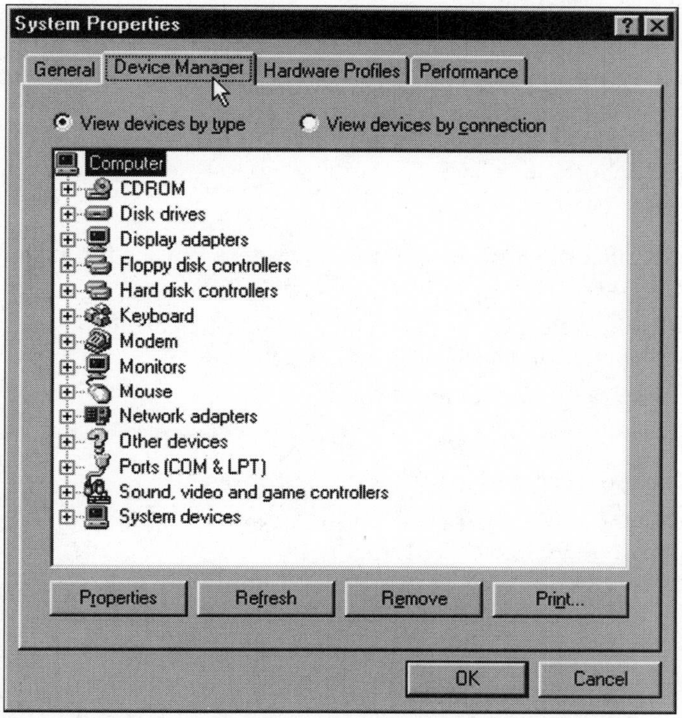

System Properties ? ✕

General | Device Manager | Hardware Profiles | Performance |

⦿ View devices by type   ○ View devices by connection

🖳 Computer
⊞ 📀 CDROM
⊞ 💾 Disk drives
⊞ 🖥 Display adapters
⊞ 🖴 Floppy disk controllers
⊞ 🖴 Hard disk controllers
⊞ ⌨ Keyboard
⊞ 📠 Modem
⊞ 🖥 Monitors
⊞ 🖱 Mouse
⊞ 🖧 Network adapters
⊞ ❓ Other devices
⊞ 🔌 Ports (COM & LPT)
⊞ 🔊 Sound, video and game controllers
⊞ 🖳 System devices

| Properties | Refresh | Remove | Print... |

OK | Cancel

Figure 17-7:
The Device
Manager
tab displays
all the
devices
connected
to your
computer.

3. **Double-click the item that needs the new driver.**

   For example, if you've downloaded a new video driver, double-click the Display adapters listing to see your current driver.

4. **Click the current driver and click the Properties button at the bottom of the dialog box.**

   Windows 98 reveals information about the current driver.

5. **Click the Driver tab, click the Change Driver button, and click the Have Disk button from the next window.**

6. **Tell Windows 98 where the new driver lurks — on your hard drive or a floppy disk.**

   Windows 98 grabs the driver, puts it in its place, and begins using it. (Chances are that you have to reboot the computer first, though.)

TIP

While you're on the Device Manager page, click the Print button. Choose the All Devices And System Summary option and click OK to send a complete technical report of all your computer's internal organs to the printer. That page may be a lifesaver down the road.

Checking the Windows 98 system and performance gauges

Afraid Windows 98 isn't working at its full capacity? You can analyze your computer's efforts to see whether they're up to snuff. Again, it's the System Properties area that comes through:

1. **Right-click the My Computer icon, choose Properties from the pop-up menu, and then click the Performance tab.**

   The System Properties dialog box shown in Figure 17-8 appears, displaying technical information about your computer.

2. **Click the File System button.**

   This step lets you change the way your computer handles files.

3. **Click the Hard disk tab.**

   Leave the Settings area box set to Desktop computer unless you're running Windows 98 on a laptop or network. Windows usually guesses correctly for the Settings area; don't change this unless you've installed a faster hard disk. Then feel free to slide the Read-ahead optimization bar to Full.

4. **Leave the Floppy Disk setting as is.**

   That way, Windows automatically searches for newly installed floppy disk drives whenever your computer starts up.

5. **If you have a CD-ROM drive, click the CD-ROM tab along the top.**

   Enter your CD-ROM drive's speed into the Optimize Access Pattern For box; Windows 98 automatically places the correct number in the Supplemental cache size box.

6. **Leave the Removable Disk setting as is.**

   Windows automatically detects a removable disk drive, like a Zip drive, and adjusts its settings accordingly.

7. **Don't bother with the Troubleshooting tab.**

   This tab is for more advanced users; beginners can often do more harm than good.

8. **Click OK and then click the Graphics button in the System Properties dialog box.**

   If your computer display has been acting weird, try sliding the Hardware acceleration knob to the left. Otherwise, let it be.

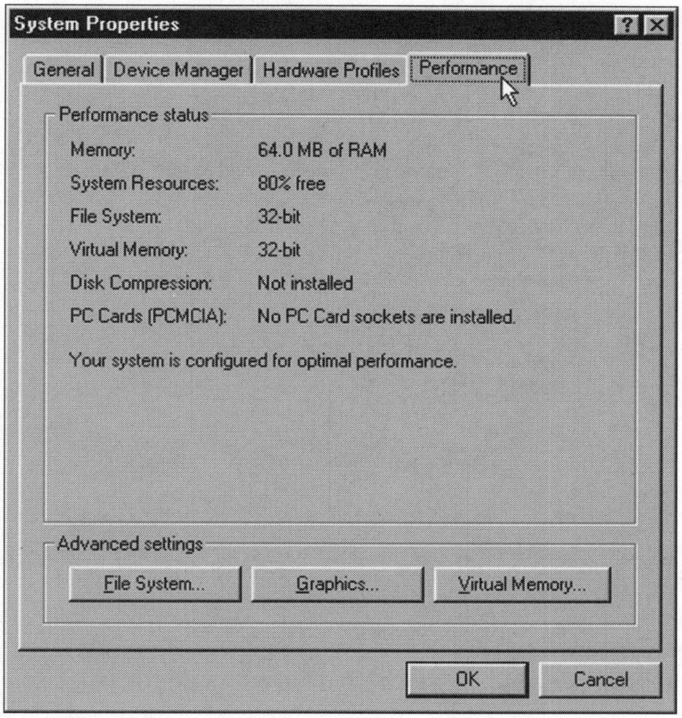

System Properties [?] [X]

General | Device Manager | Hardware Profiles | Performance

Performance status

Memory:	64.0 MB of RAM
System Resources:	80% free
File System:	32-bit
Virtual Memory:	32-bit
Disk Compression:	Not installed
PC Cards (PCMCIA):	No PC Card sockets are installed.

Your system is configured for optimal performance.

Advanced settings

[File System...] [Graphics...] [Virtual Memory...]

[OK] [Cancel]

Figure 17-8:
The Performance tab lets you customize Windows 98 software to your computer.

9. **Click OK and then click the Close button.**

   Unless you have a very good reason, don't click the Virtual Memory button. Windows 98 can almost always do a better job of juggling its own memory than any human can.

   By tweaking these options after adding new parts to your computer, you can make Windows 98 run more smoothly and with more gusto.

Finding vital statistics in the Windows 98 System Information program

Just what came installed inside your computer? This question becomes the most frightening when you're trying to answer it over the phone to a tech support person. Luckily, Windows 98 took mercy on its users with a System Information program. Here's the saving grace:

1. **Click the Start button and choose Accessories from the Programs area.**

2. **Choose System Information from the System Tools area.**

A window pops up, as shown in Figure 17-9.

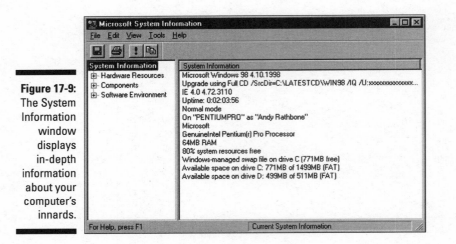

Figure 17-9:
The System
Information
window
displays
in-depth
information
about your
computer's
innards.

By poking around in this in-depth computer probe, you find out amazing details about your computer — both its insides and the parts connected to it.

The Microsoft System Information program comes with several other helpful tools, discussed in the following sections.

System File Checker

Worried that some of the files that came with your copy of Windows have gotten messed up? Microsoft's not happy about the possibility, either. To scope out the situation, use the System File Checker.

Load the System Information program, as shown in Figure 17-9, and choose System File Checker from the Tools menu.

Click the Start button, as shown in Figure 17-10, and Windows examines all its important files.

If it finds a file that's gone awry, it helps you replace it with a good version from your original Windows Installation CD.

System Configuration Utility

Although this one's perhaps the most complicated, it has one fairly easy function. The System Configuration Utility lets you pick and choose between the programs that automatically load themselves whenever Windows starts.

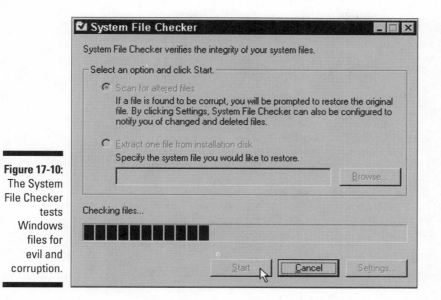

Figure 17-10:
The System
File Checker
tests
Windows
files for
evil and
corruption.

Windows likes to load programs as it starts. It lists many of these programs in the StartUp area of the Start menu's Programs menu. By clicking on any of the programs listed in the StartUp area, you can easily stop them from loading.

The sneakier programs load themselves without letting you know. After they're loaded, they push their little icons onto your taskbar, down near the Windows clock.

To get rid of them, choose the System Configuration Utility from the Microsoft System Information program's Tools menu. When the utility appears, click the Startup tab, as shown in Figure 17-11.

To keep a program from loading in the background, remove the check mark next to its name. Click OK and reboot, and the program should stop loading. (Sometimes it refuses to go away, though. Even Windows can't control itself.)

Don't get carried away and remove programs you can't identify. You don't want to accidentally remove your virus checker or other important yet unrecognized components.

If you spot any program named NetBus or BackOrifice, disable it immediately. Those are evil computer infections that let other people control your computer through the Internet. Head to www.symantec.com for more information.

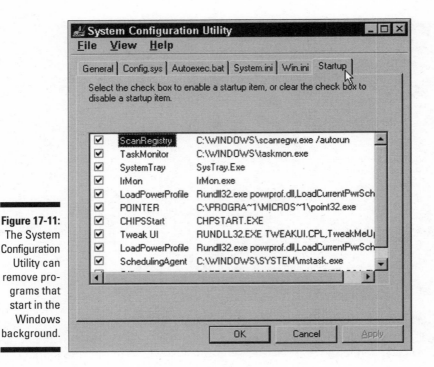

Figure 17-11:
The System
Configuration
Utility can
remove pro-
grams that
start in the
Windows
background.

Finding device conflicts in Windows 98

When two parts aren't getting along in Windows 98, you know about it sev-
eral ways. First, the computer doesn't work right. And second — luckily —
Windows 98 points out the squabbling devices and helps make amends.
Again, it's the Device Manager that rules against the unruly.

1. **Right-click the My Computer icon and choose Properties from the pop-
   up menu.**

2. **Click the Device Manager tab.**

3. **Look for an exclamation point or red X marking a particular part.**

   An exclamation point usually means that two parts are squabbling over
   the same resource — an IRQ, for example, as I explain in Chapter 18.

   A red X, as shown in Figure 17-12, means that the device is disabled.

   After you find the culprit, click the Start button, choose Help, and click
   the Contents tab along the window's top. Double-click Troubleshooting
   to see the list of possible problems, and double-click the area that's
   giving you trouble.

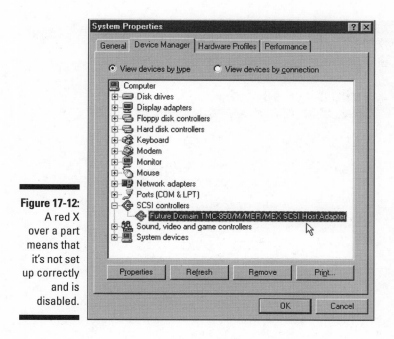

Figure 17-12:
A red X
over a part
means that
it's not set
up correctly
and is
disabled.

The Wizard walks you through the steps needed to shake loose the conflicting hardware demons.

If the Help wizard uses unfamiliar language, head for Chapter 18. That chapter tackles things like IRQs, COM ports, and other things that computer gadgets fight over.

Keeping Windows Up-To-Date

Microsoft keeps tweaking Windows or its various parts, fixing bugs, adding features, and patching holes that sick, twisted virus creators use to plant destructive forces inside your PC.

But how's a poor user supposed to keep up with all this stuff?

Microsoft took pity, and now you can update your computer with the click of a mouse. Click the Start button and choose Windows Update. Your Internet browser races to the Microsoft Windows Update Web site, as shown in Figure 17-13.

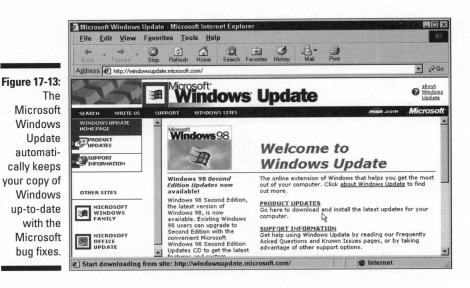

Figure 17-13: The Microsoft Windows Update automatically keeps your copy of Windows up-to-date with the Microsoft bug fixes.

If you have questions about the process, click the Support Information area. When you're ready to roll, click the words Product Updates to start the process. Microsoft begins to examine your computer to see whether Windows needs any updates.

Eventually, the Product Updates Select Software page appears, as shown in Figure 17-14.

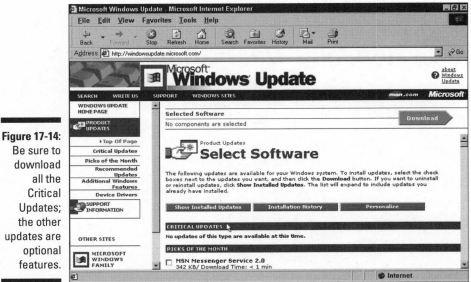

Figure 17-14: Be sure to download all the Critical Updates; the other updates are optional features.

Click the check boxes next to all the updates listed in the Critical Updates section. These features aren't optional — they're ways that Microsoft fixes things when it screws up. Choose them *all*.

When you've chosen all the Critical Updates, click the Download button. Windows automatically downloads the fixes, installs them, and asks you to restart your computer so that the fixes take effect.

✔ Feel free to peruse the Picks of the Month, Recommended Updates, and Additional Windows Features. Pay the most attention to the Recommended Updates. They're usually upgrades to programs that come with Windows: the newest version of Media Player, for instance.

✔ Some fixes are so precarious that Microsoft makes you download them separately. After they've been downloaded and installed and your computer is restarted, go back for the rest of them.

✔ Want to see what programs and fixes Windows has sent you? Click the blue Show Installed Updates and Installation History buttons shown in Figure 17-14, right above the Critical Updates sign. Windows tells you everything it's installed on your computer through the Update program.

✔ Windows offers an automatic update program, where it automatically heads to the program, downloads the goodies, and installs them. Don't sign up for it. It's always caused problems. Instead, choose the Windows Critical Update Notification. That merely tells you when Windows has posted a Critical Update. Then you can head there yourself and download it, not giving Windows a chance to mess up.

Chapter 18

Fiddling with Settings

· ·

· ·

*T*his is by far the book's scariest chapter. It's full of disturbing, psychoana-lytical words like *conflicts* and *interrupts*. If your computer's acting nor-mally, you don't need to bother with this chapter. Also, Windows 95 and Windows 98 can usually handle all this stuff automatically; those users rarely need to bother with this chapter.

But if things start to go haywire after you install a new part — or if the part simply refuses to work — you need to muddle through this conflict-and-interrupt stuff.

See, some new parts work as is, right out of the box. Your computer embraces them like old friends, invites them to dinner, and nobody spills wine on the tablecloth.

Other new parts, however, can start arguing over territory with the older parts, and the resulting brawl can get ugly fast. The solution? You need to change some of your computer's settings so that each part can get its own space.

This chapter tells you how to change the settings on your computer as well as those on some of your newest gadgets. Tweak a few settings here and there, and nobody gets snubbed, especially you.

"My COM Ports Are Arguing!"

Chapters 6 and 7 cover all you need to know about plugging a mouse or modem into a *serial* port, also known as a *COM* port. But you probably wound up in this section because of a computerized eccentricity: Computer gadgets don't always like to share serial ports.

If a gadget like a modem needs a serial port, it needs its *own* serial port. A mouse or a scanner often wants its own serial port, too. If you inadvertently set up two gadgets to use the same port, fisticuffs break out, and neither gadget works.

Gadgets that plug into the back of your computer usually don't cause much of a problem. You can plug a mouse into one port, for example, and a modem into the other. As long as your mouse and modem software know which part's plugged into which port, everybody's happy. (Chapter 6 tells how to figure out which one's plugged into which port.)

But things get trickier when you plug cards inside your computer. For example, sometimes you plug an internal modem card inside your computer and it doesn't work. Not only that, but it also knocks your once-healthy mouse or scanner out of commission.

That usually happens because the modem and mouse or scanner are fighting over the *same* serial port. They've both been told to use the same port, but when they try, they see the other part blocking the way.

If Windows can't handle the problem automatically through its Plug and Play technology during installation, the answer is to cajole the internal modem into using a different serial port. You usually do that by moving either a *jumper* or a *DIP switch* on the modem's card — a relatively simple, anesthesia-free operation that I describe later in this chapter, in the section "Jumper Bumping and DIP Switch Flipping."

Don't know what COM port to assign to your latest internal gadget? Let Table 18-1 be your guide.

Table 18-1   What COM Port Should I Give My Incoming Gadget?

If Your Computer Has These COM Ports	*Let Your Incoming Gadget Use This*
No COM ports	COM2
Only COM1 is installed, but something's plugged into it	COM2
Only COM2 is installed, but something's plugged into it	COM1

If Your Computer Has These COM Ports	Let Your Incoming Gadget Use This
Both COM1 and COM2 are installed, but something's plugged into COM1	COM4
Both COM1 and COM2 are installed, but something's plugged into COM2	COM3
Both COM1 and COM2 are installed, and something's plugged into both of them	Buy an A/B switch, described in the following section
Golly, I don't know what a COM port looks like or who's using it	Turn to Chapter 3

✔ A serial port and a COM port are the same thing: a "doorway" through which your computer passes information. If two gadgets try to pass information through the same doorway at the same time, everything gets stuck.

✔ Computers can access *four* serial ports, but there's a catch: You can use only *two* of those ports at the same time. You find two serial ports on the back of many computers. The bigger one is usually COM2; the smaller one is usually COM1.

✔ If you assign one gadget to COM1 and a second to COM2 but they're still fighting, try reversing them. Assign the second gadget to COM1 and the first to COM2.

✔ How do you assign a serial port — a COM port — to a gadget? Usually by checking its manual and moving the right jumpers or DIP switches, as I describe in the section "Jumper Bumping and DIP Switch Flipping," later in this chapter.

After you assign a COM port to your modem, you usually need to tell your modem software which COM port your modem's hogging. Some modem software is getting a little smarter, however; a few programs can find the right port all by themselves. It's about time, too.

✔ You can assign gadgets that plug inside your computer to COM3 and COM4. However, you can't use COM1 and COM3 at the same time, and COM2 and COM4 can't be used at the same time either. Short attention span, those computers.

✔ Some older internal modems like only serial ports COM1 and COM2. If COM1 and COM2 are already being used, free up a port with an A/B switch, as described in the following tip.

Don't have enough COM ports? Buy an *A/B serial port switch*. It's a little box with a switch on the front. You plug a cable from the box into one of your computer's COM ports. Then you plug two gadgets into the two ports on the box — for example, a serial printer into the box's A port and an external modem into the B port. To use the printer, flip the box's switch to A. To use the modem, flip the switch to B. Don't be surprised if you forget to flip the switch back to the printer when you want to print; everybody does.

✔ As you figure out which gadget's using which COM port, fill out Table 18-2. You can save yourself the trouble of figuring everything out again the next time this hassle comes up.

✔ Windows 98 is much more graceful about letting devices share COM ports. It usually lets them share the same port — as long as they don't try to use it simultaneously.

There's a new technology in the air, called Universal Serial Bus *(USB)*. Unlike the antiquated COM ports, USB devices get along — more than a hundred of them can share the same USB port with no squabbling. Although most of today's computers come with USB ports (pictured in Chapter 3), USB devices have been slow in coming. Keep on the lookout.

Table 18-2	Who's Using My COM Ports?
The Port	*The Owner (Mouse, Modem, Scanner, or Other Gadget)*
COM1	
COM2	
COM3	
COM4	

How to Resolve Irritating IRQ Conflicts

Like squabbling siblings, computer gadgets often argue over *interrupt* rights.

Computers, like harried parents, concentrate on one thing at a time. When a parent's cooking dinner and a kid wants some attention, the kid pulls on the parent's pant leg. Computer gadgets work the same way. Computers have pant legs known as *interrupts*.

An interrupt, often dubbed an *IRQ*, is sort of a virtual pant leg that gadgets can tug on to get your computer's attention. When you move your mouse, for example, it tugs on one of your computer's pant legs — an interrupt — and tells the computer that it moved. The computer takes note and updates the mouse arrow's position onscreen.

Just as a pair of pants has only two legs, a computer has a limited number of interrupts. And if two gadgets — a sound card and a scanner, for example — try to use the same interrupt, the harried computer doesn't know which one to listen to. So it usually ignores both of them and keeps on cooking dinner.

The solution is to assign a different interrupt — a different IRQ — to each gadget. Sounds simple enough, eh? But here's the problem: When you try to assign an interrupt to a new part, you find that gadgets such as disk drives and keyboards have already grabbed most of the available interrupts for themselves, as you can see in the horribly technical Table 18-3.

Table 18-3	Interrupts and Who Usually Gets Them	
Interrupt	*Owner*	*Comments*
IRQ 0	System timer	Your computer already grabbed this one.
IRQ 1	Keyboard	Your computer already grabbed this one. (Your keyboard interrupts your computer each time you press a key.)
IRQ 2	Programmable interrupt controller	Anything assigned here is automatically moved to IRQ 9, allowing the controller to coordinate requests on IRQs 8–15.
IRQ 3	COM 2, COM 4	These two serial ports share this interrupt. (That's why you can't use both these COM ports at the same time.) Mice or modems usually end up here.
IRQ 4	COM 1, COM 3	These two serial ports share this interrupt. (That's why you can't use both these COM ports at the same time, either.) Mice or modems usually end up here.

(continued)

Table 18-3 *(continued)*

Interrupt	Owner	Comments
IRQ 5	Second printer port	This one's usually vacant, so it's snapped up by sound cards, SCSI drive controllers, and other add-ons.
IRQ6	Floppy disk controller	Your computer's already grabbed this one.
IRQ 7	First printer port	Try this one only if you're not using a printer.
IRQ 8	Your computer's clock	Your computer's already grabbed this one.
IRQ 9	Nothing	See the IRQ2 entry. You can use IRQ2 or IRQ9, but not both.
IRQ 10	Nothing	Usually up for grabs.
IRQ 11	Nothing	This one may be free, although gadgets rarely let you choose it; laptops often snag it for PC Card slots.
IRQ 12	PS/2 mouse	Most mice today plug directly into the computer's motherboard, grabbing this IRQ in the process.
IRQ 13	Coprocessor	Your computer's already grabbed this one.
IRQ 14	Hard drive	Your computer's already grabbed this one.
IRQ 15	Nothing	This one may be free, although gadgets rarely let you choose it; it's often grabbed by hard drives as well.

✔ For such a laborious subject, interrupts have amazingly simple names. They're merely numbers, like 3 or 12.

✔ How do you assign an interrupt to a computer part? If you're not using Windows, by moving a jumper or by flipping a DIP switch (a hobby I describe later in this chapter, in its own section). Other gadgets let you choose interrupts from their installation software.

✔ If you inadvertently choose an interrupt that another part's already holding on to, nothing explodes. Your new gadget just doesn't work. Keep trying different interrupts until one finally works. It's like driving around in front of the grocery store until you find a place to park. The parking process can be bothersome, but it's quickly forgotten after you're inside looking at the fresh strawberries.

"Who's Using My Computer's IRQs?"

To find out who's grabbing the IRQs in your particular computer, follow these secret steps:

1. **Right-click on your desktop's My Computer icon and choose Properties.**

2. **Click the Device Manager tab and double-click on the word *Computer* at the top of the chart.**

   A Computer Properties chart appears, listing your computer's interrupts and which parts use them, as shown in Figure 18-1.

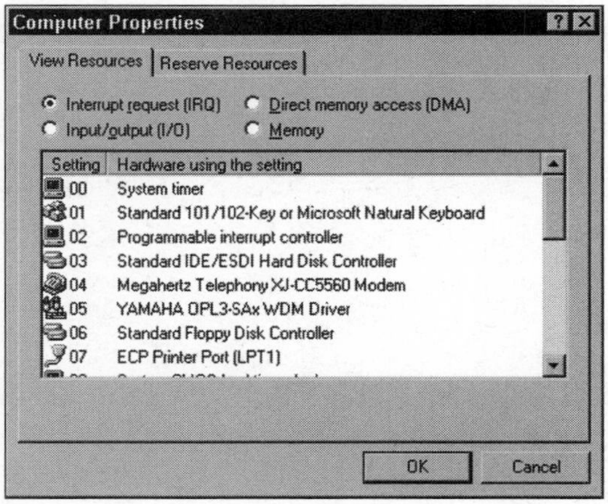

Figure 18-1: The Windows Computer Properties chart lists your computer's interrupts and the parts that are using them.

✔ Whenever you're curious about fighting interrupts, call up the Computer Properties window and take a gander at who's using what.

✔ In fact, it's wise to peek at that window before installing any cards, like network cards or sound cards. They occasionally want you to assign them a free IRQ number.

✔ Want to know everything that's in your computer? Head to Chapter 17 for the scoop on using the Microsoft System Information tool. Or, if you don't want to flip pages, choose Programs from the Start button, choose System Tools from the Accessories area, and choose System Tools.

"What's this IRQ Holder for PCI Steering stuff?"

When you pop open your Computer Profiles window, as described nearby, in the section "Who's Using My Computer's IRQs?", you'll probably spot the words *IRQ Holder for PCI Steering* in place of one of your valued IRQ numbers. What does that mean?

Well, PCI devices (the cards described in Chapter 15) can share IRQs, whereas the older, ISA devices can't. So, Windows latches on to a single IRQ, assigns it to serve PCI only, and steers it around to meet the needs of several PCI cards.

Windows also uses it for Plug and Play. By steering components to use different IRQs, Windows can find or create vacant IRQs for devices that don't use Plug and Play technology.

The point? Your IRQ isn't being wasted. Your computer is just holding it for PCI cards, not the older ISA cards. It's a good thing, despite what some "helpful" utility programs may tell you.

Address and DMA Stuff

Some gadgets get greedy. They ask not only for things like an IRQ, as described in the preceding section, but also for more arcane bits of weirdness such as an *address* or *DMA*.

Your computer assigns an address to some of its parts so that it can find them later. Not all gadgets want or need their own addresses. But some newly installed gadgets ask for their own addresses and expect you to act as a knowledgeable real estate agent.

Because your computer usually has plenty of addresses to spare, most gadgets simply choose an address at random, hoping that nobody else is using it. But if some other gadget's already living at the address, the two parts start bickering and neither one works.

The same thing happens when a newly installed gadget grabs a DMA channel that another gadget already snagged. The new gadget simply doesn't work.

DMA stands for *Direct Memory Address* channel. But who cares?

A *DMA channel* lets a part squirt information directly into your computer's memory. That's why havoc breaks out if two parts try to squirt in the same place.

The solution is to change your new gadget's address or DMA. You usually need to fiddle with jumpers or DIP switches on a card in order to do this.

But sometimes you can change the DMA and address through the gadget's installation software — you don't even need to pop off your computer's case.

Which address or DMA should you choose? Unfortunately, your best bet is the trial-and-error approach. Just keep trying different addresses or DMAs; it shouldn't take long to stumble upon a home that nobody's claimed.

You can't damage anything by inadvertently choosing the wrong address or DMA. Your gadget just doesn't work until you choose an address or DMA that's vacant.

After you choose a DMA or address, write it down on the front of the gadget's manual. You might need to give that information to any software that wants to play with the gadget.

I/O addresses for *memory* and I/O addresses for *hardware* are different. Software (spreadsheet programs, word processors, and so on) looks for addresses in memory; hardware (sound cards, scanners, and the like) looks for hardware addresses. The two kinds of addresses — memory and hardware — are on completely different streets.

Windows 95 and Windows 98 let you see who's using which DMA, giving you a clue to which ones are free. To see what's up for grabs, right-click My Computer, choose Properties, and choose the Device Manager tab. Now, here's the sneaky part: Double-click the tiny computer icon at the top of the page. When the Computer Properties window appears, click in the Direct memory access (DMA) area, and another window appears, displaying the currently used DMAs. Tricky, eh?

Jumper Bumping and DIP Switch Flipping

Most people talk to their computer by typing on the keyboard. But sometimes you need to probe *deeper* into your computer's psyche — especially when you're not using a modern Plug and Play device. To talk to your computer on a "low grunt" level, you need to move around its little *jumpers* and *DIP switches*. By wiggling these little doodads around, you can tell your computer parts to behave in different ways.

You can easily change a gadget's jumpers or switches. All you need is the gadget's manual and a magnifying glass. These little switches are *tiny*.

Moving jumpers around

A *jumper* is a little box that slides on or off little pins. By moving the little box around to different sets of pins, you instruct the computer part to act in different ways.

The part's manual tells you what pins to fiddle with. The pins themselves have little labels next to them, giving you a fighting chance at finding the right ones.

For example, see the little numbers and letters next to the little pins in Figure 18-2? The jumper box is set across the two pins marked *J1*. That means the jumper is set for J1.

If the manual says to *set jumper J2,* slide the little box up and off the J1 pins and slide it down onto the pins marked *J2*. The pins then look like the ones shown in Figure 18-3.

Quick and easy. In fact, the concept was *too* easy for computer designers, so they complicated matters. Some jumpers don't use *pairs* of pins; instead, they use a single row of pins in a straight line, as shown in Figure 18-4.

In Figure 18-4, the jumper is set between pins 1 and 2. If the manual says to move the jumper to pins 2 and 3, slide the jumper up and off. Then slide it back down over pins 2 and 3, as shown in Figure 18-5.

Figure 18-2:
This jumper
is set for J1.

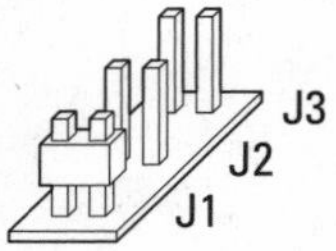

Figure 18-3:
This jumper
is set for J2.

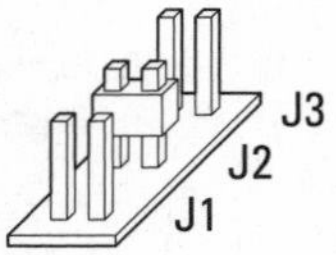

Figure 18-4:
This jumper
is set
between
pins 1 and 2.

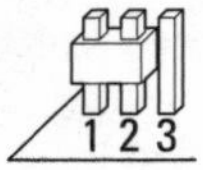

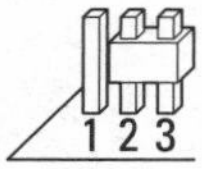

Figure 18-5:
This jumper
is set
between
pins 2 and 3.

Figure 18-5:
This jumper
is set
between
pins 2 and 3.

By moving the little box from pin to pin, you can make the gadget use different settings. It's sort of a gearshift knob for computer circuitry.

✔ The hard part of moving jumpers is grabbing that tiny box thing so that you can slide it on or off. A pair of tweezers or needlenose pliers can help.

✔ Dropped the little box inside your computer? The last section of Chapter 2 offers tips on fishing out dropped articles.

If the manual says to remove a jumper, *don't* remove it! If you slide the little box off the pins, it can camouflage itself amid the paper clips in your desk drawer, and you may never find it again. Instead, leave the little box thing hanging on *one* prong, as shown in Figure 18-6. The computer will think that you removed the jumper. Because the jumper's still attached to a pin, however, it's handy if you ever need to slide it back on.

✔ When the little box is over a pair of pins, that jumper circuit is considered *closed*. If the box is removed, that jumper is called *open*.

✔ Sometimes a jumper's little box comes with wires attached. For example, the wires leading from your computer's reset button probably push onto pins sticking up from your motherboard, as illustrated in Figure 18-7. You can pull that little wire thing on or off, just like any other jumper. The wires stay connected to the little box; the little box just slides on and off.

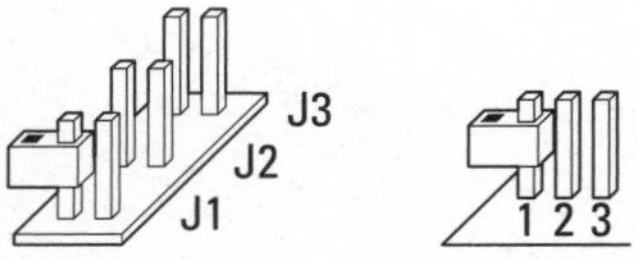

Figure 18-6:
If you're told
to remove a
jumper, just
leave it
dangling off
one pin.

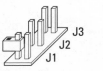

Figure 18-7:
Little wires
connect to
this jumper.

RESET

Don't know which wire should connect to which pin? Look for little numbers printed near the base of the pins. The red wire always connects to pin #1.

✔ If you don't have a manual, how do you know which jumpers relate to which setting? You don't. You have three options: Call the gadget's manufacturer and ask for a new manual, see whether the store has a manual lying around, or keep moving the jumpers around until you stumble across the combination that works.

Flipping a DIP switch

The first personal computer didn't have a keyboard. Its owners bossed it around by flipping dozens of tiny switches across the front of the computer's case. Sure, balancing their checkbooks took a *long* time, but hey, they were pioneers.

Today's computer owners still have to flip little switches, but not nearly as often. And thank goodness! The few remaining switches have shrunk to microscopic level. In fact, they're too small to flip with your finger. You need a little paper clip or ballpoint pen to switch them back and forth.

These little switches are called *DIP switches.* Figure 18-8 shows a few different switch varieties.

Figure 18-8:
The DIP
switch on
the left
has sliding
controls; the
one on the
right has
rocker
switches.

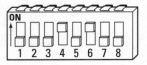 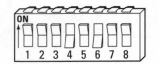

See the little numbers next to each switch? And see how one side of the switch says *On?* When you push or flip a switch toward the On side, you turn on that numbered switch.

In Figure 18-8, both DIP switches show switch numbers 4 and 6 turned on. All other switches are turned off.

- ✔ DIP switches are slowly disappearing in favor of jumpers. Some of the latest cards and motherboards let you control all the settings by using software. The process is just as aggravating, but at least you don't need a magnifying glass.

  Before flipping any DIP switches, draw a little picture of the way they're set. If something dreadful happens, you can flip them back to the way they were.

- ✔ The leftmost DIP switch pictured in Figure 18-8 has *sliding* controls. You slide the little box toward On to turn on that numbered switch. Slide it away from On to turn it off.

- ✔ The DIP switch on the right in Figure 18-8 has *rocker* controls. You press the switch toward On to turn on that numbered switch. Press the switch *away* from On to turn it off.

  Feel free to flip a DIP switch with the tip of a ballpoint pen, but don't use a pencil. The tip of a pencil can break off and jam the switch, leading to much embarrassment.

- ✔ Some manufacturers felt that labeled switches were too easy for consumers to figure out. So they left out the words *On* and *Off* and put a little arrow on one edge of the switch. Just remember that the arrow points in the On direction.

- ✔ To further confuse things, some manufacturers use the word *Open* rather than *Off* and *Closed* rather than *On*.

- ✔ Some really offbeat manufacturers label their DIP switches with a 1 for On and 0 for Off.

Nobody needs to know that the "DIP" in "DIP switch" stands for *Dual In-line Package*.

Sailing the CMOS Sea

Your computer's *CMOS* (Complementary Metal Oxide Semiconductor) memory is like the sticker in the window of a new car. It lists the machine's most important accessories.

Rather than list accessories like air conditioning and driver's side airbag, however, the CMOS (pronounced "SEE-moss") keeps track of more computer-nerdish details: the size of your disk drives, the size of your hard drive, how much memory you could afford to buy, and other geekoid facts.

Old PC and XT computers don't have a CMOS. Instead, they keep track of what's inside themselves by looking at the way the DIP switches and jumpers are set on the motherboard. (DIP switches and jumpers got their due in the preceding section.)

A CMOS provides a much more convenient system. You can update it by typing stuff from the keyboard. That's much faster than trying to figure out what DIP switches to flip after you install some extra memory.

The CMOS tells your computer how to behave, and that's why it can be dangerous. If you give it the wrong setting, your computer will behave incorrectly. Always change a single setting at a time, make a note of your change, and then make sure that your PC still runs correctly after the change.

- ✔ Your computer's CMOS remembers all this stuff even when the computer's turned off or unplugged. A little battery inside your computer keeps the information backed up on a tiny chip.

- ✔ If that little battery ever dies, however, the information in your CMOS disappears, giving your computer a bad case of amnesia. When you turn the computer on, it doesn't remember the time or the date. Computers built before 1995 may not even remember that they have a hard drive. (By the way, you can find out how to replace a dead battery in Chapter 10.)

- ✔ You may need to update your CMOS when you change your computer's battery or add a new disk drive (floppy or hard) to an older computer.

"How Do I Change My CMOS?"

Of course, it would be too simple if you could use the same method to update the CMOS memory in all computers; almost every manufacturer uses a different style.

You need to figure out what *secret access code* your CMOS uses. Although different brands of computers use different codes, the following paragraphs provide some of the more common ones. Give 'em all a shot before rooting through the file cabinet for your motherboard's manual. (The code is usually listed in the manual under *BIOS*.)

When you reboot your computer, look for words like these:

```
Press <DEL> If you want to run SETUP or DIAGS
Press <F2> To Enter SETUP
Press <Ctrl><Alt> <Esc> for SETUP
Press <Ctrl><Alt> <Ins> for SETUP
Press <Ctrl><Alt> <S> for SETUP
```

If you see messages like these that mention SETUP as the computer comes to life, quickly follow the instructions, before the message disappears. If you're quick enough, you're in: Your computer brings its master list of parts and settings to the screen. It's a boring screen of text against a solid background, and it's different for nearly every computer.

If none of these tricks works for you, it's time to grab the manual for your computer or its motherboard. Perhaps the computer maker's Web site will help.

Got the CMOS up on the screen? The following list covers things you may need to change:

Although most new computers automatically recognize their components and reset the CMOS data accordingly, it doesn't hurt to keep a copy of your CMOS settings. When you enter your CMOS Setup area, turn on your printer and press the PrtScrn key. This step will send a copy of your current screen to the printer, providing you with a paper copy of your settings.

Time/Date: Because your CMOS has a constant battery backup, it's a convenient place to keep track of the current time and date. You can change the time and date here. Or you can change the time and date simply by typing **TIME** or **DATE** at any C:\> prompt. If you've changed your computer's battery, you have to reenter the time and date in your CMOS.

Hard drives: If you're lucky, you can find a Type number for your hard drive somewhere in your hard drive's manual. Put that number — which is usually between 1 and 47 — in the hard drive's Type area within your CMOS.

Can't find a Type number? Well, if you're using an IDE drive, try choosing the Type number of any drive that comes closest to, but not over, the capacity of your hard drive. Not using an IDE drive? Windows can recognize some drives, and, luckily, most hard drives these days come with installation software. Whew!

Memory: Your CMOS occasionally needs to know when you pop in some more memory chips, but the job's pretty easy. In fact, your computer automatically counts all available memory whenever you turn it on or reset it. If your computer's quick little tally doesn't match the tally stored in your CMOS, your computer gets cautious: It sends out an error message and says to update your CMOS through the setup process.

You merely have to call up your CMOS setup and confirm that, yes, the computer *did* count up the memory total correctly — the numbers didn't match because you added some more memory! Sometimes, the CMOS already reflects the computer's new count; you just have to save the new total and exit the CMOS screen.

Motherboard: When you buy a new motherboard, you deal with a different CMOS, too. Check the motherboard's manual, and enter the settings accordingly.

Some of the latest motherboards have several pages of advanced settings that are far too authoritarian for this easygoing book. However, make sure that you turn on any memory caches. Your computer will run much faster. If you're searching for speed, try turning on some of the *ROM shadows;* if you run into trouble, change the setting back. It's important to make your changes *one at a time* so that you can identify the culprit if your computer freaks out after a change. Just turn that ROM shadow back off, and all will be well.

After you change a CMOS setting, look for a menu item that *saves* your changes. If you don't specifically tell the CMOS to save your changes, all your work will be for naught.

Part V
The Part of Tens

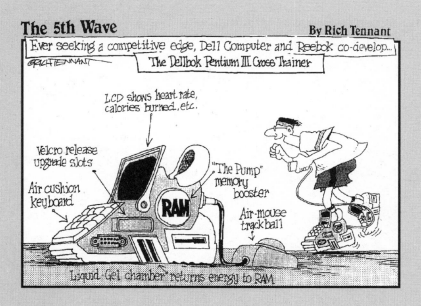

The 5th Wave   By Rich Tennant

Ever seeking a competitive edge, Dell Computer and Reebok co-develop...

The Dellbok Pentium III Cross Trainer

LCD shows heart rate,
calories burned, etc.

Velcro release
upgrade slots

Air cushion
keyboard

RAM

"The Pump"
memory
booster

Air-mouse
trackball

Liquid-Gel chamber returns energy to RAM

In this part . . .

Those of you with sharp eyes will realize something scandalous right away: Some of the lists in this section don't contain ten items. Actually, very few of them do. Most have a wee bit more information or a wee bit less.

But by the time most people get to this part of the book, they're tired of counting numbers anyway. In fact, these lists *aren't* numbered. They're just a bunch of facts tossed into the basket.

So when you read these lists, remember that it's quality, not quantity, that matters. Besides, would you want to read a fake tip about 8255 PPI (U20) just because one of the lists needed a tenth tip?

Chapter 19

Ten Cheap Fixes to Try First

. . . .

In This Chapter

▶ Making sure that the computer's plugged in

▶ Turning the computer on and off again

▶ Removing disks before booting up your computer

▶ Checking for overheating

▶ Booting from a system disk

▶ Reseating cards, chips, and connectors

▶ Cleaning card connectors with a pencil eraser

▶ Installing a new power supply

▶ Defragmenting the hard drive

. . . .

*B*efore spending any money at the shop, try these cheap fixes on your computer. You might get lucky. If you're not lucky, give yourself a good stretch and flip back to Chapter 4 for some more system-sleuthing tips.

Plug It In

Sure, it sounds silly. But industry experts get paid big bucks to say that unplugged equipment is the leading cause of "electrical component malfunction." Check your PC's power cord in *two* places: It can creep not only out of the wall outlet but also out of the back of your computer.

Sometimes a yawning leg stretch can inadvertently loosen the cord from the wall. Rearranging a computer on the desk almost always loosens cables that aren't screwed tightly into the back of the computer.

And, uh, the machine's turned on, isn't it? (That's the leading cause of printer malfunction, by the way.)

Turn the Computer Off, Wait 30 Seconds, and Turn It Back On

Sometimes the computer just gets confused for no apparent reason. If your computer drifts off into oblivion, with no return in sight, try tapping the Spacebar a few times. Try pressing Esc, or hold down Ctrl while pressing Esc. One of my laptops woke up only when I prodded an arrow key.

Still no return? Then it's time to get ugly. The next few steps may cause you to lose any work that hasn't been saved to either your hard disk or a floppy disk. Sorry!

 ✔ Try rebooting the computer: Press the Ctrl, Alt, and Del keys simultaneously. Sometimes that's enough to wake up Windows, whereupon it offers you a chance to snuff out the troublemaking program.

 ✔ If the computer's still acting like an ice cube, head for the next level of attention grabbing: Press the reset button.

 ✔ If the computer's *still* counting marbles on some virtual playground, turn off the computer. Then wait 30 seconds. (That 30-second part is important.) Finally, turn the computer back on and see whether it returns in a better mood.

You'd be surprised how much good a little 30-second vacation can accomplish.

Remove Your Floppy and Then Turn on Your Computer

Ever turn on the computer only to be greeted by a message like this?

```
Non-System disk or disk error
Replace and press any key when ready
```

Chances are, you got that message because a floppy disk is sitting in drive A, where it's confusing the computer's start-up process.

Remove the floppy and, as the saying goes, "press any key when ready." A tap of the Spacebar does the trick. Your computer returns to life.

Check for Overheating

Nobody likes to work when it's too hot, and your computer's no exception. Your computer normally works naked, but after a few months it wears a thick coat of dust.

Your first step is to look at the fan's round grill on the back of the computer. See all the dust flecks clinging to the grill, swapping barbecue stories? Wipe them off with a rag, being careful to keep the worst grunge from falling inside.

Second, check the vents on the front and sides of your computer case. Although the fan in the power supply is creating the airflow, the air is actually being sucked in these little holes and through your floppy drive doors. If these vents are clogged with crud, very little air moves across the components to cool them.

Don't just *blow* on the dust, either. The microscopic flecks of spittle in your breath can cause problems with the computer's moisture-sensitive internal components.

For best results, buy a cheap can of compressed air from a local computer store, remove your computer's case, and blow the dust off its innards every few months, paying special attention to crevices and grills.

The more parts and peripherals you add to your computer, the hotter it will run. Be sure to keep the vents clean.

Don't tape cards or "cheat sheets" (including the one from this book) across the front of your PC's case. That can block your PC's air vents, which are often disguised as avant garde ridges across the front of the case. When air can't circulate inside your PC, your computer heats up in a hurry.

Don't keep your computer pushed up directly against the wall. It needs some breathing room so that its fan can blow out all the hot air from inside the case.

Boot from a System Floppy Disk

Sometimes a computer refuses to do much more than wake up: You can hear a fan whirring inside, but the computer doesn't read enough information off its hard drive to pull itself out of bed.

If your computer's having trouble starting up and loading Windows (or even DOS, for you old-timers), pull out your system disk.

System disks, as described in Chapter 2, contain nothing but the bare-bones basics required to run your computer. Sometimes they're all you need to fix your computer's malady. At the very least, they provide ammo for any computer guru friend who looks at your failing system. He or she won't be able to do much without one.

After making your system disk as described in Chapter 2, put the disk in drive A and reboot your computer. Windows comes to the screen in a skeleton fashion, letting you change its settings until you fix the one that was messing things up. When you or your friend has fixed things, remove any disk from drive A and reboot your computer to bring things back to normal.

Reseat Cards, Chips, and Connectors

When your computer's been running for a while, it heats up and expands. When you turn your computer off, it cools off and contracts. This constant expanding and contracting can play subtle tricks on your computer's internal components. Specifically, it can make those internal parts slide out of their little compartments.

If your computer acts up, turn it off, remove the case, and give all the cards a little extra push into their slots. Give the memory chips a little extra push into their sockets as well. That can cure memory errors. While you're in there, make sure that all those internal cables are plugged snugly into their connectors.

Sometimes, taking this step clears up some intermittent problems, especially the ones that appear after the computer's been turned on for a while.

Clean Card Connectors with a Pencil Eraser

Is your computer still acting up, even after you pushed the cards a little more deeply into their sockets? Then try this:

1. **Turn off your PC, unplug it, and remove its cover.**

   If you've never gone spelunking inside your computer, check the Cheat Sheet at the front of this book. It offers complete cover-removal tips.

2. **Unscrew one of the cards and remove any cables from it.**

   You find complete instructions in Chapter 15. Basically, you need to remove that little screw along the top that holds the card in place. Then unscrew or pull out any cables connected to the card.

3. **Pull the card from its slot and clean the card's contacts.**

   Pull the card straight up out of its slot, being careful not to damage any of the electronic gizmos hanging on to it. Handling the card by its edges, using clean hands, is best.

   Now, see the little copper-colored connectors on the card "tab" that plugs into the slot? Take a pencil eraser and carefully rub it against the tab until the copper-colored connectors look shiny.

   Be careful not to bend the card while cleaning the contacts; doing so can damage the card.

4. **Replace the card and cables. Then repeat the process with the next card.**

   By removing any corrosion from the cards, you let your computer talk to them more efficiently.

Be sure to screw the cards back in. That single screw provides an electrical connection between the card and the computer.

Install a New Power Supply

When older computers simply refuse to turn on and do *anything* fun, it's probably because the power supply died.

Power supplies have become increasingly reliable over the past few years. Still, be sure to replace the power supply, which costs less than $100, before thinking about replacing the motherboard, which always costs *more* than $100.

Chapter 14 provides complete power-supply replacement instructions.

Run the Weird-Sounding ScanDisk and Defragmentation Programs

Windows 95 and Windows 98 come with a bunch of programs designed to keep Windows running trouble-free. Every few months — and immediately if Windows starts giving you some vague, unidentifiable trouble — open My Computer, right-click the appropriate hard drive's icon, and choose Properties from the pop-up menu. From there, click the Tools tab to get to the goodies.

Click the Check Now button in the Error-checking status box and then run ScanDisk, the error-checking program, on all your drives. (Use the Standard setting.)

Next, click the Defragment Now button on the same Tools tab and run the Defragmentation program on all your hard drives.

If your computer stops running during its defragmentation, it's probably because too many programs are running in the background. First, wait ten minutes to see whether the program springs back to life. The easiest cure is to restart Windows and press the F8 key before Windows comes to the screen. Choose Safe mode from the menu and run the defragmentation program while in Safe mode. When you're through defragmenting all your drives, restart your computer in its normal mode.

Windows users should also head for the end of Chapter 17 for tips on using the friendly Windows gang of built-in computer-nursing programs — especially the precision instruments included in Windows 98.

Chapter 20

The Ten Hardest Upgrades

*E*verybody wants to save money by avoiding the computer repair shop. But how can you tell which fix-it jobs you can do on your dining room table and which ones require experienced technicians who work in sterile rooms, drinking out of Batman coffee cups while holding expensive probe-things with curly wires?

Turn to this chapter when trying to decide whether *you* should hold the screwdriver or pass the job on to somebody else.

Upgrading Older Computers Like the 486

Forget about trying to upgrade your XT, AT, 386, or 486. Even if you spent the agonizing sums required to bring these oldsters to top condition, they still couldn't run most of today's software at top performance. Sure, some repairs described in this book still apply. But you lose money in the long run by keeping your old computer going.

In fact, most 486s should also be tossed in the charitable-donation pile this year because they've reached that same stage. Windows 98 runs only on Pentiums or on 486DX computers running at 66 MHz. Try to run Windows 98 on anything else, and it turns around coldly during the installation process.

Finally, an upgraded 486 comes with neither a warranty nor the latest batch of software, meaning that you won't have Windows or any of the other latest and greatest programs.

If you simply can't put away enough cash for a new Pentium, here are a few ways to keep a 486 chugging away for a little longer:

- First, if the 486 doesn't have more than 8MB of RAM, buy an additional 8MB for a noticeable jump in speed. Adding another 16MB probably won't boost speed, but it will help if you run lots of programs simultaneously.

- If you do buy RAM for a 486, however, make sure that you're buying the right style. Those 486 oldsters often use the older-style, 30-pin modules rather than today's 72-pin SIMMs. To be safe, take the old modules to the store and note the number of slots you have to work with.

- Consider a CPU upgrade chip. Manufacturers have mostly moved on to upgrades for Pentiums, not 486s, however. Your best bet might be an Internet auction house, like www.ebay.com. A quick look revealed eight 486 to Pentium-level CPU upgrades selling from $8 to $40.

- Even after upgrading the CPU and memory, you still need more computing power for today's software. Add a larger hard drive and a CD-ROM drive to your list. Better upgrade that BIOS, too, or it won't be able to handle that larger hard drive.

- If you donate your old 486 and buy a Pentium, however, first remove the video card and keep the monitor. Then plug these items into your new replacement Pentium. Remember that Windows 98 can expand your desktop across two or more monitors, giving you more room to work with.

Fixing Scanners and Printers

These sensitive bundles have too many screws and little wires. As you do with your TV, camcorder, and vacuum cleaner, take your scanner and printer to the repair shop — especially the scanner. (With the printer, at least you can try a few of the fixes in Chapter 9.)

Replacing the Motherboard

Conceptually, replacing a motherboard isn't too difficult. You merely unscrew one part and screw a new part in its place. The problem comes with all the stuff that's *attached* to the motherboard.

Replacing the motherboard is like replacing the shelves in a bedroom closet. The project sounds simple at first: Just pull out the long board that's sagging over all the shirts and bolt some newer, fancier shelves in its place. Unfortunately, you have to remove *everything* from the closet — all those shirts, hangers, and boxes of old checkbooks must come down from the top shelf. Then, after the new shelves are up, all that stuff has to go back on. And, if you upgraded the shelves, everything gets put back in a different location.

Plus, motherboards change their size as they evolve over the years. Your new one probably won't fit in the old case.

When you replace your computer's motherboard, you can simply screw it in by using the same screws that held down the old motherboard. But all the little wires plug into slightly different connectors. You have to move little DIP switches and jumpers around, too. And where does the speaker wire connect? The reset button wire?

Then you have to put all the cards back in their slots, with all the right cables plugged into the back of them. Finally, you have to fill out a new CMOS — your computer's master inventory list. Chances are, it's filled with new, upgraded words like Fast Gate A20 Option.

No, replacing the motherboard is not for the squeamish. Unless you have lots of patience, leave it for the folks at the shop.

When buying a second hard drive, make sure that the salesperson will let you bring it back for a refund if it doesn't get along with your first hard drive.

Adding Memory to an Old Motherboard

Sometimes a stroke of good fortune greets you when you lift off your computer's case and peer at its motherboard: You find some empty sockets that are ready to accept new memory chips. Other times, you're in for a disappointment — your memory sockets are already stuffed full of chips.

You can still add more memory to your computer; that's not the disappointing part. The disappointing part is that the plan costs more now. You can't just pop in some new memory chips. Now you need to pull out some existing ones, losing some existing memory in the process, which means that you need to buy an extra amount of memory to make up for the loss.

The solution? Pull out all your old chips and replace them all with the same size and type of higher-capacity chips.

Sure, this process upgrades your computer, and Windows runs much faster. But you're stuck with a handful of extra memory chips and no place to put them. If you're lucky, your local chip merchant will let you trade in your older chips, giving you a discount on the new ones. Otherwise, you'll do what everybody else does: Stick them in a plastic baggie and keep 'em in a drawer.

Or, sell 'em at the online auction house, eBay, at www.ebay.com.

If your local chip merchants won't do a trade-in for the chips, ask 'em whether they can sell you a *converter,* which is a little memory-chip-size card that plugs into a memory slot and lets you plug a few spare memory chips into it. By plugging four 4MB chips into the converter, you create a 16MB chip. (Some converters even let you use old-style chips in new sockets and vice versa.)

Connecting Computers to a Network

Upgrading computers by connecting them to a network has caused much grief and consternation over the years, especially for all those workers who have been simultaneously left helpless when their network server crashed.

Installing a network is not a job for the novice, which is why it's not covered in this book. Basically, installing a network involves placing cards in each computer and then linking them in peculiar ways with cables. After the hardware's in place, software constantly runs in the background so that the computers can talk to each other.

To get a hint at whether you'd want to tackle the task, drop by the bookstore and get ahold of my book *Windows 98 For Dummies,* published by IDG Books Worldwide, Inc. (Make sure that the book says "Second Edition" somewhere on the cover.) After reading a few sections, you should get a feel for the level of computer oomph required.

Chapter 21

The Ten Easiest Upgrades

Some of the most effective automobile upgrades are the easiest. You can simply hang some dice from the rearview mirror, for example. It looks cool, it's cheap, and you don't have to read any complicated manual to figure out which direction the dice should hang.

A few computer upgrades are almost as easy. They're collected and listed here for your upgrading pleasure.

Adding a Keyboard

By far, the easiest computer part to upgrade or replace is the keyboard. Just shut down Windows, turn off your computer, pull the keyboard's plug out of your computer, and take your old, coffee-soaked keyboard to the computer store. Buy another one, plug it back into your computer, turn the computer on, and keep typing, being careful to keep the coffee cup a little farther away this time.

You do need to make sure that the little plugs on the end of the cables match and that the number of keys matches. If your old keyboard had 101 keys, the new one should have at least 101 keys. I say "at least" 101 keys because many of the newest replacement keyboards have special Windows keys, running the total number of keys to 104 or more. The salesperson can tell at a glance what type of replacement you need, so don't bother counting the keys.

Those special Windows keys don't really do anything special, though; for instance, pressing the key with the Windows icon on it makes the Start button menu pop up. Clicking on the Start button with the mouse does the same thing. Or just hold down the Ctrl key and press the Esc key. In fact, the Windows key tends to get in the way by making the Start menu pop up accidentally if your fingers get sloppy while typing.

Be sure to check the action on those bent, *ergonomic* keyboards. (See whether the fancy fingering is worth the extra cash.) Also, if you are used to a quiet, mushy keyboard, make sure that you don't pick up one that clicks or chirps at you.

If your computer is particularly old, the salesperson also can sell you a small converter that lets your new keyboard plug into the old computer's hole.

Unlike other upgrades, adding a keyboard doesn't involve fiddling with any software, tools, or files. Just plug and play. Yay! Oh, and see Chapter 5 for some more keyboard information — you may be able to fix the keyboard rather than replace it.

Adding a Mouse

Adding a mouse can get a little tricky, but usually it's a pretty easy upgrade.

Chances are, you have a mouse port on the back of your computer. (Look in Chapter 3 for a picture of a mouse port; you're probably using the PS/2-style.) Plug in your new mouse and run the little creature's installation program. (Some don't even come with installation programs. Windows recognizes them and rolls out the red carpet automatically.) With a mouse replacement, you never have to take off your computer's case and run the risk of letting the snakes out. Quick and easy.

To replace a mouse, shut down Windows and turn off your computer. Then unplug the dead mouse, take it to the store, and buy another just like it. Plug it into the same spot, and you're through. The complete steps — as well as much more mice trivia — are dissected in Chapter 6.

Can't find a mouse with the same size connector on the end of its tail? Ask the salesperson for a *converter*. It plugs into the end of the mouse's tail, allowing the mouse to plug into the plug.

Adding Cards

Cards often get a bum rap. Adding cards sounds scary because you have to take off your computer's case. Then you have to decipher the inside-the-case vocabulary, which includes words like *slots, 8-bit, 16-bit, ISA, PCI,* and *AGP.*

For the most part, installing a card is pretty simple. Physically, it's kind of like pushing a credit card into an ATM machine. That, and tightening a single screw, is the whole procedure.

Most cards are designed to work with a wide variety of computer models from many different manufacturers. First, open the computer's case and check to see what type of slot is available. (You might have to check the computer's manual on this one. If the manual's no help, head to Chapter 3 for a pictorial identification guide.)

Then choose the type of card that fits into that slot. Today, you're usually safe with a PCI card.

Unless your computer's older and set up a little differently than most, the newly installed card probably will work right off the bat. Windows will recognize its new part and set it up so that it gets along with the other parts.

If Windows drops the ball, head for Chapter 18 for information to help you figure out what the card's manual means when it says to "set DIP switches 2, 4, and 5 to On" and "set jumpers J2 and J4."

It's *much* easier than it sounds.

Replacing a Monitor

Adding a new monitor is another easy upgrade, as long as you understand one key point: Monitors work in pairs with video cards. *Video cards* are the things that live inside your computer and give the monitor a place to plug into.

Your video card is responsible for creating an image and spitting it out. Your monitor merely grabs that image and puts it on the screen for you to show your friends. If you're looking to upgrade your monitor, you'll probably want to upgrade your video card as well. Otherwise, your new monitor probably will display the same image your old monitor displayed.

✔ Even if you buy a huge monitor to go with your old VGA video card, for example, you won't see any more information on your new screen. Your word processor will still fill the entire screen, and your windows will still overlap, just as they did on your other monitor.

✔ The solution? Buy your video card at the same time you buy your monitor. Then you can be sure that your monitor can display the highest-quality image the card can spit out.

✔ People with older computers probably have to buy a new card with that new monitor anyway because some newer monitors don't even plug into older video cards.

✔ Those new LCD "flat-screen" monitors usually won't work with just any card; they require special cards. Make sure that your card specifically states that it can handle LCD monitors before buying one.

✔ You can find more of this video card/monitor stuff in Chapters 8 and 15.

Installing a Floppy Drive or CD-ROM Drive

Floppy drives are a snap to install — *unless* you're trying to install a newer, high-capacity floppy drive into an old IBM PC or XT. Those old guys just can't stand the pressure, and you have to add a whole bunch of reinforcement parts before they can handle it.

In other computers, new floppy drives and internal CD-ROM drives simply slide on in, whereupon you connect the awaiting cables. Details abound in Chapter 12 (for floppy drives) and Chapter 13 (for CD-ROM drives).

Adding a Power Supply

Power supplies come in zillions of sizes, but even so, adding a power supply is an easy upgrade. How come? Because you install all power supplies in pretty much the same way.

Just unscrew the old power supply, making sure to save the screws. Then disconnect all the power supply's wires (write down where the different wires connect before you remove them).

For the office PC guru. . . .

These tips can help you keep the PCs running for as long as possible:

Write down your CMOS information. Although this topic is covered in Chapter 18, it's important enough to emphasize here. Your computer's CMOS works like its secretary. The CMOS keeps track of all the parts installed inside your computer. If something happens to your CMOS information, your computer will be as lost as a blue-suited executive whose secretary leaves for three weeks.

Call up your computer's CMOS and copy its settings into the chart in Chapter 18 while the information's safe. If something dreadful happens, you'll be glad you did.

Don't smoke around your PC. You can tell a lot about a PC's owner by looking inside its case. Computer repair folks can quickly tell when someone's been smoking around a PC. The PC's fan constantly sucks air into the case and blows it out the back to keep the machine cool. Smoke residue makes the internal components sticky, which encourages dust to form a kind of blanket on heat-sensitive parts. If you can't smoke outdoors, clean the inside of your PC's case regularly. Remove the case and use a can of compressed air to blow away all the gunk, as described in Chapter 2.

Avoid really cheap parts. Don't buy the *cheapest* parts. They're often made with the cheapest ingredients tossed together in the cheapest way. What saves money in the short run may cost you in the long run.

Some of the cheapest parts aren't as compatible with your other computer parts as the more expensive brands. And if something goes wrong with a cheap part, you usually find that its manufacturer has either gone out of business or doesn't have a technical-support staff who listens to you.

Don't let people flip the computer on and off a lot. A computer's most stressful experience comes when it's first powered up and a jolt of electricity flashes through it.

To ease the strain, don't turn a computer on and off repeatedly like you did to make "living room lightning" as a kid. After you turn your computer off, wait 30 seconds before turning it back on again.

Hang on to your old parts for emergencies. When you upgrade to a newer or fancier computer part, keep your old one in a closet somewhere. Then you have something to help test your computer when things go wrong. By swapping different parts one-by-one, you can eventually isolate the part that's stirring up trouble.

Store your old cards in a sandwich bag; if they're too big to fit, store them in the kind of plastic wrap you use to cover leftovers. Storing cards in this way helps prevent any damage from static electricity. If you have a little more cash, store your cards in the more durable Rubbermaid containers. Living at the Country Club? Spring for airtight Tupperware.

Haul out any old monitors and PCI video cards, too; Windows 98 lets you use up to eight monitors and PCI cards.

Buy some utility programs. The words *utility program* reek with a nerdish aroma. Utility programs aren't designed to let people do fun things; they're designed to let the *computer* do maintenance work. What a bore!

However, many utilities also contain diagnostic programs to help you figure out why your computer suddenly goes on strike. Still others can examine the way your computer's memory was set up and offer suggestions to make it run faster or smoother. These utilities are often the only way you can make your computer behave when it's acting up.

Next, drag the old power supply into the store and get another one that's exactly the same size. (Buying mail order? You may need to call the mail-order company to find the replacement power supply.) Screw the new power supply in and reconnect the wires. You're done! (You can find *complete* instructions in Chapter 14.)

While you're shopping, consider buying a power supply with a higher wattage, as I discuss in Chapter 14.

Don't ever try to repair or take apart power supplies. They soak up electricity like a sponge and can give you a serious zap if you poke around inside them.

Chapter 22

Ten Ways to Empower an Aging Pentium

The Pentium powerhouse that roared onto the desktops in the early 1990s is now whimpering with distress. It simply can't keep up. It doesn't move data around in the same size chunks or as quickly as the Intel Pentium III and Itanium models or the latest competitors from AMD. Those old Pentiums didn't support speedy graphics technology, like MMX or AGP 3D graphics, so they stumble on today's best video games.

Donate your vintage model to a charity and take the tax write-off if you have enough cash to buy a newer model. But if you're still padding your savings account, this chapter shows some simple ways to keep your old Pentium running smoothly for a few more years.

Beware, however. The upgrade tips listed here will squeeze only about another year's life from your Pentium. Don't pour too much into a dead end. Performing all the upgrades listed here will probably cost more than buying a new computer. (And those new computers come with new software as well.)

Buy More RAM

If your computer's running with less than 32MB of RAM, it's time to upgrade. Having 32MB or more will at least let Windows 98 work well with all its built-in programs. If you upgrade to 64MB, you can also run more programs at the same time, all the wile shifting information between them. And isn't that the whole point of Winows, anyway? (Chapter 11 covers memory installation issues.)

There's not much need to upgrade past 128MB, however. The chipsets on many of those ol motherboards have a memory-caching limitation that won't take much— if any — advantage of your upgrade.

Replace the CPU

Although repacing a CPU sounds terrifying, it's amazingly simple. Pull a lever, and the old CPU chip falls out. Pick up the leading-edge technology replacement at you local technoweenie warehouse and make sure that it has MMX technology for faster graphics. Line up the new chip's pins with the old chip's socket and push the new guy inside. Push down the little lever, and your computer immediately begins to run faster and have the latest multimedia technology.

These magical replacement CPU chips cost between $100 and $250, depending on their power, and get much more coverage in Chapters 3 and 10.

Intel's not the only company hawking CPU upgrades. In fact, they're the most expensive. Check out Web sites at Evergreen Technologies (www.evertech.com) and Kingston (www.kingston.com) to see how third-party CPUs push more power into your Pentium PC.

Buy a 3D and 2D Graphics Accelerator Card

Another quick way to add some spunk to Windows is to buy a 3D and 2D graphics *accelerator card.* Using the latest technology, these small, quick video cards redraw items in their new screen position as you move the items around on the screen. Plus, they perform this redrawing so quickly that your eyes register it as smooth graphical movement.

Accelerated graphics don't sound like much to get excited about. But when you see the difference it makes on your screen, you'll be surprised at all the extra zip you get from an accelerator card. Computer gamers get the most mileage for their buck from a 3D and 2D graphics accelerator card.

Don't buy a video card if the box says that it requires an AGP slot. Most older Pentiums don't have this special slot on their motherboards. (See Chapter 3 for tips on AGP slots and how to identify them.)

Add a USB Port

Those old Pentiums probably didn't come with a Universal Serial Bus port. USB devices began crawling onto the market several years ago, and they're just now reaching the shelves.

Today, mice, modems, printers, keyboards, speakers, scanners, and game pads all take advantage of USB ports — if you have one. To add USB compatibility to your old Pentium, upgrade to Windows 98 and buy a USB upgrade card, like the $30 models from Entrega (www.entrega.com).

Fine-Tune Windows

If you want to get under the hood, Windows comes with several panels of switches that help fine-tune its performance. They're all hidden in various places throughout the program.

For example, right-click the My Computer icon, choose Properties from the pop-up menu, and click the Performance tab. A System Properties window appears, displaying technical information about your computer. Here, you can optimize Windows 98 for running on a laptop or a desktop computer, change the way Windows 98 handles files, speed up the way your computer reads compact discs, and tweak other aspects of performance.

You can find many more system tweakers hidden on the System Tools menu, which you can call up through the Start button. (Click the Start button, choose Programs, and choose Accessories to find the System Tools area.) In the System Tools area, Windows 98 hides a handful of programs for backing up your computer, clearing away unnecessary files from your hard drive, scanning your disks for errors, and performing other valuable tasks.

Finally, be sure to defragment your Pentium's hard drive regularly, a topic covered in Chapter 19. If you run into troubles with Windows, head for Chapter 17 for a complete description of Windows settings and utilities.

Chapter 23

Ten Baffling Things Your Computer May Say When You Turn It On

In This Chapter

▶ Bunches of confusing little messages

▶ that pop up on your screen

▶ when you first turn on your computer

▶ as well as tips

▶ on what you're supposed to do to fix them

*W*hen you first turn on your computer and it wakes up, it scurries around looking at all its parts. If your computer finds something wrong, it tells you. Unfortunately, it doesn't tell you in English. Instead, your computer sends you some complicated observation about its internal mechanics and then stops working.

This chapter offers some translations for some of the most foreign-looking boot-up messages you may see frozen on your screen.

"When My Computer Boots Up, It Spits Out Weird Words"

We're talking gut-level error messages here — the kind your computer spits out as a welcome when you first turn it on.

These types of error messages are stored in your computer's *BIOS,* the base-level chip that serves as your PC's nervous system. (Check out Chapter 10 for more BIOS basics.)

Different brands of BIOS chips spit out subtly different error messages. However, Table 23-1 shows some key words and phrases that all BIOS chips use when they find something wrong with your PC.

Table 23-1   Common Bootup Messages and How to Get Rid of Them

These Key Words	*Usually Mean This*
Bad or missing command interpreter	Your computer's looking for a file named COMMAND.COM, which is supposed to be in its root directory. Copy that file back to your root directory from your system disk, as described in Chapter 2.
CMOS, Configuration	When your computer mentions CMOS, you need to change some of its settings. Head to Chapter 18 to read about CMOS settings.
Diskette seek failure	A cable may be loose, or your computer's CMOS may have an incorrect setting. Check the cable, and head to Chapter 18 to read about CMOS settings.
Drive Failure	Head for Chapter 13 and make sure that your hard drive's cables are plugged in snugly. Is the drive getting power from the power supply? Also check out Chapter 18 to make sure that the drive is listed correctly in your computer's CMOS.
Invalid configuration information — please run SETUP program	While booting up, your computer probably noticed that somebody had swiped or added a piece of hardware; because the part inventory didn't match its expected list, the computer wants you to run the SETUP program to confirm what's what. Hit Chapter 18.
Memory and Failure	When combined in the same message, these two words usually mean that something's wrong with one or more of your memory chips. First, reseat your memory chips (Chapter11); if that doesn't help, have them professionally tested (Chapter 11). You may need to replace the motherboard (Chapter 10).

These Key Words	*Usually Mean This*
Non-system disk or disk error	Take out the disk that's in drive A and press the spacebar for a quick fix. If your computer sends this message about your hard drive, you need to copy COMMAND.COM over to the hard drive from your system disk, as described in Chapter 2.
Parity	Your memory's acting up. Head for Chapter 11 and try pushing the chips more firmly into their sockets.
Partition table	Your hard drive's acting up. Your best bet is to buy a hard drive installation utility, as described in Chapters 13 and 18, and let the utility try to fix the problem.
Sector not found or Unrecoverable error	These words mean that a disk is starting to go bad. Windows ScanDisk or programs such as Norton Utilities or PC Tools can help recover any information before it's too far gone to retrieve.
Timer	Problems with timers usually mean that your computer's motherboard is defective.

If the computer spits out a particularly puzzling error message, check out Chapter 4 for ways to diagnose your problem over the Internet. Chapter 25 lists other error codes.

"What Do Those Little Numbers Mean?"

Some of the genuine IBM computers and a few older clones just flash some code numbers on the screen when they're having problems getting on their feet. They don't bother listing any more helpful details about what's bugging them and what they want you to do about it. Table 23-2 explains what some of those cryptic numbers mean and also tells you which chapters offer more information about fixing the problem.

One note about the table: See how the codes have the letter *X* in them, as in *1XX?* The X stands for *any* number. The code 1XX can mean any three-digit number starting with the number 1, such as 122, 189, or something similar.

Table 23-2	Numeric Codes and What They Mean	
This Code	*Usually Means This Is Acting Up*	*Comments*
02X	Power supply	You may need to replace your power supply, as described in Chapter 14.
1XX	Motherboard	These numbers often translate into expensive problems. Look up any of your computer's other symptoms in Chapters 24 and 25; Chapter 4 may help as well.
2XX	Memory	Try pushing your memory chips more firmly into their sockets (Chapter 11). If that doesn't work, you probably need to ask a professional to test your memory chips.
3XX	Keyboard	Is a book lying across the keyboard, pressing some of the keys as your computer boots up? Another possible solution is to turn off your computer, unplug the keyboard, shake out any dust, and try rebooting the computer. See Chapter 5.
4XX	Monochrome video or adapter	Only XTs complain about this problem. Your monochrome video card is acting up. See Chapters 8 and 15.
5XX	Color video or adapter	Only XTs complain about this problem. Your CGA video card is acting up. See Chapters 8 and 15.

This Code	*Usually Means This Is Acting Up*	*Comments*
6XX	Floppy drive or adapter	Could a bad floppy disk be in the drive? Is your CMOS set up for the right type of disk? Better start with Chapters 12 and 18.
7XX	Math coprocessor	Is your math coprocessor seated firmly in its socket? Does your computer's CMOS know that the chip's there? Chapters 10 and 18 should help you fix this one.
9XX	Printer port	Your I/O card may be at fault. See Chapters 3 and 15.
10XX	Second printer port	Your I/O card may be at fault. See Chapters 3 and 15.
11XX	Serial port	Your I/O card may be at fault. See Chapters 3 and 15.
12XX	Second serial port	Your I/O card may be at fault. See Chapters 3 and 15.
13XX	Game card	Your I/O card may be at fault. See Chapters 3 and 15.
17XX	Hard drive or controller	Better give Chapter 13 the once-over: Make sure that your hard drive's cables are securely fastened and that its jumpers are set correctly. See Chapter 18. Also make sure that the controller card is set firmly in its slot. See Chapters 15 and 19.

Chapter 24

Ten Common Warning Beeps and What They Mean

In This Chapter

▶ Lists of little beeps

▶ that fill the air

▶ when you first turn on your computer

▶ and what, for goodness' sake,

▶ you're supposed to do about them

*A*nybody who's watched television in the past decade has seen computers that can talk to their owners. Your little desktop computer can talk, too. Rather than use the more common vowels and consonants, though, your computer does the best it can: It strings together some beeps.

By carefully counting all the beeps, you can figure out what your computer's trying to say. Although your computer is no opera singer, it can give you a clue to what's wrong even if you can't see any error messages on your monitor.

What's This BIOS Beep Business?

Sometimes your computer freaks out while it's booting up or being turned on. But if it finds something wrong before it gets around to testing the video card, the computer can't flash an error message on the screen. So the computer beeps to say what's wrong.

Unfortunately, no clearly defined "beep standard" exists. All PC manufacturers know that their computers should beep when something's wrong, but because there aren't any hard-and-fast rules to follow, the manufacturers all assign different "beep codes" to different problems.

The secret beep codes are stored in your computer's BIOS chip (which I describe in Chapter 10). By figuring out what BIOS your computer uses, you can tell which beep codes your computer uses.

Watch the screen carefully when your computer first boots up or is turned on. Look for some words about BIOS copyright — that legalese stuff you usually ignore.

Do you see a company name? It's probably AMI — short for American Megatrends — or else it's Phoenix. These two companies are the biggest BIOS makers. Don't be confused by the *video card* BIOS copyright stuff that may pop up on the first line; you're looking for the computer's *real* BIOS information. Can't figure out what BIOS you're using? Chapter 10 has more tips.

When your computer makes some beeps and then stops working, count the number of beeps you hear. Feel free to turn the computer off, wait 30 seconds, and turn it back on again. When you're sure that you've counted the right number of beeps, look in the table in this chapter that corresponds to your brand of BIOS. The table translates different beep codes for you.

- ✔ If your computer's down to the beep stage and you've tried all the cheap fixes I list in Chapter 19, something's usually seriously wrong.

- ✔ Many of the errors mean that a chip is bad on your computer's motherboard. Unfortunately, it's usually easier to replace the entire motherboard than to isolate the problem chip, remove it, and solder another one in its place.

- ✔ Still, if you have computer hacker friends, see whether you can cajole them into giving you a hand. If you explain the specific problem — a bad timer chip, for example — they may know whether it's something they can fix or whether the whole motherboard's a goner.

AMI BIOS Beeps

Normally, computers using the AMI BIOS don't bother with beeps. When they can't muster the energy to boot up, they flash an error message on the screen. To figure out what the computer's trying to tell you, look up the message in Chapter 23.

But if something's wrong with the video card or the computer's so confused that it can't even put any words on the screen, the computer falls back on the ol' beep trick. Table 24-1 explains what your AMI BIOS beeps are trying desperately to tell you.

Don't take these beep codes as the absolute truth. Although they provide a clue to why your computer's acting up, they don't always finger the exact culprit.

Table 24-1	AMI BIOS Beeps and What They Mean
Number of Beeps	_What It Means_
No beep	You're _supposed_ to hear one beep. If you don't hear anything, your computer's suffering from a bad power supply, a bad motherboard, or a speaker that doesn't work.
1 beep	Normally, computers issue one self-assured beep when everything's working fine. But when nothing appears on the screen, you had better check your monitor (Chapter 8) and your video card (Chapter 15). If those two parts appear to work well, the single beep can mean that your motherboard's struggling with some bad chips. This job is for the people in the white lab coats. You probably can't fix it yourself.
2 beeps	Your computer's complaining about its memory. Make sure that the chips are seated firmly in their sockets (Chapter 11). If that doesn't fix the problem, you probably need to pull out the chips and have them tested at the chip store. If the chips are good, you may need a new motherboard. Again, this problem may be beyond your help.
3 beeps	Same as the 2-beeps message.
4 beeps	Almost always the same as the 2-beeps message.
5 beeps	Your motherboard's acting up. Try reseating all the chips, especially your CPU (Chapter 10). If that doesn't work, you may have to spring for a new motherboard.
6 beeps	The chip on your motherboard that controls your keyboard is acting up. Try reseating the chip (if you can find it) or try a different keyboard. You may want to take this one to the shop.
7 beeps	Basically, it's the same as the 5-beep warning: Your motherboard's acting up. Try reseating all the chips, especially your CPU (Chapter 10). If that doesn't work, you had better spring for a new motherboard.
8 beeps	Your video card may be incorrectly installed. Better hit Chapter 15; you may need to replace your old video card.
9 beeps	Your BIOS (Chapter 10) is acting up; you probably have to replace it.

(continued)

Table 24-1 *(continued)*

Number of Beeps	What It Means
10 beeps	Your motherboard (Chapter 10) is acting up; if this problem persists, you have to replace the motherboard.
11 beeps	Your motherboard's cache memory has problems. You'd best take this one to the shop.

Genuine IBM BIOS Beeps

If you have a true-blue IBM computer, the kind that says *IBM* on its case, Table 24-2 lists some beep codes you may hear.

Don't take these beep codes as the absolute truth. Although they provide a clue to why your computer's acting up, they don't always finger the right culprit.

Table 24-2	Beep Codes for *Real* IBM Computers
These Beeps	*Mean This*
No beep	You're supposed to hear one beep. If you don't, your computer has a bad power supply, a bad motherboard, or a speaker that's broken or not connected.
Constant beep	Your power supply (Chapter 14) isn't working right.
Short, repetitive beeps	Your power supply (Chapter 14) isn't working right.
One long beep, one short beep	Your motherboard (Chapter 10) isn't working right.
One long beep, two short beeps	Your video card (Chapters 8 and 15) or its cables are messing up.
One long beep, three short beeps	Your EGA card (Chapters 8 and 15) or its cables are messing up.

Phoenix BIOS Beeps

If you see the word *Phoenix* on the screen when you reboot or turn on your computer, your system uses the Phoenix BIOS.

So? Well, Phoenix honed the beep code concept to a fine art. Listen to the beeps carefully: The computer gives you *three* sets of beeps, with a pause between each set.

For example, if you hear BEEP BEEP, a pause, BEEP BEEP BEEP, another pause, and BEEP BEEP BEEP BEEP, that translates to two beeps, three beeps, and four beeps. That all boils down to this code: 2 – 3 – 4. You need to look up 2 – 3 – 4 in Table 24-3 to find out what your Phoenix BIOS is complaining about this time.

Don't take these beep codes as the absolute truth. Although they provide a clue to why your computer's acting up, they don't always finger the right culprit.

Table 24-3	Phoenix Beep Codes
These Beeps	*Usually Mean This*
1 – 1 – 3	Your computer can't read its CMOS (Chapter 18), so your motherboard's complaining (Chapter 10).
1 – 1 – 4	Your BIOS probably needs replacing (Chapter 10).
1 – 2 – 1	A timer chip on your motherboard is acting up; you probably have to replace the motherboard (Chapter 10).
1 – 2 – 2	The motherboard is bad (Chapter 10).
1 – 2 – 3	You have a bad motherboard (Chapter 10) or bad memory (Chapter 11).
1 – 3 – 1	The motherboard (Chapter 10) or memory (Chapter 11) is bad.
1 – 3 – 3	The motherboard (Chapter 10) or memory (Chapter 11) is bad.
1 – 3 – 4	You probably have a bad motherboard (Chapter 10).
1 – 4 – 1	You probably have a bad motherboard (Chapter 10).
1 – 4 – 2	Some of the memory is bad (Chapter 11).
2 – ? – ?	Any beep series starting with two beeps means that some of your memory is bad (Chapter 11). Better get the chips tested professionally.

(continued)

Table 24-3 (continued)

These Beeps	Usually Mean This
3 – 1 – 1	One of the chips on your motherboard is acting up; you probably have to replace the whole thing.
3 – 1 – 2	One of the chips on your motherboard is acting up; you probably have to replace the whole thing.
3 – 1 – 3	One of the chips on your motherboard is acting up; you probably have to replace the whole thing.
3 – 1 – 4	One of the chips on your motherboard is acting up; you probably have to replace the whole thing.
3 – 2 – 4	Your keyboard (or the chip on the motherboard that controls it) is acting up. Visit Chapter 5.
3 – 3 – 4	Your computer can't find its video card. Is there one in there? (See Chapter 15.)
3 – 4 – 1	Your video card is acting up (Chapter 15).
3 – 4 – 2	Your video card is acting up (Chapter 15).
3 – 4 – 3	Your video card is acting up (Chapter 15).
4 – 2 – 1	Your motherboard has a bad chip; you probably have to replace the whole thing (Chapter 10).
4 – 2 – 2	First, check your keyboard (Chapter 5) for problems; if that doesn't fix the problem, your motherboard's probably bad.
4 – 2 – 3	Just as with the beeps in the preceding table entry, first check your keyboard (Chapter 5) for problems; if that doesn't fix the problem, your motherboard's probably bad.
4 – 2 – 4	One of your cards (Chapter 15) is confusing your computer. Try pulling your cards out one-by-one to isolate the culprit.
4 – 3 – 1	Your motherboard has probably gone bad.
4 – 3 – 2	Again, your motherboard has probably gone bad.
4 – 3 – 3	One of the timer chips died. You probably have to replace the motherboard.
4 – 3 – 4	Try calling up your CMOS (Chapter 18) and checking the date and time. If that doesn't fix the problem, try changing your computer's battery (Chapter 10). Still acting up? Try a new power supply before breaking down and buying a new motherboard.

These Beeps	*Usually Mean This*
4 – 4 – 1	Your serial port's acting up; try reseating (or replacing) your I/O card (Chapter 15).
4 – 4 – 2	Your parallel port's acting up; try reseating (or replacing) your I/O card (Chapter 15).
4 – 4 – 3	Your math coprocessor's acting up. Run the program that came with it to see whether it's *really* fried or just pretending.

Chapter 25

Ten Common Error Messages (And How to Avoid Them)

In This Chapter

▶ Oodles of error messages

▶ that seem to pop up

▶ when you're trying to finish

▶ up some work

▶ and turn off the darn computer.

Computers come with great gobs of error messages. You find the ten most popular — actually, the most *un*popular — error messages in this chapter. You also find some tips on how to shut 'em up.

Puzzled by a recurring error message? Head for Chapter 4 and find the section about using the Internet to diagnose your computer. The section on newsgroups shows how to identify and purge the most dastardly error messages.

Insert disk with COMMAND.COM in drive A. Press any key to continue

If you haven't moved up to Windows, this message usually means that your computer can't find its life-giving pieces of DOS. Stick a system disk in drive A and press Enter. Or, if your computer usually boots off your hard drive, remove any errant floppy disks that may be sitting in drive A and press Enter. (Dunno how to make a system disk? Troop back to Chapter 2.)

Invalid Media or Track 0: Unusable Format Terminated

When your computer hides its most important files on a system disk, it sticks them in some front-row seats called *Track 0*. If those seats are damaged — they're full of gum or something even worse — the computer can't stick its important stuff on them.

That's what happens when this message appears. Throw the disk away and try another. If you get this message when you're trying to format your hard drive, you're in *deep* trouble. Head for Chapters 12 and 13 for some possible fixes.

Sector not found

DOS is having trouble finding information on a disk. Try running ScanDisk, which I describe in Chapter 19. If you haven't backed up your disk — whether it's a hard disk or a floppy — do it as quickly as possible. Your hard drive (covered in Chapter 13) may be on its last legs or in need of reformatting.

Access denied

You're probably trying to write (or delete) something on a write-protected floppy disk. If you're *sure* that you want to change the disk, disable its write-protection. If you're working with a 3½-inch disk, slide the little tab away from the hole in the disk's top corner. (On a 5¼-inch floppy, remove the little piece of tape from the edge of the disk.)

You may also receive this message if you try to delete a protected file on the hard disk. Or perhaps you're trying to read or write to a file that is used or manipulated by another program in Windows.

Divide Overflow

This one leaves you no choice but to reboot the computer. Your computer's fine, but the software did something that has confused everybody since their first math course: It tried to divide by zero.

Try reinstalling the software onto your hard disk from the original disks. If that doesn't work, try cajoling the folks on the software's tech-support line to send you a new, working copy of the program. Also, make sure that you have the most current drivers, as discussed in Chapter 17.

Drive not ready. Abort, Retry, Ignore, Fail?

The computer's probably startled because it tried to find a file on a drive but couldn't even find a floppy or compact disc in the drive. If you *did* put a disk or a CD in there, is the drive's latch closed? Is the disk or CD right-side up? Make sure that the disk or CD is in the correct drive and press R for Retry. (You may have to give the drive a few seconds to recognize the disk, especially with CDs.)

A:\ is not accessible. The device is not ready.

Windows usually shoots this message out when you shut down your computer while displaying the contents of a floppy drive. Then if you remove the floppy disk and restart Windows, it tries to reread the information from the disk in order to display it on the screen again. When the disk's not there, Windows complains.

The moral? Don't leave the contents of a floppy disk on your monitor when you shut down your computer.

"My computer puts that C:> thing on the screen, not Windows!"

When Windows refuses to come out on stage, it has usually broken a leg — and not in a good way. If you recently installed some software, the incoming software may have damaged some Windows files. Or, if you just tried to install Windows, the installation process may not have worked all the way.

To fix everything, run the Windows Setup program again — the one that installs Windows on your computer. When Windows asks during the installation process, choose the Verify option to make Windows check all files and replace any that are missing or damaged.

Track 0 Bad — Disk Unusable

If you get this message when you're using an older computer, you're probably trying to format one of those high-density, 1.2MB floppies in a 360K floppy drive. It just can't be done.

If you get this message when you're *not* using an old, 360K drive, the floppy disk itself is probably bad.

Finally, if this message refers to your hard drive, it's particularly bad news. Head to Chapter 19 for a possible cheap fix, and then see Chapter 13 for some more detailed tips.

Insufficient disk space

When you see this message, your disk — hard drive or floppy disk — doesn't have enough room on it to store the incoming files. You have to delete some files from it to make room. Of course, you can just put in a clean floppy disk or buy another hard disk, as I describe in Chapter 13.

Insufficient memory

Your computer doesn't have enough memory to run this particular program. Or perhaps the memory that you do have isn't set up right.

If you're using DOS or trying to run a DOS game, put your system disk (described in Chapter 2) in drive A and reboot your computer. When your computer reboots from the boot disk, it comes up "clean" of anything that's sucking memory from the available pool. Don't try to run Windows after this trick, though.

If your Windows programs complain of "Insufficient memory," you have two options: First, try shutting down all your extraneous programs so that all your memory is available for your current program. Second, buy more memory and install it, as I describe in Chapter 11.

Bad command or filename

You probably typed something at the C:\> prompt, and your computer can't figure out what you are trying to do. You may have spelled something wrong or typed the name of a program your computer can't find.

If you see these words when your computer's first booting up, one of the lines in your AUTOEXEC.BAT file is confusing your computer. (That weird-sounding file's described in Chapter 16.)

Bad or missing filename

If you see this message when you boot up your computer, it probably means that the computer couldn't find a driver listed in your CONFIG.SYS file. Look at Chapter 16 and then check your CONFIG.SYS file to see what's amiss. Otherwise, your computer's telling you that it couldn't find a file. Check out the information on *paths* in Chapter 16.

Parity Error

Any message containing the unpleasant words *Parity Error* can pop up on just about any computer at any time. Windows frames the words in a pleasant blue background; its grandfather, DOS, just slaps the words on the screen. Either way, the solution's the same: Restart your computer.

Parity errors usually mean your memory's acting up, meaning you should head for Chapter 11.

Chapter 26

Ten Years of Computer Antiques . . . and What to Do with Them

*T*his chapter's for the people with the garage sale computers — or the computers they're considering selling at the garage sale.

Here, you find the make and model of computers since their birth in 1981. Check your computer's case or receipt to find its model, look it up here, and decide who gets it for Christmas.

Original IBM PC (1981)

The PC that started the whole craze more than a decade ago isn't worth much today, even to antique dealers. A Model T Ford still gets a raised eyebrow of respect in Sunday parades, but the original IBM PC is probably worth less than a Brady Bunch lunch box.

Identifying characteristics: The original IBM PC, shown in Figure 26-1, has big, black floppy disk drives, which are almost four inches tall. It has no reset button and has the letters *IBM* across the front. It's heavy — and probably dusty, too. The original IBM PC has space for no more than five cards. It has an 8088 CPU.

Why you should care: This computer is way too old for any serious upgrading. Many replacement parts simply aren't available.

Upgradability: One guy made a lamp out of his.

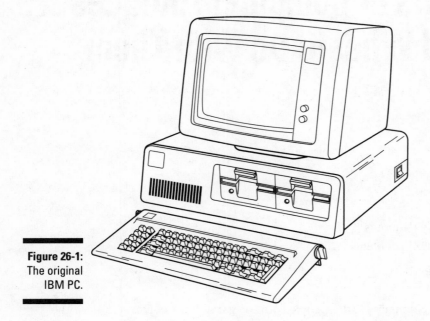

Figure 26-1:
The original
IBM PC.

IBM XT (Early 1980s)

IBM dumped its original IBM PC for the flashier XT model, which introduced the *hard disk* (also known as *hard drive*). Rather than store all their programs and files on little floppy disks, people could simply copy their information to the huge hard disk inside the computer. Well, the hard disk was huge for those days, holding 10MB of information — the equivalent of seven 3½-inch floppy disks, by today's standards.

Identifying characteristics: It has an 8086 or 8088 CPU and slots for eight 8-bit cards. But who wants to get technical? Don't bother upgrading an XT model, either.

Why you should care: Don't even bother trying to sell it if you consider getting it out of the garage.

Upgradability: Thinking of building a new computer from scratch? You can't even salvage the case from this one — it's the wrong size. Make this computer into a lamp for the *other* side of the couch.

Because the old XT computers don't have 16-bit slots, they can't handle the latest, fanciest sound cards, video cards, and other goodies. Also, some really picky old XT computers don't like just *any* card in the slot closest to the power supply. Save that slot for last.

IBM AT (Mid-1980s)

The IBM AT is the XT's replacement. The AT model finally added a little oomph to the desktop. In fact, all future computers copied this model. Today's computers are sometimes called *AT-class* computers, to separate them from the anemic XTs and PCs they replaced.

New life through NewDeal

Those old AT or better computers aren't dead yet. Since they can't run Windows, a company named NewDeal wrote its own graphical interface. The program has the Windows "point and click" graphical interface, but it runs on a 286 with 640K of memory, a CGA graphics card, and at least 9MB of hard drive space.

What do you get? A system that runs several programs at once, swaps data with most PC applications, supports most printers up to 24-bit color, networks with other PCs, and browses the Internet.

Toss in a full-featured word processor, spreadsheet, graphics program, and Web page editor to make your old PC run like Windows but without Microsoft's demanding computing horsepower requirements.

The following figure, for instance, shows NewDeal's NewBanker, a bookkeeping and check-writing program. NewBanker is running a Windows-like interface on an old 286 computer with only 640K of RAM. Before throwing away that old computer, check out NewDeal. It may be the tonic your computer's been waiting for.

Identifying characteristics: The IBM AT is up to five times faster than the XT; this computer's Intel 286 CPU set the standard for computers to come. Plus, it has 16-bit slots for more powerful 16-bit cards.

Why you should care: This computer can do many of the things today's powerhouse computers can do, with one big exception: It can't run Windows or any Windows software. It can't even run decent games.

Upgradability: There's hope. You don't need Windows to run a computer. Instead, check out the NewDeal suite of products, at www.newdealinc.com.

PCjr

Many, many years ago, IBM tried to make a *home-size* computer for the home market, but nobody bought it. Rumor has it that several thousand PC*jr*s are sitting in a warehouse somewhere back east. The PC*jr* is not built to the same hardware standards as a *real* PC. Leave any PC*jr*s (yours included) sitting on the shelf with the 8-track players at the Salvation Army.

PS/2 (1987)

IBM, upset that so many other companies were making bucks off its computer design, decided to change the design. IBM added something called Micro Channel Architecture (also known as *MCA* for the nerds who like to sling letters around).

Why you should care: Watch out, because these guys differ from *normal* computers. Most important, they use special MCA versions of *cards,* like video cards or internal *modems.*

Upgradability: No way.

IBM pulled a fast one: Not all PS/2s use that MCA stuff anymore. The only way you can know for sure is to pull out the manual and peek: Does it say MCA or *ISA?*

386, 486, and First-Level Pentium (Late 1980s to the Present)

Until a few years ago, these computers worked fine. Now, with Windows 98, they don't cut the mustard. The 386 class of computer includes the 486 (1989) and all the Pentiums. Although the 386 and 486 class of computers don't have much life left in them, Pentiums are better equipped for an upgrade.

The chip designers finally got it right with the 386 chip used for these CPUs. In fact, that CPU spawned a whole new class of computers, sometimes called the *386 class*. This group includes the 386, the 486, and all the Pentium chips, even to this day.

Identifying characteristics: If your computer can run any version of Windows, it's running this type of chip.

Why you should care: First, the bad news. Upgrading an aging 386 or 486 computer to the Windows level will cost more than a new computer and never deliver the horsepower. The good news? If you're *really* tight for cash, Chapter 20 offers advice on what you can get by slipping another hundred bucks into a 486.

Upgradability: Own a Pentium machine? No problem! These machines are the easiest to upgrade and can handle almost anything you throw at them. Most common upgrades include bigger hard drives, more memory, and faster video cards. The latest craze is to plug in faster CPU chips (covered in Chapter 10), which is one of the best ways to push a Pentium into working a little faster.

Y2K Problems

The year 2000 has passed. Has your computer passed out? In case you missed the fuss, computers were supposed to freak out at the year 2000. That's because programmers used to program their years as only two digits. In computer language, the programmers wrote the year 1986 as 86.

Most newer model computers didn't have much trouble recognizing the new year as 2000 rather than as 1900, although some oldsters still have problems known as "Y2K." (That's a secret code for Year 2000 because K stands for "thousand" in the metric system.)

The problem lies in those computers' BIOS chips, which hold CMOS information. Chapter 10 describes how to replace your BIOS chip with an updated model that should bring your computer's time schedule back in synch with the rest of the modern world.

If you're having trouble finding a BIOS replacement, check out the Evergreen Year 2000 Upgrade (`www.evertech.com`). Plug in the card, and it automatically fixes your BIOS to handle the year 2000-date-change rollover — if your computer's compatible.

There's more. Windows 3.1 isn't Y2K compatible, so you might encounter problems if you're still running that operating system. If your computer can't handle the move to Windows 95, check out NewDeal, described earlier in this chapter.

Index